The ABCs of DPC:
A Primer on Design-Procurement-Construction for the Project Manager

The ABCs of DPC:
A Primer on Design-Procurement-Construction for the Project Manager

A Project Management Institute Book

Project Management Institute

130 South State Road

Upper Darby, Pennsylvania 19082 USA

610–734–3330

www.pmi.org

Library of Congress Cataloging-in-Publication Data

The ABCs of DPC: A Primer on Design-Procurement-Construction for the Project Manager
      p.   cm.
   Includes bibliographical references
   ISBN: 1–880410–07–9 (pbk. : alk. paper)
   1. Industrial project management. I. Project Management Institute
TA190.D45   1997
658.4'04 – – dc21   97-49802
                                                                                            CIP

Published by:

Project Management Institute, 130 South State Rd, Upper Darby, PA 19082
Phone: 610–734–3330 or Visit our Web Site: www.pmi.org

ISBN: 1–880410–07–9

Copyright ©1998 by the Project Management Institute. All rights reserved. Printed in the United States of America. No part of this work may be reproduced or transmitted in any form or by any means, electronic, manual, photocopying, recording, or by any information storage and retrieval system, without prior written permission of the publisher.

PMI Book Team

James S. Pennypacker, *Editor-in-Chief*
Toni D. Knott, *Editor*
Bobby R. Hensley, *Acquisitions Editor*
Michelle Owen, *Graphic Designer*
Mark S. Parker, *Editor, Production Coordinator*

Design-Procurement-Construction Specific Interest Group Contributors

Mark Owen Mathieson, *PMP, Chair*
Norman F. Jacobs, Jr., *Editor*

PMI books are available at special quantity discounts to use as premiums and sales promotions, or for use in corporate training programs. For more information, please write to the Business Manager, PMI Publication Division, 40 Colonial Square, Sylva, NC 28779. Or contact your local bookstore.

The paper used in this book complies with the Permanent Paper Standard issued by the National Information Standards Organization (Z39.48—1984).

10 9 8 7 6 5 4 3 2 1

Contents

vii	Preface
1	Caution: Project Management Professional at Work!!!
13	Successful Utility Project Management from Lessons Learned
23	Staff Responsibilities of the Project Manager
29	The Great Juggling Act
37	Job Set-Up by Project Manager
49	Project Management and Job Administration
55	Partnering: A Tool for Communications Management
67	Paperwork by Project Managers
69	Job Documentation: A Project Manager's Responsibility
79	Project Management Control, Computers, and Software
85	Pre-Project Planning for Capital Facilities
97	Communications for High Performing Project Teams
103	Philosophy and Critical Path Method Communications
109	Critical Path Method Updates and Control
115	Today's Needs in Project Management *The Project Management Technique: Manage, Schedule, and Cost*
119	Using Project Finance to Help Manage Project Risks
131	Assuring Excellence in Execution in Construction Project Management
139	The Residual Costs of Inferior Project Management
145	An Architect's View
149	Construction Delay Communication Computer System
161	Appendix A: AIA Document A201-1997: General Conditions
231	Appendix B: Effective Project Management in Bureaucracies
255	Appendix C: Project Manager's Book List
257	Appendix D: PMI and Design-Procurement-Construction Specific Interest Group (SIG)
261	Appendix E: The Authors

Preface

By Mark Owen Mathieson, PE, PMP
Chairperson, Design-Procurement-Construction Specific Interest Group

The ABCs of DPC: A Primer on Design-Procurement-Construction for the Project Manager was an idea developed by the reconstituted Design-Procurement-Construction (DPC) Specific Interest Group board of directors at its August 1996 meeting. The primary purpose of the meeting was to develop an educational and professional advancement vehicle or forum for members in the field of project management at the entry, intermediate, and advance levels. The primer idea was nurtured and endorsed at the DPC's annual business membership-at-large meeting held in Boston on October 6, 1996, and the project was guided by the able stewardship of Publication Co-Chair Norman F. Jacobs, Jr., and Project Management Institute's Publisher/Editor-in-Chief Jim Pennypacker.

The message received by our Design-Procurement-Construction board of directors at the Boston meeting was loud and clear. We must not only survive as a specific interest group but also establish a leadership position in the Project Management Institute and be a specific interest group of choice. In order to accomplish these goals, we have to meet the educational requirements of the DPC membership at a two-tier level.

The first tier of education is what we call, in generic terms, "entry" or "undergraduate level." Entry level involves two types of practitioners, one being the typical young entrants or technically trained transplants into the project management field and the other including international corporations or countries entering into project management for the first time.

The second tier of education is what we call "graduate level" for the long-time members of the Project Management Institute, those who know the project management body of knowledge, find it boring, and are looking for leading edge education.

Our intermediate and advance level handbooks, coupled with executing cooperating agreements with such entities as Construction Industry Institute and Design-Build Institute of America, will go a long way toward meeting our mission statement for our graduate-level membership.

Our mission is to provide participants with the highest quality information, education, training, skills, and opportunities to successfully identify, plan, manage, and participate in design, procurement, and construction for projects involving building and facilities in the residential, commercial, and industrial sectors of the worldwide economy.

Our series of practical application handbooks are intended to be valuable ready references for both entry level and long-term project management careers in design, procurement, or construction.

Our success is tied to your commitment to your profession!

Caution: Project Management Professional at Work!!!

PM Network (October 1993)

One day the joint venture's construction management executive vice president asks you to assist another project manager by managing the field work. As one dutifully says, after the usual basic questions are satisfactorily answered, I said, "Yes."

On a sunny October day in 1992, with my PMP tools and a positive attitude in hand, I stepped onto the project site and instantly felt my feet, then my stomach, and finally my neck become wet with perspiration. My feeling of gratification on starting a new project was swept away by an instant state of depression. It had become quite evident that I had stepped onto and inherited full helm responsibility of a badly sinking and severely listing vessel with water breaking simultaneously over the bow and stern. Compounding the situation was a strong tide shoving the vessel onto the rocky shoreline directly ahead.

I had accepted total responsibility for a federal government project that had already been shut down twice; was five months behind schedule—going on nine months; was 50 percent over budget with no end in sight; was run by a frustrated general contractor and subcontractors who were dealing with low field morale; had provoked deep, vocal community resentment; possessed no project coordination with county and state officials; contained a serious deficiency in the original scope of work generation and sign-off by the local user; and had no real leadership or manager at any level. If matters were not bad enough, the client had a new tough-minded and very successful chief executive officer/president, and the project location was virtually in his business backyard. And, and, and . . . and, over the next eight months the site would be subject to a constant killer weather pattern that the locale had not experienced in the last twenty-five years.

What does a project manager do? Walk away and cut his losses? No!!!

The answer is: "Caution: Project Management Professional at Work!!" Step back and watch what happens.

History

The project is a sixty thousand square foot (about the size of a football field) automated United States Postal Service (USPS) mail processing facility (delivery distribution center) located on eight acres in Anne Arundel County, Maryland. The prototype documents were developed by a master architect hired by the USPS's Philadelphia Major Facilities Office using the Postal Service's Kit-of-Parts program. Once the Postal Service granted project authorization for this particular location, a local architect/engineering firm was selected to modify the documents to meet local codes; review the plans with other agencies to ensure that all requirements for services, such as utilities, were adequately met; review local postal needs; and adapt project requirements to the unique site configuration and soil conditions.

Delivery distribution center projects are typically $3 million in value (excluding automated equipment, utility rough-in, move-in, phone system, professional services, and site acquisition costs) and are delivered in three hundred calendar days, from notice-to-proceed to final acceptance and occupancy.

Management of the project was assigned to Sverdrup-Gilbane, a joint venture (a United States Postal Service (USPS) construction support contractor). Sverdrup-Gilbane is under contract to provide a full array of planning, design, construction, and real estate support services throughout the USPS Philadelphia Major Facilities Office's operating region. These services are provided for each project on a work order basis for a period of three years.

Upon the issuance of the notice-to-proceed to the general contractor on February 14, 1992, the state-of-the-project was as follows:
- The local postal user had not completed a review of the documents.
- County and state reviews had not been completed.
- The local community (residential and government business campus) was unaware of the project.
- Bid documents were incomplete.

Twice the State of Maryland and the United States Army Corps of Engineers had shut down the project. One shutdown was erroneously caused by the state when an unregistered and dislocated storm-water retention pond, which was thought to be on United States Postal Service property, conflicted with the bid document sediment control sequence of events and building footprint. The pond turned out later to be on the adjacent owner's property. As a direct result of the project shutdown and its extended duration, the general contractor lost its superintendent and steel erector, several smaller subcontractors went out of business, material prices had increased, and the project was now subject to winter conditions.

On October 1, 1992, the state-of-the-project was as follows:
- Quality of fieldwork was marginal.

- The general contractor had been issued two time extensions revising final completion from December 10, 1992, to April 30, 1993.
- County/state/local postal users were still reviewing the documents and issuing continuous changes to the general contractor via the Postal Service.
- The general contractor had submitted a bona fide revised critical path method schedule requesting final completion date be revised to July 23, 1993.
- Subsequent changes to documents resulted in the general contractor posturing for a September 1, 1993, final completion date.
- It took an average of two weeks to resolve errors/discrepancies on monthly invoices after formal final submission, thus creating a periodic cash problem for the general contractor and subcontractors.
- The contracting officer had agreed to pay extended overhead once project duration was known, and an audit rate was established.
Is this a hopeless situation? It could be, but not in this case.

Management Approach

The only approach that would solve this serious dilemma was to load the Project Management Institute's nine building blocks of knowledge (i.e., framework, scope, quality, time, cost, risk, human resources, contract/procurement, and communication management) into a shotgun and fire in all directions.

The first order of business was to instill instant leadership and market the framework for the project's recovery corrective action plan. The framework took the shape of establishing management and project direction, esprit de corps, project momentum, and quality, safety, cost/time recovery; reducing bureaucracy, revising methods and means to suit contractor and working environment; and eliminating general contractor and subcontractors from subsidizing the project.

The second order of business was to clean our internal house and bring order to the field files and project control documents. The field files were reorganized. The executed contract, addenda, certificates of insurance, bonds, notice-to-proceed, pre-construction and job site meeting reports, bid documents, correspondence, daily reports, and so on were thoroughly reviewed.

A serious and frank "state-of-the-project" status meeting was held with the Postal Service. It was advised of the extreme at-risk exposure (100 percent!) and vulnerability to all types of claims. The United States Postal Service (USPS) was also advised that it was impossible to establish either a completion date or the USPS' overall financial obligation. Initially, the USPS was advised to either stop issuing changes or just issue a blank check to the general contractor and indicate the completion date desired. It was requested that the project manager be permitted to screen desired changes, issue critical changes only, and hold all other changes and release them to the contractor at a later appropriate time once project control was regained and responsibility to perform had been transferred back into the contractor's lap. It was also suggested that the USPS permit as much as possible of the decision-making process to be held at the field level. The USPS agreed.

The cause and general magnitude of the primary changes inflicted on the project fell into three basic categories: local USPS user program requirements and sign-off, state/county plan review requirements, and community appeasement.

To satisfy local USPS user program requirements, the following changes were executed:
- Eliminated grass field on west side of building and added a twenty-three-stall covered carrier loading dock and forty-six-stall carrier parking lot for $163,000
- Added a $146,000 fuel island
- Brought the building design up to USPS current program requirements for security-safety-fire-handicap, provided power-air for automated equipment, and met move-in requirements, all for an order of magnitude of $200,000.

Also, Maryland's Department of Environment issued valid plan review comments, subsequent to the issuance of notice-to-proceed, which required the adjacent property owner's storm-water retention pond to be enlarged and re-graded. The United States Postal Service (USPS) had previously obtained the adjacent property owner's approval to use the storm-water retention pond for USPS storm-water runoff. This was reflected on the bid documents. But the adjacent property owner would not grant the USPS permission to modify the pond. The USPS was forced to add three on-site below-ground infiltration structures and redesign/relocate all utility line approaches to the building for $358,000.

Finally, to obtain local community approval, the USPS added a $262,000 brick/concrete masonry unit/precast wall to screen the building from adjacent neighbors. The USPS also committed another $300,000 for future county infrastructure improvements in the neighborhood. These dollars were not contractually committed through the general contractor's contract.

Historically, it has been difficult for a project manager to have the Postal Service accept a building as scheduled for a variety of reasons. Having accomplished this task on two other recent postal projects, the author was aided in preestablishing mutual trust and patience for some unorthodox methods for achieving project recovery and mitigating dollar and time damages.

Trust had initially been established by taking the initiative and becoming fully knowledgeable in United States Postal Service (USPS) design, construction, acceptance, closeout guidelines and handicap, security, boiler, and safety regulations. Next, a relatively easy concept was initiated: all branches of the Postal Service were invited to the site. Surprisingly, this had not been done often in the past. Members of postal branches that held responsibility for final acceptance of the project were requested to visit the site at key strategic times during the construction phase, which afforded them an opportunity to establish and understand their concerns, requirements, and, more importantly, their buy-in for final acceptance.

As an example, the USPS tests and certifies all of its boilers and pressure vessels. Upon receipt of the approved boiler shop drawings from the architect/engineer, but prior to the contractor receiving them, the USPS boiler inspector was invited to the job site to review bid documents, shop drawings, and the physical progress to date. The boiler inspector generated comments, and a sit-down meeting with the contractor was held to discuss pertinent issues. In most cases, no dollars were involved and absolutely no time was lost. Items that had been identified by USPS boiler inspector review, if caught at substantial completion, would certainly have compromised the final completion date and generated serious dollar implications.

Similar positive impacts had been realized from key field meetings with the United States Postal Service inspection (security) service. Postal security requirements impact all facets of the project (e.g., door/frame gauges and system of construction, glass type, hardware type, exterior/interior sight lines, unsecured openings in the roof and exterior walls, fence construction, site lighting levels, and landscaping placement).

Meetings were held with the architect/engineering team, resulting in securing similar agreements. An example of a problem experienced by the architect/engineer was the large number of changes being processed by the architect/engineer team, created by the owner and field demands. This created unbearable pressure on the architect/engineer and field staff. The architect/engineer flooded the field staff with incomplete scope-of-work change packages. The architect/engineer would then reissue them (two to five revisions per package) on what appeared to be a three-day cycle. The contractor and subcontractors lost control of what drawings they were quoting or what, in fact, eventually ended up in the change order.

A similar meeting was held with the general contractor, but a relationship of trust and leadership had been quickly established between the general contractor and the project manager with the first step onto the job site on October 1, 1992. The general contractor had submitted a "request for information" for authorization to soft-cut the building's 200-foot by 240-foot slab-on-grade control joints. The request had already been denied, and the contractor was forced to place concrete in twenty-foot by twenty-foot sections. This method was labor intensive, consumed valuable calendar days, and extended the duration that the subgrade would be exposed and therefore vulnerable to adverse weather conditions. Observing firsthand that the contractor was laying out pour stops in a twenty-foot by twenty-foot pattern, the situation was reviewed, the architect/engineer overruled, and the contractor permitted to place slabs in forty-foot by 240-foot single-pour strips.

At the first official meeting with the general contractor the cards were laid on the table, and the discussion was honest and to the point. After a thorough review of documents and site and team players, the existing April 30, 1993, completion date was deemed attainable if control of the project could be re-established. The entire project team agreed that the established schedule was attainable through good management, by revising the methods used by the contractor, issuing partial or full notices-to-proceed prior to completing negotiations, modifying non-critical scope of work items, expediting owner processing of overdue changes, and permitting the contractor to bill for negotiated change orders not fully executed. The latter was allowed only if the invoice's total earned to date was less than the official contract amount.

In an effort to establish a cooperative atmosphere, there was no attempt made to squeeze every penny out of the contractor's quotations. Since time was of the essence, and the United States Postal Service (USPS) was subject to extended overhead claims, any savings accrued through constant protracted change order negotiations would be lost tenfold in extending the project duration and additional claims dollar exposure. The USPS was already in a defensive posture. This method was less confrontational and would establish an attitude that the USPS wanted a fair and reasonable quote up-front, had no hidden agendas, played no games, and was not mandated to reduce every quote by "X" percent.

The next step was to have the entire project team bring all the control systems up to date, improve their accuracy, and enforce a collective buy-in on their constructive value. Submittal, RFI, and change logs had not been maintained with accurate and current information and dates. To facilitate a project team attitude adjustment, all logs were discussed in detail and became attachments to the job site meeting reports. With responsible party turnaround times preestablished, everyone was held accountable for returning submittals, answering RFIs, or negotiating changes. It did not take long before the rank-and-file fell into place by eliminating themselves from the hot seat at each job site meeting.

The contractor, acting as a broker, required additional management oversight and guidance to help ensure that the cited project goals were reached; properly pressure the subcontractors to perform; identify and expedite closure on numerous scope of work loopholes not consummated during buy-out; and adjust the temperament of all team members. Additional concern was the ultrashort leash the general contractor held over the superintendent by overburdening and over-restricting the superintendent from being truly effective out in the field. To an uninformed eye, it would appear that the superintendent was acting more like a lead foreman, only managing one ball at a time. The superintendent would focus onsite and drop the building "ball," and vice versa. Active advertising of this problem created more field participation by the general contractor's president, resulting in resolving this issue to a manageable level.

An offer was made to support the cost of an assistant contractor project manager for a one- to three-month period. It became apparent that the contractor was getting overwhelmed with the volume of changes, changes upon changes, processing of quotes, and writing hundreds of subcontractor change orders. That in itself would cause a serious schedule slippage. Although the offer was declined, a proactive position was maintained and provided a cost-effective insurance policy against schedule slippage caused by administrative change orders.

Over the next four months, the goals that the initial management framework held for the project recovery corrective action plan were achieved. Scope of work and community, county, and state issues were resolved. The Postal Service readily observed that the quality of workmanship had improved greatly compared to a recently completed comparable nearby facility. Observing substantial progress between monthly site visits had recaptured project momentum and schedule attainment. Finally, positive United States Postal Service (USPS) feedback was generated by the periodic site visits by different project-accepting branches of the Postal Service.

During the period of our construction, the Washington metropolitan area was subjected to the worst all-encompassing weather that the area had seen in the last twenty-five years. Just during the month of March 1993, the site received seven inches of rainfall, and then there was the infamous blizzard of 1993. During the February/March time frame it became evident that the building's completion date was good, but the killer weather was beating us on site work. The project team was now looking at a site (and project) completion date of July 9, 1993. To facilitate project closeout and reduce exposure to extended overhead claims, the USPS and the contractor agreed to split the project's single final completion date into two completion dates; one for building and one for site. The USPS and the contractor agreed to use the building's final completion date to key-off for all contract-related issues (i.e., extended overhead calculations, the USPS assuming responsibility for building and related utility costs, reducing contractor's bond exposure, and releasing a substantial amount of the retention, which equaled 2.5 percent of the contract value, at any one time).

Results

By using the Project Management Institute's body of knowledge functional areas, all the cited objectives were achieved to everyone's expectations and satisfaction.

Framework. A clear, concise line of legitimate and referent authority was laid out; a viable corrective-action-plan was developed; measurable goals were established; project control tools were re-instituted; and a collective esprit de corps was instilled among the project team members. We focused on the "process" as an "offensive tool" to support the delivery of the product of the project.

Scope. The true critical scope of work and the appropriate construction methods and-means to accomplish program requirements were clearly established.

Quality. Established up-front that quality (and safety) would not be compromised under any circumstances. An instant casualty would have been the United States Postal Service (USPS) buy-in and support of a variable acceptance schedule. The quality of workmanship was substantially improved and readily evident to the USPS. The issuance and quality of drawing changes to the contractor was expedited.

Cost. The 50 percent over-budget ratio was frozen and controlled at that level. Turnaround time on invoices and change orders was expedited. Due to the substantially increased project momentum, wish list changes were identified and deleted to prevent the contractor from inadvertently executing these changes.

Schedule. The building was completed within two weeks of goal.

Risk. The USPS' at-risk exposure to extended overhead dollars, field costs associated with maintaining site an additional five months, material and wage rate increases, and further delay claims by subcontractors were substantially mitigated. Except for the extended overhead claim, no other claims were submitted by the general contractor or any of their subcontractors.

Human Resources. Under the circumstances, since it was not possible to change any project team personnel, the project manager had to perform as if coach and manager of a baseball team. The primary goal was to identify everyone's strengths and channel them in the appropriate directions. It was continuously necessary to educate or reeducate, encourage, reward, and admonish field and office crews.

Contract/Procurement. The change order process was revised from sketchy undocumented scope-of-work references to a very definitive descriptive scope, using the contractor's change-log control numbers. Basic document control principles were strictly enforced, whereby all documents were identified with the firm's letterhead, date, project reference, number of pages, and subject.

Communications. Communication was the cornerstone to the successful recovery of this project. A tremendous amount of trust was placed in the spoken word. A project cannot be built with paperwork alone; those resources were re-channeled to positive field contributions that facilitated the delivery of the project.

In short, the United States Postal Service (USPS) was able to extract itself from an untenable situation with a quality facility that met and exceeded their expectations.

As Phil Schreiner cited in a *Building, Design & Construction* editorial, "If the '80s were focused on salesmanship, the '90s are all about stewardship. Those CMs who can instill genuine confidence in their results-oriented capabilities will thrive. You must stress demonstrable control through procedures, processes and tools that can be identified and proven. Good intentions won't be good enough" (3).

Conclusion

The project and construction management profession has performed a disservice to its clients by encumbering a project's delivery process (crossing every "t" and dotting every "i" syndrome) to the detriment of the delivery of the product of the project. This not only holds true for the well-publicized project failures but also for the successfully delivered projects. Lack of strong and aggressive leadership, unnecessary defensive posturing, unwieldy and unnecessary paperwork, and the associated staff that accompanies this process inevitably lead to unsatisfactory performance.

It is our inherent responsibility as the construction project manager to maturely evaluate the project's scope and quality management requirements in order to ensure that all aspects of the project and its results fully meet the needs and expectations of the owner, user, architect/engineer, and construction community.

In addressing the issue of "process," this article reviewed how a trained project management professional used commonsense approaches to management, leadership, and communication. From this he gained an all new respect for the institution of project and construction management and the certification of key project management personnel as project management professionals (PMPs). Through these skills and knowledge, this PMP became the public agency's cost effective insurance policy in a project's successful total delivery.

According to Peter F. Drucker, in *The Effective Executive*, "Time is . . . a unique resource. Of the other major resources, money is actually quite plentiful . . . People, the third limiting resource, one can hire, though one can rarely hire enough good people. But one cannot rent, hire, buy, or otherwise obtain more time" (1). Time on this project was our number one enemy; the completion was not a goal, it had to be a reality.

Over the last twenty years, the construction management process has unfortunately been allowed to grow and mature as a defensive rather than as an offensive process. Using the process as an "offensive" tool pays immediate dividends by advertising that "we" are working together as a shared-risk team to the benefit of the project and each respective company's interests—a win-win situation. A byproduct of the offensive approach is the automatic elimination of the project's collective oversized staffing and administrative (paperwork) deadwood, to the benefit of the project. Non-critical activities that have no value or direct benefit in achieving or ensuring the successful delivery of the project are eliminated. All parties need to wrestle the defensive nature out of the process and manipulate it to function in an offensive role.

Process, according to the *Project Management Body of Knowledge (PMBOK Exposure Draft)* (4), is the set of activities by means of which an output (product of the project) is achieved. It is a formal approach to sorting through numerous and varied activities in order to identify the critical issues and provide contingencies for the difficulties that may arise. It is at this juncture that the project management profession has lost sight of the commonsense approach to the process and what the process supports—the project (2).

A Postal Point of View

The realization of the Anne Arundel and Severna Park, Maryland, projects were the result of a Postal Service consolidated ten-year effort to find suitable sites to resolve serious postal operational deficiencies in the subject area. The local political climate contributed to and escalated the detrimental project environment outlined in this article.

Our real estate personnel and local operational staff were continuously frustrated in finding suitable sites in politically correct locations that still met postal requirements. The sites that were eventually selected were in a remote location yet still within the postal operations envelope. The initiation of a project in this area was compounded by the fact that the county reacts quickly to any political pressure. We happened to bear the brunt of community frustration and anxiety. This situation was going on, in parallel, while community contacts were made, and informal reviews were proceeding with the county plan review officials.

Existing local traffic and sewer problems were exacerbated by our location, particularly at the Anne Arundel project site, and hence the road and sewer settlement, to the tune of $300,000. The other site changes were side issues (i.e., screen-wall and landscaping, and so on), due to the fact that the

Postal Service was caught up in the county's need to satisfy the community on greater non-project-oriented issues.

If we had pursued a normal course of business for project planning and approval prior to our start date, the Postal Service would have brought on the wrath of the community and very likely would not have built the two buildings. By attempting a low-profile project scenario with county officials, we avoided an early project kill but brought on a lot of unreasonable project criteria demands from the community leaders and added cost. The flip side, however, is that the Postal Service will be operating where we are obviously needed and considerably sooner than if we had followed a routine approach.

Politics make strange the most innocent of situations. Given the history, climate, and other factors, the path chosen was a conscious and correct decision by our organization. The risk far outweighed the alternatives and necessitated the actions for taking on these projects.

References

1. Drucker, P.F. 1990. *Timeline User Manual,* Preface: V. Quotation, Symantec Corporation.

2. Mathieson, M.O. 1991. "Revolutionizing the Concept of 'Process' in Working with and Facilitating the Project Delivery 'Product' to the Benefit of all Public Agencies." Project Management Institute's Annual Seminar/Symposium, Dallas, Texas.

3. Schreiner P. 1992. "Start Now to Develop Your Post-Recession Action Plans." *Building, Design & Construction* (October): Editorial, 5.

4. Project Management Institute. 1994. *Project Management Body of Knowledge (PMBOK Exposure Draft).* Upper Darby, PA: Project Management Institute: 11.

Successful Utility Project Management from Lessons Learned

Project Management Journal XXI:3 (September 1990)

Introduction

The management value of reviewing project histories is not in learning about people, places, and things but in learning the project management lessons taught by previous business experiences. Large, multiyear utility and government energy programs present a number of management challenges. Within this family of projects on state, municipal, and commercial utility plants and federal energy facilities, some successes have occurred, as well as numerous cases of failures, large cost overruns, schedule slippages, and performance compromises. Therefore, to enhance the project management processes for new energy and waste projects, we can look to previous utility industry and government energy projects for applicable lessons learned.

Many companies, agencies, and project managers are beginning to take advantage of these "lessons learned" in developing their project organizations and selecting their project management tools. Utility commissions and regulatory agencies are also beginning to realize the economic value of applying lessons learned and may require that lessons learned be incorporated into the management strategy for each new energy project. However, a review of many current project organizational structures and project control methodologies raises concerns that the mistakes of past projects may in fact be repeated on many utility projects because the past lessons learned are not being heeded.

Project management experience information has been extracted and summarized from reviews of technical literature, utility assessment experience, Institute of Nuclear Power Operations construction assessment experience, Atomic Industrial Forum reports, Nuclear Regulatory Commission inspections results, American Nuclear Society reviews, the Ford Amendment study, and the professional experience of senior project personnel. Examination of this large body of historical data on past projects provides clear bases for explaining the various successes and failures. A study of those experiences also provides lessons learned and key insights into the factors leading to project success. These major lessons learned and success factors related to the project management process are described in the following paragraphs and can be used to guide the structuring and development of a project management strategy to avoid repeating costly errors.

Project Management Lessons Learned

A number of the project management lessons learned establish requirements that are fundamental to the success and effectiveness of whatever project management and organizational approach is adopted. The following are six of the major lessons learned.

Apply Centralized Project Management

Several significant trends have developed in the utility industry and the government over the past twenty years. These trends reflect responses to such severe pressures as unfavorable economic factors, the inflationary spiral, the large magnitude and long duration of construction projects, bureaucratic growth, increased and unpredictable regulatory and environmental requirements, and the too often mediocre performance of the organizations that utilities and government have historically looked to for managing major projects.

One of the more identifiable trends has been the swing toward strong, formalized central project management, including either self-performed construction or construction management. Today's utility project manager must coordinate and integrate large aggregates of human and non-human resources. Often, most of these personnel resources are outside the control of traditional management patterns, leading to matrix management relationships that cut across interior organizational flows of authority and responsibility and radiate outside to autonomous organizations. Adopting centralized project management provides the managerial unity required to achieve specific project goals within a functional-type organizational structure and with minimal disturbance to the organization's other ongoing business.

Two other possible management alternatives have been attempted in the utility industry, but with little success. These alternatives are:
- The project activities remain functionally separated. This choice has not been effective because the functional managers are provincial by nature, and the overall support of the project, as well as the responsibility for long-range planning, has characteristically been inadequately coordinated.
- A senior executive of the organization performs the project integration. This has not worked either because the senior executive's time is usually diluted by the necessity of providing support to other projects or duties.

Traditional utility management, with its functional type of organization, cannot realistically be counted upon to provide the management and involvement required in a large construction project. On the other hand, project management has no organizational or functional constraints or politics and can provide the management involvement required to effect the organizational changes necessary for managing complex activities such as power plant construction. Therefore, each individual utility owner can mold and develop his own individual project management organization to satisfy the unique existing functional organizational capabilities and constraints.

Use Strong Project Management

A project management structure may be defined as being comprised of individuals who are appointed to integrate internal and external organizational and functional elements in order to complete a project on time, within budget, and to the utility owner's satisfaction. The project management organization must be an integrator of widely diverse disciplines. It must balance the relative factors of engineering, construction, schedule, cost, and human resources. The supporting functional organizations should provide the basic foundation upon which to carry out project-oriented activities. The project organization must perform all of the management functions with heavy emphasis placed on functional coordination or synchronizing activities, with respect to time, cost, and location.

Certain features that have contributed to project success set apart the strong matrix project management organization from the traditional, or function-oriented, organizations. These are:
- The project manager must be both strong and dedicated only to the project.
- One central point for timely decision-making must be established, involving diverse interests in the organization, with limited organizational reporting levels.
- Project management must be directly, and by charter, involved in managing the participation of organizations and agencies normally outside its direct control. It must pull together such diverse activities as site feasibility studies and acquisitions, obtaining licenses and permits, engineering, construction management, construction, and plant start-up and operation. All of these activities must be time-phased over the life of the project, and all require coordinated planning, scheduling, and control.
- The project organization's authority and responsibility must cut across functional and organizational lines. Natural organizational conflicts must be brought into the open and dealt with by the project management organization.
- The project organization must determine the "when" and "what" of the project, thus providing a focal point for project activities. The functional managers, in supporting many projects, must determine how and where the support will be given.

- The project organization's life must be finite. After the project is complete, the personnel directly supporting the project should be assigned to other activities.
- Because the project organization contains a high proportion of professional personnel, managerial techniques different from the simple superior/subordinate relationship must be developed. The work situation for project personnel is fluid, and project team members tend to feel uncomfortable because they have little direct authority. Therefore, in the project organization, increased motivation, persuasion, and human relations must augment the normal functions of management.

Assign a Single Project Manager Authority

There must be only one person in charge. The project manager must have the necessary managerial authority to ensure responsiveness to her requirements within the parent organization and must be accepted as the authoritative agent of the utility organization in dealing with outside organizations. The project manager must have sufficient authority and capability to control the allocation and expenditure of funds and human resources and should actively lead budget and schedule deliberations. The project manager must be the responsible and single formal contact with the various outside agencies for the project. Major features of this position include:

- The project manager must be a senior-level macro-manager who can also manage up the organizational interfaces.
- For major projects, the project manager must have a strong deputy project manager who can manage down the project organization.
- All participants must understand the project manager's responsibility and authority.
- The project manager must manage cost and schedule performance against a predefined baseline.
- All major technical, cost, schedule, or performance decisions must be made with the project manager's participation.
- The project manager, on complex regulated projects with state-of-the-art technology, must manage relatively independent technical and quality assurance personnel.
- The project manager must have sufficient managerial and signature authority to discharge responsibilities. However, project managers seldom have organizational authority commensurate with their overall project responsibility and must supplement that lack of authority with diplomacy, persuasion, team building, logical decisions, integrity, and so on.

Enlist Senior Management Support

Successful projects show that senior utility management must demonstrate support for strong central project management and the single project manager authority. There must also be organizational commitment by all project participants to successful project completion if the project objectives are to be reached on time and within budget.

Use a Controlled Acquisition Procurement Process

On major commercial projects, severe acquisition problems have resulted from interface mismatches among requirement specifications, regulatory requirements, engineering, procurement, construction, operations/maintenance, architect/engineers, construction management, and owners (licensees). Government nuclear plant acquisitions have suffered from the same problems as commercial plants. In addition, state and municipal government plants built to meet federal regulatory licensing requirements have incurred additional cost and schedule impacts because of contracting methods and contract administration that were constrained by state laws and regulations not adequate for today's large projects. This situation, coupled with inadequate owner/operator involvement in project procurement management and implementation, created a negative impact on project execution and completion.

A primary reason for these project problems is the failure to adequately develop and understand the full scope of the project acquisition strategy (the "plan for the plan") and the subsequent failure to prepare and issue (at the start of the project) the key documents implementing that strategy. The primary objective of the acquisition strategy and process is to provide a comprehensive guide for all actions involved in the total acquisition cycle for the project. Key elements of any successful acquisition include the following.

A complete and comprehensive acquisition strategy and plan are developed and documented. The strategy effectively covers technical, business, scope, schedule, economic, management, organizational, quality, and public issues. The plan is issued prior to performance of any technical work or prior to placing any contract, other than small-scope, specific specialty services contracts.

Development and operation of a procurement planning and control process that integrates procurement with the latest project plan and schedule to avoid delivery-related project work delays, thereby reducing and controlling otherwise unmanageable cost increases; assigns proper priority to elements of front-end engineering to avoid downstream procurement delays and costly excess design margins; and uses a procurement control system that provides reporting to senior management is necessary.

Firm control of the procurement process is established. The procurement process is placed under the direction of the project office and supports the project plan and schedule. The process passes along, with each initial project procurement contract or initial change order that adds the project work to an existing contract, all project requirements, top-level project documents, and a project management structure along with a definitive scope of work, including roles, responsibilities, and authorities.

The project management organization and structure includes and uses a strong centralized acquisition management process. All organizational interfaces, as well as a timely decision process, are carefully planned and executed to support implementation of uniform procurement methods and procedures. The project office uses and controls the contract administration process.

Employ Project-Wide Management Systems and Controls

Experience shows that the dollar magnitude, scope, and inherent complexities of major utility projects dictate the need for using a formally structured project management system. The need for a project management system is also dictated by uncertainties that arise because of a lack of familiarity or precedent on how the project should be managed to successfully achieve its objectives. This is especially true in the areas of cost and schedules. Without precise guidance and direction as to what is specifically expected, personnel at the lower and middle echelons continually make value judgments beyond their expertise. Top-level management executives are justifiably troubled by greater than usual feelings of uncertainty and, therefore, are concerned about the realism of initial as well as interim cost estimates, cash flow (funding) projections, time commitments, schedules, and so on.

Historically, a formally structured project management system implies a measure of totality; that is, it includes the entire collection of organization, planning and control tools, and associated management and information systems needed to manage a complex, one-time task. The project management system forces a logical approach to management and facilitates decision-making and thus enables project management to readily handle increased responsibilities. From a utility owner's perspective, the project management system provides for the monitoring of project planning and execution, ensures evaluation of real project progress, and supports timely resolution of problems in relation to specific milestones.

On successful projects, these systems can be characterized as follows:
- Project documentation is developed that clearly establishes roles, responsibilities, and authorities.
- A clear definition of the work effort is provided through a complete work breakdown structure.
- A well-defined, traceable baseline for the costs, schedule, and scope is established at the beginning of the project and carefully maintained throughout the life of the project to ensure complete tracing ability of any changes.
- The process produces an integrated network schedule, including milestones; provides front-end loading of engineering; uses a budget apportioned against the schedule; provides an overall plan for performance and sufficient selective reporting to stay aware of progress; and requires periodic management review to ascertain project status.

- A configuration management process is established, including formalized and documented change management. This process places special emphasis on preliminary and critical design reviews for excess margins, documentation, maintainability, constructability, produceability, interfaces, and so forth. Change management anticipates the special needs of start-up and test without losing control.
- A strong corrective action process is implemented across the project.
- Information systems required for operations, such as records management, document control, and commitment management, are developed and used during design and construction by all participants.

Factors Affecting Project Success

Assembling, documenting, and applying those successful project management lessons learned is not enough, in itself, to ensure project success. A study of the background of the lessons learned shows that the root causes for problems or failures of a project can seldom be explained by technological issues. In fact, the review of the technical and management literature and of the summary of results prepared from many management assessments and quality assurance assessments for the commercial utility industry shows that the major cause of project failures is usually sociological.

The sociological issues include: dysfunctional organizational cultures, destructive politics, unqualified/inadequate staffing, lack of personnel motivation, high personnel turnover, poor vertical and horizontal communications, inappropriate or inadequate organizational structures, inadequate training, inexperienced management, and poor public relations.

These sociological issues are the root cause of the poor project/business management processes responsible for most project problems. For example, owners, due to inexperience, have failed to implement strong project management at the beginning of the project and prior to placement of any key contract. The sociological issues are then reflected in business and project management problems in the acquisition, design, procurement, development, construction, test, and operation of a facility. The business and management problems within the project then result in:

- Incomplete project objectives and acquisition strategies
- Ineffective project management and lack of integrated planning and control
- Ineffective communication and integration of project activities
- Inappropriate contracting methods and poor contract administration
- Lack of design control and inadequate configuration management and change control
- Untimely, incomplete, and inadequate procedures and lack of procedural compliance

- Poor control of documents and information and inadequate records management
- Non-certifiable quality assurance program or non-verifiable quality assurance program activities.

Therefore, projects that succeed generally do not do so because they use, or fail to use, any particular advanced technology. Their success can be explained by their use of more effective ways of:
- Developing a complete acquisition strategy
- Planning the work and contracting the tasks
- Completing designs prior to construction
- Using and controlling information
- Managing the project
- Utilizing organizational development processes, such as team building, management of change, and positive reinforcement, to focus the diverse project talent on project objectives
- Modifying the work place and organizational culture in response to changing project needs
- Administering the contracts
- Establishing public and institutional interactions.

In addition, whether a project will succeed, fail, or have major problems is usually determined early in the life of the project. Consequently, it is particularly important in the initial phase of the project to focus on those management factors that lead to project success. The review of project management lessons learned provided eight sets of those factors influencing project success, which are summarized in the Ishikawa Diagram provided in Figure 1.

Conclusion

The project management lessons learned and the success factors from utility and government energy projects, based upon a review of the literature, management assessments, and the professional experience of senior personnel, show that:
- Success of most major projects depends significantly on the strength of the project organization.
- Project infrastructure and top-level project documents need to be established early in the project life cycle.
- Project success is highly dependent on the project management actions taken during the initial phases of the effort.
- Reviewing and using applicable lessons learned can contribute to the successful management of the project.
- Project failure is seldom due to technical problems; rather, the underlying reasons for failure tend to be the result of sociological problems related to culture, politics, organization, staff qualifications, or management. These

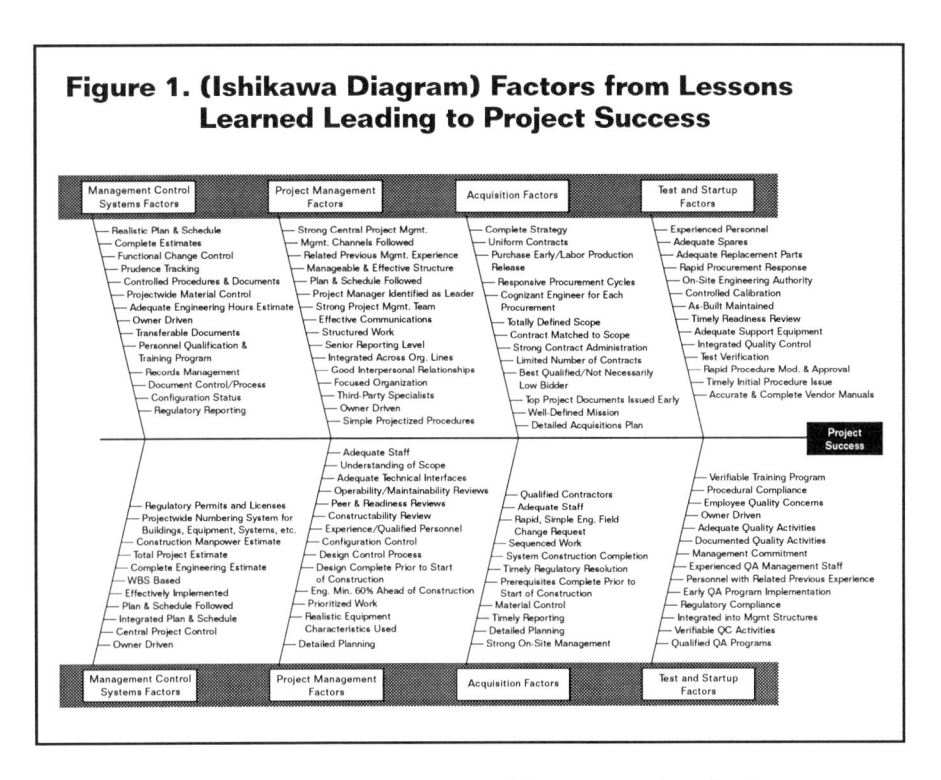

Figure 1. (Ishikawa Diagram) Factors from Lessons Learned Leading to Project Success

Management Control Systems Factors	Project Management Factors	Acquisition Factors	Test and Startup Factors
Realistic Plan & Schedule Complete Estimates Functional Change Control Prudence Tracking Controlled Procedures & Documents Projectwide Material Control Adequate Engineering Hours Estimate Owner Driven Transferable Documents Personnel Qualification & Training Program Records Management Document Control/Process Configuration Status Regulatory Reporting	Strong Central Project Mgmt. Mgmt. Channels Followed Related Previous Mgmt. Experience Manageable & Effective Structure Plan & Schedule Followed Project Manager Identified as Leader Strong Project Mgmt. Team Effective Communications Structured Work Senior Reporting Level Integrated Across Org. Lines Good Interpersonal Relationships Focused Organization Third-Party Specialists Owner Driven Simple Projectized Procedures	Complete Strategy Uniform Contracts Purchase Early/Labor Production Release Responsive Procurement Cycles Cognizant Engineer for Each Procurement Totally Defined Scope Contract Matched to Scope Strong Contract Administration Limited Number of Contracts Best Qualified/Not Necessarily Low Bidder Top Project Documents Issued Early Well-Defined Mission Detailed Acquisitions Plan	Experienced Personnel Adequate Spares Adequate Replacement Parts Rapid Procurement Response On-Site Engineering Authority Controlled Calibration As-Built Maintained Timely Readiness Review Adequate Support Equipment Integrated Quality Control Test Verification Rapid Procedure Mod. & Approval Timely Initial Procedure Issue Accurate & Complete Vendor Manuals

→ **Project Success**

Management Control Systems Factors	Project Management Factors	Acquisition Factors	Test and Startup Factors
Regulatory Permits and Licenses Projectwide Numbering System for Buildings, Equipment, Systems, etc. Construction Manpower Estimated Total Project Estimate Complete Engineering Estimate WBS Based Effectively Implemented Plan & Schedule Followed Integrated Plan & Schedule Central Project Control Owner Driven	Adequate Staff Understanding of Scope Adequate Technical Interfaces Operability/Maintainability Reviews Peer & Readiness Reviews Constructability Review Experience/Qualified Personnel Configuration Control Design Control Process Design Complete Prior to Start of Construction Prioritized Work Realistic Equipment Characteristics Used Detailed Planning	Qualified Contractors Adequate Staff Rapid, Simple Eng. Field Change Request Sequenced Work System Construction Completion Timely Regulatory Resolution Prerequisites Complete Prior to Start of Construction Material Control Timely Reporting Detailed Planning Strong On-Site Management	Verifiable Training Program Procedural Compliance Employee Quality Concerns Owner Driven Adequate Quality Activities Documented Quality Activities Management Commitment Experienced QA Management Staff Personnel with Related Previous Experience Early QA Program Implementation Regulatory Compliance Integrated into Mgmt Structures Verifiable QC Activities Qualified QA Programs

sociological issues are the root cause of the poor project/business management processes that are, in turn, responsible for or generate most project problems.

- Most project problems are created early in the project life by failing to consider the sociological and related process issues. Therefore, the project manager fails (or is not allowed) to address the root causes for project difficulties, often resulting in stop work orders, as a minimum, or, in extreme cases, project cancellations.

In addressing the root causes for the problems encountered in major utility and government energy projects, specific steps must be taken to increase the likelihood of project success. The sociological issues are most easily addressed by establishing a strong centralized project management organization and process located at the project site. The organizational components—including the owner/operator and the owner/operator's agent—must have clearly established roles, responsibilities, and authorities. This project organization can then effectively and efficiently complete the project strategy, which provides the guidance necessary to adequately address other root causes for project failure.

In supporting a strong project management system, utility project managers are urged to pay particular attention to the planning aspects of the project. This includes preparation of various plans (such as a project plan, project management plan, system engineering management plan, quality assurance plan, and so on), which provide the basis for the project strategy. It is essential that the project management processes—including project baseline management, work breakdown structuring, configuration management, quality assurance, and project reporting requirements—be specified clearly and early for incorporation into contractual documents.

Utility managers need to review and understand the lessons learned on their own past projects and act upon the success factors identified in Figure 1. By giving proper and timely attention to those factors leading to project success, utility managers can help ensure success of their future projects. The time and effort invested in thoroughly and systematically examining all management, regulatory, commercial, legal, and technical lessons learned as they relate to a project will yield insurance for successful project completion and is an investment that history shows will also yield large early monetary returns.

Staff Responsibilities of the Project Manager

The project manager is responsible for motivating herself and the staff "team" to complete a given project on time and within budget. This individual needs to have and show a rekindling of spirit and a rededication to the profession of construction project management.

As the project manager so very well knows, the responsibilities for the completion of any project are many, indeed, and considered by novices as awesome. For the benefit of those who may not be appreciative or cognizant of the heavy demands on a manager, we are listing below single thoughts that would apply to one's duties, in order that they may be incorporated into one's mind in one sitting:

Project Manager's Responsibilities

1. Plan, schedule, and control.
2. Manage people (prime mission).
3. Contact, interview, hire, supervise, coordinate, evaluate, train, and give guidance to staff.
4. Use the purpose and broad company objectives, goals, and standards; formulate in greater detail "goals" and standards for your specific project responsibility.
5. Allow time to "listen to people problems."
6. Develop detailed job descriptions and people responsibilities.
7. Negotiate "time"—and liquidated damages.
8. Promote good public relations.
9. Review manpower requirements of critical path method schedule.
10. Update equipment requirements.
11. Code purchases.
12. Coordinate subcontractors.
13. Plan overtime critical path method schedule activities.
14. Direct staff members.
15. Plan and monitor special critical path method activities on the critical path.
16. Expedite completion by weighing new ideas.
17. See that all personnel are familiar with letters to and from the architect/engineer.

18. Inform staff of change order status.
19. Hold daily "planning" meetings with staff.
20. Know safety requirements and follow up with staff.
21. Devise systematic follow-up system.
22. Submit monthly progress reports to management.
23. Review outstanding contracts not finalized.
24. Expedite mock-ups, submittals, and samples.
25. Hold weekly subcontractors meetings.
25. Control "labor" cost.
26. Approve engineering field designs.
27. Obtain approval of monthly billings.
28. Manage back-charge data.
29. Supervise office manager and procedures.
30. Forecast material needs.
31. Manage "updating" of critical path method schedule.
32. Review weekly payroll.
33. Approve subcontractors' monthly billings.
34. Maintain proper relations with architect/engineer and owner.
35. Critique record-keeping program.
36. Analyze critical path method narrative report.
37. Evaluate the daily use of critical path method by "team" members.
38. Document "delays" and time impact analysis.

General Superintendent's Responsibilities

1. Know all specifications 100 percent.
2. Know all "plans" and plan requirements.
3. Study approved shop drawings.
4. Critique critical path method—quantify, manpower and activity durations.
5. Project and obtain adequate "manpower."
6. Supervise job superintendents.
7. Coordinate subcontractors—plan and follow up.
8. Plan concrete forming and pours.
9. Follow up on rebar requirements.
10. Review "labor" cost and crew sizes.
11. Security—supervise guards.
12. Quality control of concrete—update daily.
13. Be familiar with letters to and from architect/engineer.
14. Review letters to and from subcontractors.
15. Plan all phases and monthly reports of equipment.
16. Plan ahead—all critical path method activities.
17. Know revisions by letter or otherwise.

18. Forecast materials needs.
19. Hold "daily" planning meeting.
20. Attend weekly safety meetings.
21. Plan "winter" concrete and form protection.
22. Know architect/engineer requirements.
23. Complete mockups for architect's approval.
24. Review scaffolding and critique same.
25. Investigate equipment for special use.
26. Hold weekly rebar meetings.
27. Know change order status and subcontractors involved.
28. Educate on first aid.
29. Code invoices.
30. Follow-up with architect/owner representative.
31. Organize weekly "scheduling" meeting.
32. Attend staff meetings.
33. Record activities by node numbers on daily reports.

Office Engineer's Responsibilities

1. Expedite, log, and follow-up on all submittals.
2. Design scaffolding, shoring, and forming.
3. Keep "as built" drawings up to date.
4. Know critical path method schedule—study all activities.
5. Record pictures and movies—job progress.
6. Know architect/engineer requirements.
7. Review and critique specifications for errors and omissions.
8. Coordinate equipment by owner.
9. Attend staff meetings.

Quality Control Engineer's Responsibilities

1. Critique mechanical and electrical submittals.
2. Coordinate all concrete tests.
3. Review, submit, and file all test reports.
4. Coordinate mechanical tests and inspections.
5. Make log of specified tests required.
6. Prepare preliminary punch list.
7. Record pile-driving data.
8. Monitor water table data.
9. Gather project closeout data for owner.
10. Attend staff meetings.

Engineer's Responsibilities: Change Orders and Back-Charges

1. Work up and obtain approval of all change orders including cost and time.
2. Record and submit back-charges.
3. Make cost studies as directed.
4. Review critical path method schedule as directed.
5. Study overtime requirements.
6. Estimate quantities and manpower as directed.
7. Review labor costs.
8. Attend staff meetings.

Engineer's Responsibilities: Scheduling and Labor Costs

1. Prepare project critical path method schedule and distribute sorts to proper team members.
2. Monitor critical path method schedule.
3. Provide weekly report of critical path method schedule for superintendents and project manager.
4. Review critical path method "manpower" requirements.
5. Provide daily reports on critical path method as directed.
6. Make "fragnets" of critical path method as directed.
7. Make milestone critical path method schedule.
8. Make detail bar charts as directed.
9. Monitor weekly labor units.
10. Critique labor cost.
11. Record daily starts percent complete and completion dates of every critical path method activity.
12. Write monthly narrative report.
13. File critical path method schedule sorts.
14. Assign responsibility codes to critical path method activities.
15. Educate staff in the daily use of critical path method.
16. Evaluate critical path method schedule use by team members.
17. Monitor submittal schedule.
18. Critique delivery schedule.
19. Study all critical path method schedule sorts.
20. Post critical path method schedule at site.
21. Record all concurrent and other delays.
22. Provide monthly updates.
23. Define critical path method input requirements.
24. Attend staff meetings.

Office Manager Responsibilities

1. Organize office management procedures.
2. Supervise all secretaries except project manager's secretary.
3. Supervise material receiving clerk.
4. Manage payroll personnel.
5. Coordinate purchase orders.
6. File accident reports.
7. Provide payroll checks.
8. Manage petty cash account.
9. Record materials receiving reports.
10. Complete and file daily reports.
11. Organize records of documentation.
12. Maintain file of all correspondence.
13. Manage records of change orders.
14. Keep file of critical path method schedule documents.
15. Attend staff meetings.

Expeditor's Responsibilities

1. Develop daily log of materials requirements.
2. Organize follow-up system.
3. Review submittal log and materials needed.
4. Expedite subcontractors as directed.
5. Fill out "materials forecast" report weekly.
6. Visit suppliers as directed.
7. Be involved in record of job pictures.
8. Know critical path method schedule.
9. Project next month's schedule of materials.
10. Attend staff meetings.

The Great Juggling Act

Some project managers may work for owners, architects, or general contractors. No matter which role you play, you must know similar management techniques in order to be a contributing construction team member.

Project managers gather information on design and construction to provide the owner, architect, and contractor with many useful guidelines so that they can successfully initiate and complete a project within the allocated funds and time estimates. Management of any project can be made easier for the project manager if he takes complete advantage of organized management.

The term, "project manager," is used to describe many functions, but, for our purposes, she does exactly what the word says: manages the project. Her prime function is to see that the project gets done on time and within the budget. Project management might be described as the judicious allocation and efficient usage of resources to achieve a desired end. Astute project management requires at least as much art as science and as much human engineering as organizational management abilities.

Guidelines and Project Management

Professional project management guidelines include, but are not limited to, the following:
1. Review of design criteria on day one
2. Critique of budget parameters and cost estimates
3. Plan, schedule, and control; use of critical path method; define game plan
4. Review of designs versus cost control; and evaluate time
5. In-depth review of plans and specifications
6. Administration of contract bids and negotiation
7. Project inspection and quality control
8. Project payments and "S" curve projections
9. Actual construction management of projects (coordination)
10. Completion checklist and project closeout
11. Instruction and education of people; staff responsibilities
12. Definition of the project game plan and work it.

In cases when the project manager also is responsible for the engineering or architectural design, he, of course, will be wearing two hats. When this happens, he must strive to maintain absolute objectivity. One of the advantages of having a project manager who is not a member of the design team is his ability to function as an objective reviewer of the design. He also may function as an arbiter when the design is questioned or must be modified because it does not meet the established criteria or allow construction within the budget and time.

Review of Decision Criteria
The astute project manager has to find out from those who are supposed to know exactly what they really want. She should be sure that those involved in engineering, operations, traffic safety, insurance, and others who may design requirements are given an opportunity to have their input at all times.

Budget Parameters and Cost
The term "budget parameters" means nothing more than establishing guidelines for how much is to be spent for the project. These parameters let everyone involved know how much money is available for each part of the project.

Detailed checklists, such as those published by The Construction Specification Institute, give a good outline of divisions to cover in cost. Cost control is a daily job and responsibility of the project manager, and he should be involved in all cost decisions.

Every item of cost should be classified and given a cost code in the estimate and also coded to the activities on the critical path method schedule. The estimator then prepares his "quantity survey," coordinated with his cost code list. Later, when purchased, the cost code is used on all purchase orders and invoices received by the project manager. Also the original cost code system serves as a checklist for the estimator. Once one has set up the cost code, one has begun a systematic organization.

Project Manager's Critique Quantities versus Durations for Critical Path Method

Construction Estimates
The "estimate" comprises input from all team members and other cost data available to the project manager. The current working estimate is a report showing what the project budget is, what has been spent against the budget, and what remains to spend. The estimate is kept up to date by modifying it regularly with each change order and each purchase order or contract that the project manager initiates. Each updated estimate must include a contingency.

Planning, Scheduling, and Control
The overall schedule for the project must take into consideration the time required for planning, designing, and construction of the project. In preparing the original master schedule, after the preliminary schedule, the

punctilious project manager should keep in mind that this is not a detailed construction schedule for the total project. The schedule also outlines the project manager's game plan.

For large projects, the master schedule may consist of a complex critical path method network diagram to be prepared with the assistance of a consultant. Such a network should show activity responsibilities, cost, manpower, durations, logic and sequence, restraints, and interrelationships for decision-making of all those involved in the project.

The master schedule should also have fragnets prepared for each phase of the design process to help control the flow of information between various engineering disciplines and those involved in reviewing and expediting the work. Do not forget the specification writer; she too may be on the critical path.

The construction schedule serves the project manager as the yardstick against which he can measure progress. It lets him know if the project is on time and, if not, what is lagging behind. In the event the project falls behind, the project manager should determine whether the delays are caused by lack of management information, manpower, materials, or lack of action on his part or that of the design team or owner. Daily record actual critical path method dates. The critical path method schedule shows the duration of each activity, manpower requirements, start dates, sequence and logic, and "float" time. The activities on the critical path must be completed on time or the project will be delayed.

The project manager must daily monitor each and every activity on the schedule, and plan ahead for the next month's work. Each subcontractor, the architect/engineer, the owner, and the contractor must be informed of the schedule in writing at timely meetings. The monthly update evaluates the project status.

Time documentation must be a daily record of "actual" critical path method schedule activities start and completion dates. The risk analysis of not having good documentation leads to a time enigma.

Design versus Cost Control

As design goes through various steps from schematics to final drawings, the project manager should be sure that as each phase is completed, the design criteria are being adhered to in detail. It is up to the project manager to move the project by seeing that information and decisions flow to completion.

An important part of the review procedure is to see whether the limits established by the project budget parameters are in line. New estimates should be made at each design stage, review, or phase. In the event the review shows a higher budget cost, the project manager should determine why and take the necessary steps either to reduce cost or get approval for budget increases.

Coordination of plans and specifications are a must for cost control so that both say the same. The specification writer must be involved in cost control when she is writing the project specifications.

Project Inspection and Quality Control

Unless the project manager is technically competent and experienced in detailed inspection of construction projects, it is best for him to leave technical inspection of the work to the architect or engineer who designs it. As the project nears completion, it is common practice during the project closeout phase to prepare a "punch list," a list of items requiring correction by the contractor. The architect and the project manager must make a joint inspection of the project before final acceptance. Quality control is the responsibility of the project team members.

Project Manager Critique Submittals

Contractor's Project Manager

Today's construction project manager depends on people to function with action, follow up on new processes, excel in performance, study new methods, educate personnel in updated systems, and establish profit-motivated procedures. The astute project manager must keep up to date on all construction functions. Do not impede progress!

An effective project manager needs to be involved in seminars to keep up with the times, know the latest computer software packages that may help in the job, and be willing to take the time to read industry publications and journals to keep abreast of current trends. Project managers are expected to project an enthusiastic attitude to have an integrated, systematized, compatible, and balanced organizational management team. To function thoroughly all team members need to have a daily programmed approach to organize plans and use individual efforts and abilities 100 percent.

Building an astute construction organization must take into consideration the talents, experience, abilities, and versatility of key personnel. Versatility includes the ability to do more than one job. After you have mastered one skill, you learn another.

Time Equals Money

The professional project manager needs to be as versatile as a businessman, lawyer, financier, management specialist, labor relations expert, schedule engineer, and production person. Good business methods guide the overall functions of construction by providing accurate business records, company ground rules, financial plans, performance measurement indexes, profit improvement systems, and quality daily reports.

To function as a project manager in today's competitive business world, each of us needs updated planning, scheduling, and control of projects. For years we functioned with projects controlled by bar charts. Today, we must incorporate better controls of time with schedules, such as the critical path method as a functional management tool to keep project completions on time.

Project safety also is a concern for all contractors, owners, and architects. In-house seminars on project safety are needed for all team members.

Construction Law and the Project Manager

Construction law is becoming a bigger issue for the project manager. In the event of litigation, the attorneys will depend on complete records for either defense or prosecution of a claim. This documentation must include updated schedules, expert witnesses, knowledge of specifications, weather records, warranty responsibilities, acceleration cost, time impact studies, concurrent delays, float time, record of labor inefficiencies, analysis of delays, record of disruptions and interference, effect of economic duress on overall operations, change conditions during construction, early completion rights, awareness of schedule milestones, and people involvement in daily activities of the project.

Project Management Organization

Standard practice procedures should be set forth in detail showing exactly how each function (company manual) is to be performed and, most importantly, by whom. Organization is simply planned direction. It is a procedure or system, a planned schedule of events or activities, a list of things to do, one after the other, that gets something done in the shortest possible time with the least amount of waste, and, in turn, produces an adequate profit.

Policies and objectives stated in the company manual should be reviewed by the project manager since it lists each person's responsibilities, team functions, and the geographic location of projects. The prudent project manager must understand good cost control methods and maintain good relations with the owner, architect, engineer, subcontractors, and vendors. She should have basic information on what has been done and how, but she must also be imaginative (think) and flexible in her operations so she can adjust to new situations when they appear.

One of management's big problems is the development and advancement of young people. Not only must the project manager know his job, but he must also be able and willing to take the time to teach it to others. Delegation is a key requirement of good project management, to give counsel to and create a loyal organization that will work as a team. Project management requires creative management on the job daily. The dynamic project manager must provide and prepare the construction schedule. He must arrange for and direct the services of specialists. He must provide for and superintend the handling of deliveries of materials and equipment. Also, he checks storage, protection, preparations, and placement of materials and equipment. He keeps people productive.

Management Guidelines for Project Managers

The professional construction project manager can be a qualified general contractor who performs management under a professional services contract with the owner. Working with other team members, the manager guides the project from design to completion. She will provide the team with information and recommendations on construction technology and economics, and she needs to propose construction alternatives to be studied and evaluated by the team during the planning phase. She also will accurately predict the effects of these alternatives on the project's cost and schedule.

Analyze Game Plan

Once the project's budget and schedule have been established, the project manager will monitor the subsequent development of the project to ensure that those targets are not exceeded without the knowledge and concurrence of the owner. He will manage the procurement efforts, coordinate the work of subcontractors, assure conformance to design requirements, provide current cost and progress information as the work proceeds, and perform other construction-related services as required by the owner.

Professional Project Management

Essentials for success of a professional construction project manager include:

- Thoroughly analyzing a job before bidding and taking into consideration the special conditions of the project; the bid should include a profit
- Carefully estimating, basing the bid on previous experience and cost records; have systems of checking in-house work and subcontractors involved
- Closely supervising operations by qualified personnel; having good cost control of labor and materials
- Maintaining good relations with owner's subcontractors, vendors, labor, and architects
- Always seeking improvement in methods and procedures; being open-minded to new techniques of placing materials
- Keeping close purchasing and accounting controls; updating and following up on all systems
- Being adequately financed; the cash flow should be projected for each project; contract conditions of retaining should also be known
- Planning and maintaining the critical path method schedule and all updates
- Maintaining an up-to-date educational program for all personnel

- Planning for public relations, human relations, and sales; company policies and objectives should be defined in a written manual; define responsibilities of personnel as to team functions
- Organizing planning to prevent the ripples of the lack of good planning
- Keeping daily documentation to provide the status of your project
- Evaluate your communication system
- Managing time and esprit de corps
- Planning your safety program.

Project Management during Planning and Design

During the planning and design phase of a project, the project manager provides a wide range of professional services. Specific assignments include the following:

1. Consulting with, advising, assisting, and making recommendations to the owner and architect or engineer on all aspects of planning for the project construction.

2. Reviewing and evaluating the architectural, civil, mechanical, electrical, and structural plans and specifications as they are being developed and advising and making recommendations with respect to such factors as construction feasibility, possible economics, availability of materials and labor, time requirements for procurement and construction, and projected costs.

3. Preparing a budget estimate based on a quantity survey of the plans and specifications at the preliminary stage of development. She will continue to review and critique and refine these estimates as the development of the plans and specifications proceeds and will advise the owner and the architect or engineer if it appears that the budget targets for the project cost or completion will not be met. She will prepare a final cost estimate when plans and specifications are complete.

4. Recommending for purchase and expediting the procurement of long-lead items to ensure their delivery by the required dates.

5. As working drawings and specifications are completed, she will take competitive bids on the work. After analyzing the bids thus received, she will either award contracts or recommend to the owner that such contracts be awarded. The exact procedure will depend upon the contract with the owner.

6. At an early stage in the project, she will prepare a detailed project schedule for all project activities by the owner, architect, engineer, subcontractors, submittals, deliveries, and himself. The project manager will closely monitor and update the schedule during both design and construction phases of the project and be responsible for providing all parties with periodic reports as to the status of the work with respect to the project schedule.

Principles of Budgetary Control and Project Managers

The efficient use of budgets and budgetary controls is a key to successful forecasting, profit planning, and overall operation. Top management must first have a respect for facts. Secondly, managers must have clearly defined organizational responsibilities. Controls should be policed by the financial officer. Prepare your annual budget early in the last quarter of the preceding year.

Cost Control and Profitability Analysis by Team

Profitability analysis is a management tool that offers perhaps even greater opportunity for cost control than that which resulted from pioneering work on time and motion studies and cost accounting. Teamwork is a must with all persons involved in cost control in order to sell its importance. Establish team techniques for cost analysis.

Project Management: A Commonsense View

On any project, adequate and timely controls are necessary if top management is to delegate responsibility to the degree desirable, and, at the same time, be assured that the functions delegated are being carried out in accordance with agreed upon standards. Admittedly, the project manager has to be a hardheaded realist who puts first things first. Foremost among these "firsts" are planning and making a profit in order to stay in business.

Job Set-Up by Project Manager

You, the project manager, are the one person who controls each and every activity of your particular project. The "game plan" is yours, and its complete success or failure lies in your hands. The responsible project manager is the chief motivator of people and positive actions and must take the initiative for all operations.

Today we find bold, complex, and vigorous architectural concepts and technology that influence our activities in many ways. The project manager must plan and organize orderly sequences of construction activities dependent on time and resources.

Project Manager's Contract Review and Critique

Know what contract responsibility you, the project manager, have with the owner. Review each subcontract and purchase order, and keep a copy in your files. During this review, go over the specifications and drawings to be aware of the specific contract document content. After you are thoroughly familiar with each contract, go over them with each subcontractor's representative on the job site before work begins to avoid misunderstandings. Remember, every contract includes specification requirements, general conditions, special conditions, addendum requirements, and plan requirements.

Project Manager's Planning

The number one priority on any project is in-depth planning. During the planning phase the project manager must know all submittals and the delivery of every item, as well as the project resources. Do not proceed into any other part of the project until you have confirmed delivery dates.

Diagram and know the logical sequence of all activities. Work items are called "activities," and each activity requires a duration in work days in order to time your schedule. The sequence of submit, approve, fabricate, and deliver must precede the erection or installation of work activities.

During scheduling you will have certain activities that must be completed 100 percent before starting other activities. For example, steel must be erected before the roof deck can be installed.

During planning make rough drafts of your schedule. Remember, you are controlled by restraints, such as those imposed by management, deliveries, submittals, approvals, specification, manpower, and logic.

During the planning process, you have had time to think out the project. Now put this thinking on paper in the form of a network diagram to get a visible picture of your game plan. This (network) picture identifies the problem areas and raises a flag on activities that are critical to completion time. Also, you should analyze and evaluate activities that are near critical and plan to keep them on time as well to prevent placing more activities on the critical path.

After you have completed your rough drafts, you should review them with all major subcontractors to obtain a good team effort. Critique all procedures and methods to complete each activity so you will know equipment and manpower needs. You, as the author of your schedule, should be aware of the legal consequences before you issue the final network diagram to the owner, architect, and subcontractors.

- Punctilious planning
- Query critical path method planning
- Tactical planning
- Dynamic critical path method planning
- Critical path method daily planning
- Methodology of critical path method planning
- Astute critical path method planning
- Philosophy of critical path method planning
- Critique of planning resources
- Planning restraints
- Criticality of planning
- Milestone planning
- Scrutinized planning
- Feasibility planning
- Conceptual planning
- Vigilant critical path method planning
- Systematized planning
- Submittal planning
- Sequence and logic planning
- Entrepreneurial planning
- Strategic planning
- Coordinated critical path method planning
- Problem avoidance planning
- Insightful people planning
- Thought planning
- Evaluation of project planning
- Team and candid planning
- Critique of planning

- Implementation of "game plan"
- Assiduous planning
- Follow-up planning
- Synergistic planning
- Magnanimous planning
- Esprit de corps planning
- Management planning
- Delivery planning.

Critical path method schedule planning also is complete project management. The planning and analysis by the astute project manager requires that the whimsical attitude towards critical path method schedules be removed. This also requires that the project manager use daily vigilance and meticulous management abilities. The project manager should be dynamic and articulate in communication of critical path method methodology. The meticulous project manager must resolve the "enigma" of timely critical path method input. The collection of the input data requires detailed and intimate knowledge on the part of the project manager about the project to which critical path scheduling is to be applied. The project manager must organize, methodize, and systematize all critical path method input data to complete the animus. List all activities by the month of start during the planning phase.

Evaluate Game Plan and Know Contract Documents

Job Start-up Checklist
- Contract review
- Project manager planning
- Plan of development approval
- Notice to proceed by owner
- Complete plans and specifications
- Building permit
- Temporary service: electric
- Temporary service: water
- Temporary service: heat
- Temporary service: toilets
- Establishment of documentation format
- Insurance: builder's risk
- Building inspector: inspection
- Engineering: layout, benchmark
- Subcontractors' and suppliers' lists
- Signs (company, no trespassing, and so on)
- Owner's separate contractors
- Study of game plan

- Bond on subcontractors
- Time enigma
- Program photos
- Mobilization
- Communication of schedule
- Barricades
- Field office
- Security
- Fire extinguishers
- Safety
- Preliminary schedule
- Staff and responsibilities
- Site meeting agenda
- Evaluation of concurrent activities
- Define goals and objectives.

Pre-Construction Meeting

The project manager must hold a pre-construction meeting before the notice to proceed. Attendance should include all contract parties. An agenda for the pre-construction meeting may include schedules, submittals, payment breakdown, contract documents, and change orders. Considerations for schedules are: type required, who submitted it, date of submittal, input required, date of approval and who approved it, and frequency of updates. During the submittal process, lists of names of parties to submit and specification requirements should be made, and a submittal schedule and log need to be established. The payment schedule should be defined during payment breakdown, and contract documents need to be reviewed. During the change orders process, procedures should be established.

The Project Manager at the Fulcrum Point

The pivotal role—the fulcrum—in the project management system is the project manager. A summary of some project management activities include:
- Project planning, organization, and staffing
- Work plan: schedule
- Start-up
- Directing and controlling
- Documentation and coordination
- Submittals and approvals
- Monitoring and control
- Delivery status
- Project closeout.

The project manager is involved in sources of conflict over the project life cycle, such as priorities, schedules, manpower, cost, technical issues, procedures, and personalities.

Project Managers and Time Wasters

The possibility of time wasters exists in any of the areas of project management, such as critiquing, planning, organizing, staffing, directing, decision-making, communicating, and controlling. Advance planning can minimize the possibility.

Job Layout

Before starting construction on projects, a job layout should be made to scale showing the areas for excavation cut and fill; utilities; roads; permanent buildings and areas available for the field office, warehouse, and storage spaces; and access to building for steel erection. Provisions should be made immediately for job signs in an effective location.

Establish two benchmarks and retain them throughout the project. After the layout of all building lines and levels, check the dimensions against all structural and mechanical drawings so that no conflict develops.

Give an in-depth study to field dimensions required by the shop drawings. Review window and door head heights as to masonry coursing and know the size of the equipment that must go through these openings at a later date. Critique general conditions and field dimensions!

Coordinating Subcontractors

Know the names of each subcontractor on day one of your contract and the name of each contact person. Also, know the division of her contract work. Obtain schedule input from each subcontractor during the planning phase; the subcontractor can help you "put the pieces together" on any project. Subcontractors comprise your committee enabling construction of your project, so use them to their fullest potentials.

Subcontractors can make or break you, so you, the project manager, must use all of your diplomacy, control, judgment, and experience in order to obtain and keep them on the project when you need them.

Review and analyze each subcontract and be sure the division or divisions of the project and any special conditions in the contract leave no question in your mind.

Keep the telephone number of each subcontractor contact person on file for daily use. Communicate your game plan and critical path method schedule updates to each and every subcontractor.

Special Considerations by the Project Manager

Submittals

Review, critique, analyze, and evaluate the specification and list all submittals required so you can log them as received and always know the exact status of same. Study your submittal schedule.

Remember that neither fabrication can begin nor can deliveries be made until submittals are complete on a given item. Memorize the sequence of submit plus approve plus fabricate and deliver. Follow up on re-submittals and see that each subcontractor completes them according to your submittal schedule. When the specifier wrote the specifications, he had a purpose in requiring submittals. It is your contract responsibility as the project manager to follow those specifications to the letter.

During your review of submittals (update monthly), coordinate them with all trades involved so that all team members will be aware of the details. Check all submittals as to the supplier's or subcontractor's contract requirements and critique with a lot of thinking. All notes that say "by others" could mean you.

Keep your files up to date with a copy of all approved submittals and see that each required subcontractor has a copy. Also, the copy of submittals and log of same will be very useful during the project closeout phase.

Change Orders

Be aware of proposed change orders. Advise the home office immediately when any proposed change order may hold up the project or if the proposed change affects any work you have completed or any materials on the job site.

Review all papers under the proposed change order and work with the office in determining their cost. Once the change order is approved, you will receive copies of it to send to the affected subcontractors and suppliers. Go over them carefully. Document time and cost on each change order.

Critique Game Plan and Know Timely and Adequate Critical Path Method Input

Purchasing and Project Managers

All field purchases require a purchase order from the home office. Your project has a budget for each item. When you are buying an item, you need to obtain the best price to meet delivery requirements and specification data. Each purchase order has a number to help in accounting upon invoicing. Also, you need the job number, name of company you are buying from, quantity of materials, unit price, total cost, and discounts, as may apply.

Plan your purchases so you can buy in quantities to save delays, delivery cost, and panic when you needed a special item yesterday. Do not duplicate purchasing.

Equipment

You can't expect your equipment to take care of itself. Know the operating instructions for each piece of equipment. Are you aware of the importance of employee attitudes toward the equipment? Have a program for making equipment last longer, including set-up, procedures, training, adjusting the equipment to fit the operator, and preventive maintenance.

Give one person full responsibility for operating the equipment. Plan your equipment use and schedule well ahead of your actual needs. Buy, rent, or lease; weigh the cost of each.

Cost Control

A thorough review and evaluation of the cost report showing labor and materials costs should be made weekly on the project. Discuss all items and activities that have overrun the estimate in order to affect improvement recommendations. In cases when the unit price estimate is too low, the vice president of operations should be advised. Then the information and detailed analytical supporting data may be discussed thoroughly with the estimating department to correct future estimates.

Cost control numbers should be tied to the schedule activity listing by nodes and updated monthly as planned versus actual cost. Critique the planned crew sizes as to actual crew sizes used versus the activity durations that control cost.

Survey work hours spent on given activities as to quantities in place. Conduct a monthly assessment of labor cost to date against the same estimated work items, and project the cost of completion. Control equipment costs to avoid going beyond their estimated costs. Check the ratio of journeyman to foreman supervision cost when small crews are involved.

Management and Job Set-up

Your role as a construction project manager is one of management. As a manager, you must be willing to get involved. Don't be defensive; make learning your goal. Be willing to change your mind and take risks. You need to develop your management philosophy to guide you in your decisions.

Set goals and objectives. Good managers set goals and reach for achievement. Goal setting demands reflection on organizational purpose. When making a decision, know what you're trying to accomplish.

What is your game plan? Goals increase a manager's confidence, especially when plans for their attainment have been developed. Goals save time, and time equals money. Develop a plan for management action. Top managers grow through analysis and feedback.

As project manager, use your time effectively, set priorities, delegate whenever possible, control interruptions as much as possible, learn to concentrate intently on the task at hand, make lists of the items you need to discuss with superiors, associates, and subordinates and communicate clearly.

Correspondence and Communications

Paperwork cannot be avoided in today's construction business. Paperwork will not go away, so work out a plan to conquer it. Write it; don't say it. Review all memos, letters, and transmittals daily. Know who will follow up on all correspondence, and communicate with your team members so no loose ends are left hanging. Communicate the job site meeting minutes to people for their information.

Manpower Leveling and Project Managers

Review, critique, evaluate, and analyze your project schedule weeks ahead of time so you will know which activities are to begin in the near future. Plan your crew sizes for future activities so you will know your project manpower needs. Chart your manpower levels from the beginning (monthly) to the end of the project.

You, the project manager, must know which activities are on the critical path of your schedule to know where your manpower level is critical. Manpower on other activities may be shifted to keep your level close to the same total crew sizes.

Study your project needs and know when and where you can use your time most efficiently. Review the abilities of your staff members and delegate specific duties to them. Encourage your team members to take on additional responsibilities. Obtain input from your superintendent as to manpower leveling of crews working under him.

Be a Knowledgeable Project Manager

Daily Reports

Use management tools such as daily reports. Daily reports reinforce the project manager's documentation and update company files. Information needed on each daily report includes:
- Date
- Job name
- Contract days
- Contract days used
- Contract days left
- Weather: temperature AM or PM
- Subcontractors working and manpower
- Company manpower by craft
- Description of activities worked
- Reference to critical path method nodes
- Materials received
- Visitors
- Job needs, materials, and submittals
- Project manager's signature.

Knowledge of Concrete

Many good books have been written about concrete. Read one or more to update your knowledge. Know the specifications and notes on the structural drawings that cover concrete. Review your concrete design mixes, and be sure you order the correct mix. Test cylinders must be taken on all pours. Visit a concrete testing laboratory. Some people do not follow specification requirements on a slump test; however, keep in mind that the engineer had a good reason for specifying a given slump.

Order your concrete early (plan ahead) to help promote a good relationship with your concrete supplier. Plan your manpower and equipment for placing and finishing concrete. Time spent waiting to begin pours costs money and pushes into night work.

Review all reinforcing steel drawings and submittals, and know the plan and specification requirements for them. Also, be aware of any inserts or openings needed in your concrete work.

Critique plans to determine special forms required. Make detailed drawings showing how you plan to form all concrete items shown on the estimate. Plan to reuse forms four to six times. Form materials cost money. Also, time spent to fabricate special forms is a costly item and to redo them is money spent twice.

Order form materials, including ties and specialty items, early. Review and study rent cost on forms and accessories. Analyze form handling. Is it more economical to set and strip with manpower or equipment? When cleaning up and hauling away forms, don't get rid of any forms or accessories that you can use at a later date.

Knowledge of Masonry

Review and analyze the drawings showing the masonry details early. Go over masonry submittals and provide the specified samples and mockups. Obtain all items, such as door frames, early so you won't hold up your masonry subcontractor. Plan your work so you can close in portions of your building early. Be aware of masonry crew sizes and daily production as to your project schedule.

Knowledge of Steel

Structural steel submittals and fabrication plus erection may be by a subcontractor; however, it is still the project manager's responsibility to see that it is erected properly. Know the safety and bracing requirements for steel erection, and be sure your subcontractor follows details as shown and specified.

Plan your steel erection so that it will not hold up other critical activities. Be sure to check all steel members for plumb and level before releasing the subcontractor. Follow up on paint requirements on all steel, and know specification requirements on grout for columns.

Knowledge of Mechanical Submittals
Coordinate all mechanical submittals with structural dimensions and other trades. Review the mechanical drawings and specifications. Going over the mechanical submittals will help you obtain a better picture of the project.

Study with the mechanical superintendent the location of supply and waste to the building, underground piping, piping in masonry, sheet metal work, insulation, controls, equipment, and fixtures. Know storage requirements of mechanical materials. Analyze sprinkler layouts, and coordinate same with ceiling heights and reflective ceiling plans.

Knowledge of Electrical Submittals
Know the electrical drawings and specifications since these, too, are a part of your project. Go over the electrical submittals to obtain a better picture of the project.

Study with the electrical superintendent the location of your main service, special panels, grounding in concrete, equipment, transformers, and wiring of HVAC equipment and switch gear. Know storage requirements of electrical materials.

Knowledge of Security
Analyze the specifications and special conditions as to requirements for security. Provide protection of materials and equipment. Some projects require twenty-four-hour-per-day watchmen so plan ahead for personnel needs. Review and study the need for an effective lighting and fencing system.

Knowledge of Weather
Because weather can be an important factor affecting project time and production, always allow for bad weather days when planning a work schedule. Plan ahead for hot and cold temperatures, and have the proper equipment on the job. Be aware of the specifications reference to weather, and follow through accordingly.

Knowledge of Safety and First Aid
Each project manager should have a current "first aid card." Also, she needs to have emergency telephone numbers in case of an accident. Keep a record of all accidents, and file copies of reports to the home office. Have a first aid kit on the job, and keep the kit well supplied.

Knowledge of Architect's Relations
The architect may be the owner's agent or management representative. Review the "general conditions" in the specifications, and know the architect's role in construction.

Also, certain specification divisions outline in detail requirements that must be approved by the architect, such as samples, submittals, mock-ups, and punch list. Architects may have inspectors on the site daily or who visit the job from time to time. You will need to cooperate with the inspector to the full extent of the contract.

Knowledge of Follow-Up System
Write it down; document now! Every building project has hundreds of items you need to know tomorrow, next week, next month, and even next year. Keep all of your notes. Documentation can save you hours of searching at a later date.

Update Your Game Plan Monthly
Work out your own follow-up system to obtain submittal approvals and deliveries. Follow up on your planning and scheduling so you can advise subcontractors that they will be required on the job site well in advance of their actual start dates. Follow-up is a daily special value when you are completing punch list items; use it wisely.

Project Management and Job Administration

Risk Avoidance

The owner's responsibility for astute planning, project mobilization, a submittal program, and a team scheduling system are growing daily. The owner's obligation and opportunity to avoid conflicts and litigation do not end once the contracts are signed and the contract funds allocated. The contract documents provide the rules by which the "game" will be played and the rewards for playing well. The selection process identifies the players. Without a good set of rules and a competent group of players, a successful outcome may be impossible. However, the combination of a good set of contract documents and a good group of project participants does not, in itself, ensure a successful project. The owner must honor the rules of the game and hold others to those rules as well.

Many of the rules of project administration/project management are implicit and not expressly stated anywhere in the contract documents, such as the owner's duty to coordinate and the owner's duty not to unreasonably interfere with the contractor's performance. Also critique the owner's duty to maintain proper schedule updates.

For a successful project, all participants must recognize, remain mindful of, and faithfully adhere to their respective obligations. Make it a goal to daily orchestrate the critical path method schedule! If each player performs, the project will be a success, and litigation should be avoided. Many disputes arise out of a lack of understanding. The owner or architect's duty as to coordination and/or approval of the project schedule is not completely defined in the contract documents. Often, the owner does not fully appreciate the needs of the contractor, and the contractor does not fully appreciate the needs of the owner. The same can be said of any pair of participants in the process. The owner's responsibility begins with the duty to provide the contractor a place to work. This may seem obvious, but many construction delays are caused by the owner's or agent of the owner's failure to timely provide the necessary property rights or completion of performance of a preceding contractor.

The owner should also be aware of the enormous role coordination and scheduling play in a complex construction project. Just as the owner, contractor, and architect/engineer all have differing interests, various contractors on the same project have differing interests and if someone does not coordinate schedules and referee their efforts, chaos will prevail. Whether the owner has elected the general contractor method of construction—in which case the general contractor has coordination responsibilities—or has employed a construction manager to coordinate and schedule the project, or has delegated coordination responsibilities to the architect, or has the in-house capabilities of performing such coordination scheduling and is undertaking to do so, the party charged with coordination scheduling responsibilities must carry it out.

The construction schedule has become an integral and indispensable "tool" in major commercial construction. In its simplest form, a construction schedule establishes the "time and sequence" within which the various activities of the various contractors will perform. The schedule also establishes the architect's time and sequence with respect to approvals and timely decisions and, too, the owner's time and sequence of activities related to the owner's equipment.

The development of a schedule and strict adherence to it facilitate efficient completion of the project. The schedule plans contract performance, delivery of equipment and materials, and manpower requirements in relation to time. The schedule update provides the status of the project. The critical path method schedule narrative report defines the problem areas.

It is difficult for the non-contractor to fully appreciate the sanctity of the construction schedule. Both the order in which the various subcontractors perform their activities and the sequence in which a subcontractor performs particular activities (for example, a plumbing contractor building from the bottom up) are the results of centuries of experience and training that have developed the most efficient and productive means of construction. A contractor bases a price on the assumption of being allowed to perform the contract as efficiently as possible. Any deviation from the "schedule" can result in unanticipated costs to the contractor and in claims. Any acceleration of the project performance "time" also causes the contractor to incur additional cost, such as overtime, labor cost, and loss of productivity and can result in claims.

With regard to scheduling, the owner or owner's representative also has a duty to timely consider contractor request for extensions of contract performance time for delays beyond the contractor's control. The exact grounds by which a contractor is entitled to a time extension and the mechanism for granting one should be addressed in the contract documents. Do your contract documents require a "time impact analysis"? Often, even on the advice of experienced architects or construction managers, the owner will advise the contractor that no request for an extension of time will even be considered or the subject of a decision until after project completion. Such a position can give rise to contractor claims based on constructive acceleration. The gist of this theory of recovery is that by refusing to grant "time extensions" when they are warranted, the owner has placed the contractor in a position of needing to accelerate work in order to make up the "time" lost to the original

50

schedule. This is done in an effort to avoid the assertion of liquidated damages in the event no time extension is eventually granted.

Time Equals Money

Thus, the refusal to consider and grant time extensions at the time they occur, when required by the contract, can constitute a constructive order by the owner to the contractor to accelerate. The owner can avoid "claims" of construction acceleration by fully considering meritorious time extension requests and approving them by negotiating an agreed payment for acceleration that will result from denial of the request.

Another frequent basis for contractor claims, which can be avoided through proper contract administration, is delay by the owner, the architect/engineer, or other owner representatives in responding to contractor questions or request for clarifications or to needs for design changes. Often during construction the contractor will become aware of a design problem or ambiguity, which requires some clarification or perhaps redesign. If the architect/engineer, construction manager, or the various other parties who may be involved in the process of resolving such a situation do not act expeditiously, the project can be "delayed," causing damages to both the owner and the contractor and potentially resulting in claims and litigation.

Resolve Enigma

Quality control is a major concern of most owners and must be initiated from the first day of the project. A qualified construction inspector—whether the project design architect/engineer, another architect, a construction manager, an independent consultant, or an in-house employee with construction experience—must be involved in the day-to-day performance of the project to ensure contractor compliance with the design specifications and standards of good workmanship. Inspection and acceptance of unsatisfactory work can in some cases preclude the owner from later asserting a "claim" against the contractor on the basis of those deficiencies.

The inspection process must be even-handed, however, and in tune with the practical realities of construction. Construction is not a precise science. Phases, such as substantial compliance and reasonable tolerances, are very prominent in the construction vocabulary. The degree of variance from the precise contract requirements that is acceptable depends on the nature of the project and the particular work involved. In almost all cases, some variance must be expected and, in fact, may be unavoidable and will not diminish the integrity or value of the finished product. Trade customs and practice permit reasonable deviations from contract plans and specifications, such as, for example, a one eighth inch of sag in ten feet in a concrete slab. Today's two-by-four measures more like 1 ½ by 3 ½. A contractor bases a bid on the assumption that the owner understands this, and an overly zealous inspector can cost the contractor enormous "time and money" and expose the owner to claims for over-inspection and harassment, requiring work beyond the reasonable requirements and fair meaning of the contract. It should be recalled that any forced deviation from the contractor's anticipated method, time, or sequence of performance can, under proper circumstances, constitute a constructive change. This is not to say that the owner cannot insist on perfection, or, for that matter, anything desired for which the owner is willing to pay. But the owner must make his demands clear in the contract documents in order to bind the contractor to it.

The owner, by the power of his purse, can exercise a great deal of control over the project administration process. The owner must be careful not to abuse this power, for to do so can result in as much damage as the failure to exercise the power at all. Owners should be aware of their obligations in the construction process and of their powers to require adherence of obligations on the part of all contract parties.

The owner's ultimate control over a wayward contractor is the right to terminate the contract. Such a right should be provided in the contract documents for the case when a contractor fails significantly to fulfill obligations under the contract. The wrongful termination of a contractor, however, can expose the owner to severe liability. At the same time, even when there is a valid basis for termination, the cost of exercising that right and employing a substitute contractor, in terms of both time and money, may be prohibitive. Nevertheless, there are situations when this remedy of last resort is called for, and the owner should be aware of this. It is sound advice always to consult an attorney prior to terminating a contractor because this action inevitably leads to serious disputes and litigation.

The owner should stress to the architect/engineer and contractor the need to take preventive measures at each step of the construction process in order to minimize the risk of litigation. The value of avoiding litigation can be great. However, even while all these actions are being undertaken, the owner should be maintaining accurate and thorough records of the project in the event disputes do arise.

Project Manager and Critical Path Method Updates

Contemporaneous records of any factual occurrence that later becomes the basis of a claim are invaluable in defending against a construction claim or preparing an affirmative claim. To maintain accurate records, keep the critical path method schedule updated on a timely basis. Keep all contract personnel informed of daily record keeping. An "astute" project manager or contract administrator will plan to keep her project on schedule by using critical path method updates monthly.

Esprit de Corps of Contract Administration

- Document your game plan of project management and job administration.
- Systematize your project managers as to contract administration.
- Canvass your project team and its philosophy as to the proper contract administration.
- Does your project manager have the mind to be meticulous, assiduous, querist, synergistic, punctilious; or does she acquiesce?
- Study the risk analysis of the use of the new A201-1987 General Conditions of the Contract for Construction document. (**See Appendix A: AIA Document A201-1997**)

Partnering: A Tool for Communications Management

Project Management Institute 26th Annual Seminar/Symposium (October 1995)

Introduction

Project communication management deals with providing "the critical links among people, ideas, and information that are necessary for success" (1). In order to optimize project communications, project managers should use every available cost-effective tool in order to maximize the communications process between all key stakeholders. The United States Army Corps of Engineers has found that project partnering, or teambuilding, is one process that greatly enhances communications among stakeholders on construction projects.

Research Methodology

The authors recently conducted a three-phased study of project partnering in the Corps of Engineers. First they studied responses to a Corps-wide data call from the Office of the Chief of Engineers regarding lessons learned in partnering. The authors used a database to organize 188 observations from the responses into seventeen different topic-categories. Next the authors conducted twenty telephonic interviews with construction contractors who have entered into partnered contracts with the Corps. Finally, the authors interviewed twelve professional facilitators who have led partnering sessions for the Corps. This comprehensive study is unique in that it is the first time that the Corps of Engineers has examined project partnering using subjective input from all key players in the partnering process. The results of the interviews and data were analyzed to provide a thorough list of techniques and practices that should either be explored or abandoned in order to improve the Corps' performance in project partnering.

Partnering provides many benefits for projects, only one of which is enhanced communications. However, the authors discovered that project partnering adapted itself well into the four processes for managing communications as defined in the *Project Management Body of Knowledge (PMBOK Exposure*

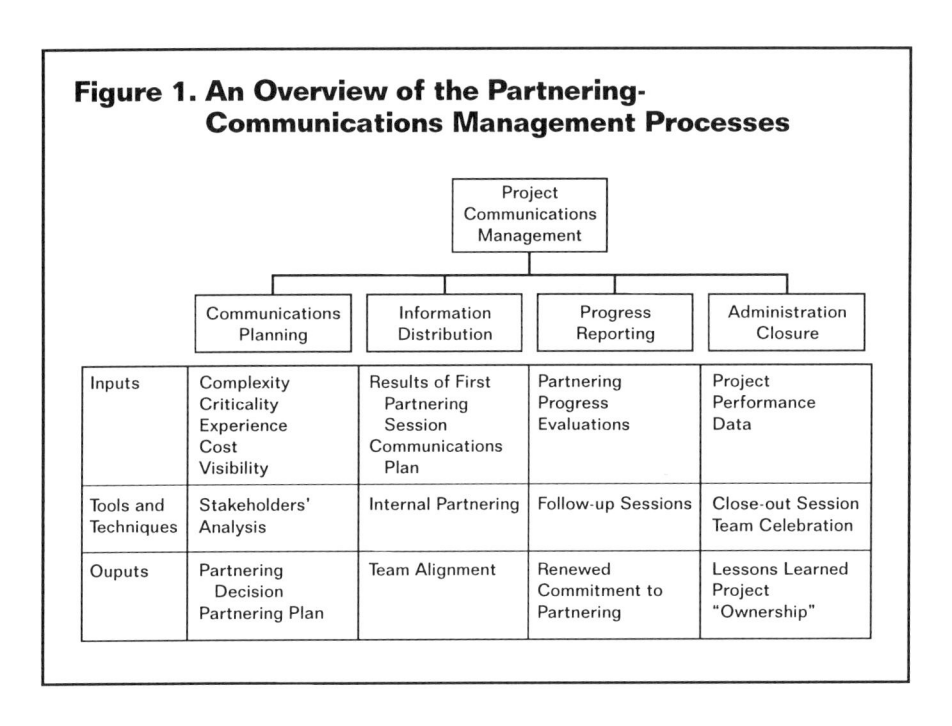

Figure 1. An Overview of the Partnering-Communications Management Processes

	Communications Planning	Information Distribution	Progress Reporting	Administration Closure
Inputs	Complexity Criticality Experience Cost Visibility	Results of First Partnering Session Communications Plan	Partnering Progress Evaluations	Project Performance Data
Tools and Techniques	Stakeholders' Analysis	Internal Partnering	Follow-up Sessions	Close-out Session Team Celebration
Ouputs	Partnering Decision Partnering Plan	Team Alignment	Renewed Commitment to Partnering	Lessons Learned Project "Ownership"

(Parent: Project Communications Management)

Draft): communications planning, information distribution, progress reporting, and administrative closure. Figure 1 presents an overview of how project partnering fits into the project communications management process.

Project Partnering versus Strategic Alliances

It is important to distinguish between project partnering or teambuilding and strategic alliances, another form of collaboration between owners and contractors. Strategic alliances do not focus on a single project but rather on a long-term relationship between two or more organizations. In this sense, partners actually combine or share resources for the purpose of achieving mutually beneficial goals and objectives (2). Project partnering, on the other hand, is defined as "a project-focused process that builds and develops shared goals, interdependence, trust and commitment, and accountability among team members and seeks to improve team members' problem solving skills"(3). This type of partnering is a short-term arrangement intended to reinforce common goals, build a project team, establish a formal dispute resolution process, and improve project communications. The team management styles matrix (see Figure 2) is often used by facilitators to show the association between the project's issues and the project team's relationship (4). The goal of project partnering is to operate in the upper right quadrant, in an environment where the key stakeholders can

Figure 2. The Management Styles Matrix

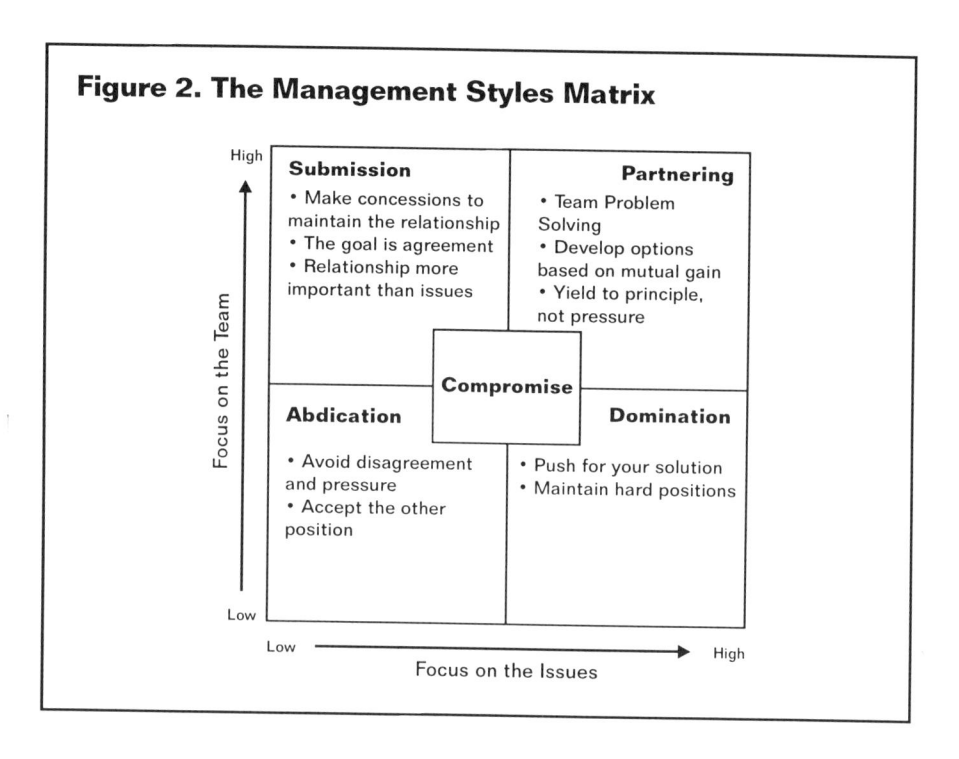

Focus on the Team (High ↑ / Low)
Focus on the Issues (Low → High)

Submission (High Team, Low Issues)
- Make concessions to maintain the relationship
- The goal is agreement
- Relationship more important than issues

Partnering (High Team, High Issues)
- Team Problem Solving
- Develop options based on mutual gain
- Yield to principle, not pressure

Compromise (center)

Abdication (Low Team, Low Issues)
- Avoid disagreement and pressure
- Accept the other position

Domination (Low Team, High Issues)
- Push for your solution
- Maintain hard positions

focus on both the issues at hand and the team relationship while seeking "win-win" or "least loss" solutions to any disputes that may arise during a project.

The United States Army Corps of Engineers is one of the agencies credited with proliferating, if not inventing, partnering. In the late eighties, the Corps' construction projects were extremely adversarial. Many projects ended in claims or litigation, and project costs were skyrocketing. In 1988, in an effort to improve construction project performance, the Corps of Engineers' Mobile, Alabama, District solicited several consulting firms to prepare a model for a process that the district could use to reduce the adversarial nature of its construction projects. The Synergistic Group, Inc., of Mobile, Alabama, won the contract and provided the initial model for the project-partnering process. The first Corps project that used the partnering process was the Oliver Lock and Dam.

Partnering in the United States Army Corps of Engineers

Replacement, located on the Black Warrior-Tombigbee Waterway at Tuscaloosa, Alabama, is an example of partnering in the Corps. Since then, the use of the partnering process on Corps projects has increased dramatically. Currently hundreds of projects have been partnered worldwide.

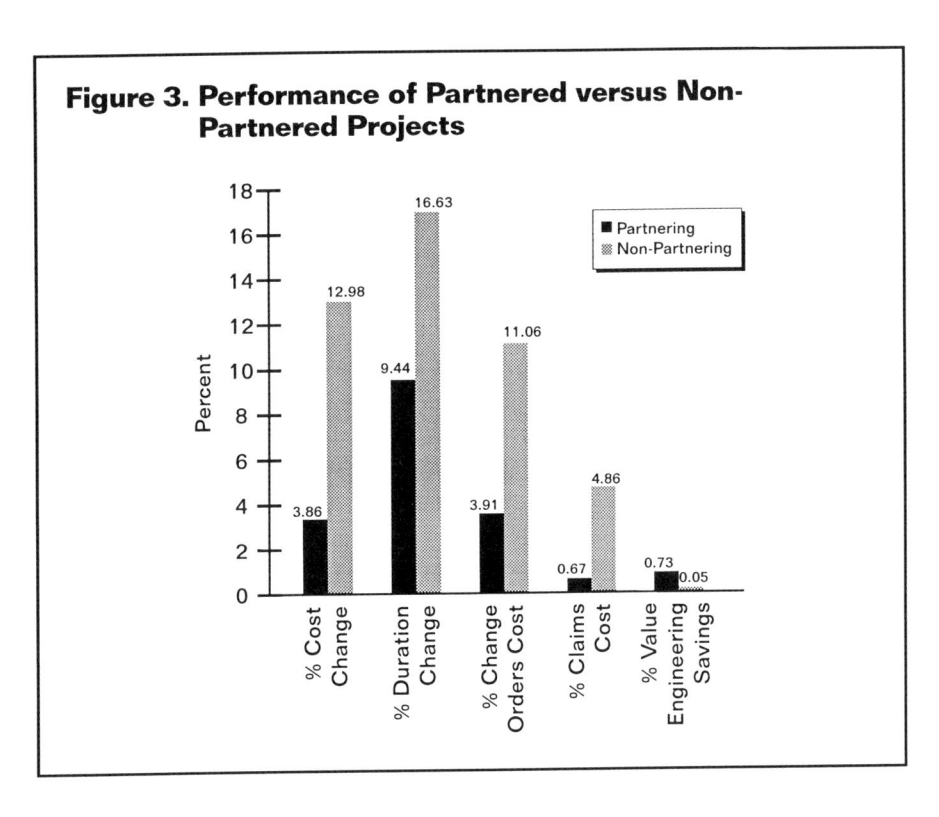

Figure 3. Performance of Partnered versus Non-Partnered Projects

Metric	Partnering	Non-Partnering
% Cost Change	3.86	12.98
% Duration Change	9.44	16.63
% Change Orders Cost	3.91	11.06
% Claims Cost	0.67	4.86
% Value Engineering Savings	0.73	0.05

Partnering has been widely credited with changing the very nature of construction projects in the Corps. Construction-related litigation has decreased in the past seven years from an annual cost prior to 1989 in excess of $1 billion to the 1994 total, which was less than $600 million (5). Project benefits are equally impressive. In a 1992 study, Weston and Gibson compared the performance of the nineteen projects that the Corps had partnered to date with the performance of a sample of non-partnered projects within the same range of contract amounts. The results are presented in Figure 3. On partnered projects, cost increases were reduced by 9.12 percent; schedule growth by 7.19 percent; change order costs by 7.15 percent; claims costs by 4.19 percent; and value engineering was nearly fifteen times as great when compared with non-partnered projects (6).

Both empirical and subjective data indicate that partnering, when performed correctly, can dramatically enhance the overall success of a construction project. The authors found that all twelve interviewed facilitators answered affirmatively the question: "Should the Corps of Engineers continue to partner in the future?" Also, eighteen of twenty contractors' representatives answered "yes" to the question: "Do you want to partner with the Corps in the future?" Both of the contractors who did not answer affirmatively gave a conditional "yes," based on a better defined alternative dispute resolution process than they had on a previously partnered project. The following sections discuss partnering in terms of the model presented in Figure 1 and the research results outlined in this study.

Partnering during Communications Planning

Communications planning involves determining the information and communications needs of the stakeholders. This involves deciding who needs what information, when they will need it, when they will receive it, and how it will be provided to them. In terms of partnering, this process involves deciding whether or not to formally partner a project, developing a partnering plan, and conducting the initial partnering session.

Inputs

While planning for project communications, the project team should base the communications plan on a thorough cost-benefit analysis. Project teams have an abundance of very costly systems available that are designed to enhance communications. If the project management team does not foresee that a system will yield benefits to the project, which are proportional to its costs, it would not be prudent to employ the system. Correspondingly, the project team must decide whether to utilize partnering on the project based on a similar analysis. Through analysis of the interviews, the authors discovered five factors that should be considered in analyzing the necessity of partnering. The five inputs to the cost-benefit analysis are the:

- Project's criticality
- Experience of the stakeholders in working together and in partnering
- Project's cost
- Project's visibility.

Tools and Techniques

The five inputs affecting the partnering decision must be carefully weighed when conducting the stakeholders' analysis. Simply stated, formal partnering is not for everyone or for every project. However, if any of the five factors increase the project's risk, then the stakeholders should consider investing the time and resources into a formal partnering agreement as a means of improving the project's overall performance and communications.

Outputs

The stakeholders' analysis will yield three important decisions regarding partnering. First, the stakeholders should decide whether to use partnering on the project. In the Corps of Engineers, some form of partnering is required on all construction contracts, as discussed by the Chief of Engineers Lieutenant General Arthur Williams in his 1993 policy memorandum: *Therefore, it is the clear policy of the Corps of Engineers to develop, promote and practice partnering on all construction contracts, and to universally apply the concept to all other relationships* (7).

Second, the decision must be made whether to conduct formal or informal partnering. Although the Corps' policy is to partner all projects, regardless of the project's size, scope, complexity, or criticality, the decision whether to formally or

Table 1. Responses from Facilitators Regarding Success Factors in Partnering

"What Are the Three Most Important Contributors to a Successful Partnership?"	Number of Times Cited
Committed and Personally Involved Executives	8
Effective Follow Ups	5
Common Goals	5
Good Communications and Candor	5
Well-Defined Dispute Resolution Process	4
Willingness to Make Partnering Work in the Field	4
Dedication to the Partnering Process	3
Trusting the Other Parties	3
Being Fair Minded and Professional	2

informally partner is left to the discretion of the project team. If the contracting parties have a great deal of experience partnering together and are committed to the principles of partnering throughout all levels of their organizations, then the partnering process may not require a significant investment of time. For example, the partnering process can be initiated relatively quickly and may not require an external facilitator. However, based on the results of the stakeholders' analysis, if one or more of the input factors increase the project's risk, the stakeholders should strongly consider employing a professional facilitator to formally lead them through the partnering process.

The third decision in the stakeholders' analysis should involve agreement on a partnering plan. The project team should agree upon how the partnering effort will be executed. If the formal partnering approach is selected, they must agree upon a location for the initial meeting, its duration, the primary attendees from each organization, and whether or not to employ a professional facilitator for the process. If the informal approach is selected, the project team must decide how it will produce the partnering spirit on the project without the benefit of a formal partnering process.

During the research, the authors found that 92 percent of facilitators interviewed preferred to conduct formal partnering sessions at a neutral site, while 80 percent of contractors preferred neutral sites. A neutral location such as a meeting facility at a hotel allows all partners to "get away" from their respective organizations and concentrate on the partnership. The authors also found that all twelve of the professional facilitators who were interviewed and 88 percent of the contractors prefer to have professional facilitators lead the initial partnering session rather than a member of one of the project organizations or a jointly led effort. Regarding the attendees at the partnering sessions, 92 percent of the facilitators agree that attendance should be limited to individuals who can "make things happen" during the project. The facilitators placed the optimum number of attendees at the sessions between twenty and thirty, with no single partner dominating the sessions. Additionally, the personal involvement of executives of all key organizations in the partnering process was cited most frequently by facilitators as being one of the three most significant contributing factors to a successful partnership (see Table 1).

At the initial formal partnering session, the key players from all sides are introduced, their roles in the project are explained, common goals for the project are discussed and agreed upon, team-building exercises are conducted, and a problem resolution process is mapped for all attendees. Finally, all attendees sign a "partnering agreement." In this agreement, the project team members make a personal pledge to work together in a spirit of cooperation, trust, and respect. The partnering agreement will then become a vital part of the project communications plan, the overall output of the planning process.

Partnering during Information Distribution

The goal of the information distribution process shown in Figure 1 is to make needed information available to project stakeholders in a timely manner. It includes implementing the communications management plan, as well as responding to unexpected requests for information. In terms of partnering, this process involves "spreading the word" about partnering to the individual employees of each organization who are members of the project team and reinforcing the partnering concept within each organization.

Inputs

After the initial partnering session, the project team should document and disseminate the dispute resolution "map" and the identity and role of the key players and plan how to operate their organizations within the context of the agreed upon communications plan. In fact, all organizations that are involved in project partnerships must internalize the partnering concept into their company cultures. Companies that cannot operate internally in the spirit of partnering are doomed to make the project a miserable experience for themselves and the other members of the project team.

Tools and Techniques

Internal teambuilding exercises comprise an outstanding method of internalizing good organizational team skills. Similar to project partnering sessions, internal teambuilding exercises promote a better understanding of the functions and roles of other departments in the organization. They also promote a trusting environment in which the organization will operate during the project. During these sessions, a facilitator can reinforce the project's problem resolution methodology by defining an internal dispute resolution process and an internal communications plan.

Internal partnering and teambuilding exercises are excellent means of implementing the precepts of partnering in an organization. The facilitators

Table 2. Responses from Facilitators Regarding Failure Factors in Partnering

"What Are the Three Most Important Contributors to Failure In a Partnership?"	Number of Times Cited
Close Minded to New Ways to Approach Business	8
No Follow Ups	5
Partnering for the Wrong Reason	4
No Dispute Resolution Process Defined	3
Leadership That Is Not Committed	3
No Trust Among Partners	2
Ineffective Teambuilding	2
Adversarial Relationships at the Job Site	1
Indecisiveness	1
Mistakes In Bidding	1

interviewed discussed the factors that contribute the most to failed partnerships (see Table 2). A close-minded attitude toward accepting a new way of conducting business was the reason facilitators cited most frequently for why partnerships fail. Organizational teambuilding sessions will help employees who are entrenched in the old adversarial paradigm to "open their minds" to a new way of operating.

Outputs

This process will result in a project team that is aligned from top to bottom. The team will fully understand the spirit of partnering, the project's goals and objectives, the communications plan, and a dispute resolution map, both within and outside of the individual organizations.

Partnering during Progress Reporting

The progress reporting process provides the key stakeholders with a report of the project's status and performance indicators. In terms of partnering, this process involves assessing the general health of the partnership, identifying trends that may be destructive to the partnership, and proposing solutions to any problems that may exist. The importance of this step in the partnering process simply cannot be overstated.

Inputs

In order to identify trends in the partnership, the key stakeholders periodically complete a "grade card," which measures the partnership in terms of the goals set forth in the initial partnering session. These objectives are difficult to measure since they deal with subjective issues, such as trust, teamwork, and the reduction of administrative requirements. However, the objective of the partnering evaluation is not to precisely measure the "soft" issues of the project but to create discussion, identify trends, and bring to the surface issues relating to the health of the partnership.

Tools and Techniques

When the decision to partner a project is made, the key stakeholders should recognize that partnering is a process, not an event. Following up on the progress of the partnership is absolutely essential to success. Follow-up partnering sessions are held periodically and may be led by the same professional facilitator who led the initial session, by a representative of any of the project partners, or jointly by representatives of the project team. The concept of conducting follow-up sessions was very succinctly explained by one of the Corps' district chiefs of construction as follows: *Follow-up is easy to forget, but probably is one of the most important aspects of partnering. The follow-up evaluations are a simple process of evaluating to see if each partner is living up to its original commitments. The original tenets of the partnership are used as the basis of the evaluations.*

These sessions are most effective if they are held separately from the weekly project progress meeting. The meeting must focus on the objectives of the partnership, not on any ongoing disputes of the job. The goal of follow-up is to solve any threats to the overall health of the partnership before they threaten the entire working environment of the project. Conducting effective follow-ups was the second most frequently cited reason for successful partnerships. Correspondingly, failing to conduct effective follow-up was the second most frequently cited reason for why partnerships fail. Additionally, thirteen out of twenty contractors stressed the importance of following up on the progress of the partnership, while seven out of eleven of the Corps' divisions that provided input to the study discussed the importance of follow-ups.

Outputs

The benefits of the follow-up sessions should include a renewed commitment to the spirit of partnering, a better understanding of the other partners' particular situations in the project, and an increase in the partners' ability to communicate about the tough issues of the job.

Partnering during Administrative Closure

During the administrative closure process, the project team verifies and documents project results, collects and archives project records, and institutionalizes lessons learned regarding the process. During this process, the project team officially brings the partnership to a conclusion and celebrates its success.

Inputs

Final project data and a final partnership evaluation provide the inputs to the administrative closure process.

Tools and Techniques

A final, after-action review at the end of the project will provide valuable insight into the successes and failures of the partnering process. After the project is complete, key stakeholders will have a more impartial view of the partnership; since the majority of controversial issues will have been settled, it is hoped, with a "win-win" solution.

Finally, the team should celebrate the project's success. Partnering is planned by managers but executed in the field each day of the project. Every employee who contributed to the partnership should feel as though his contributions were noteworthy. Making a partnership work requires patience, flexibility, and the unique ability to shed the old paradigms of project relationships. Everyone who contributes to the process—from the chief executive officer to the clerk in the contracting office—should be given the opportunity to reflect on a job well done.

The authors found that administrative closure is the most neglected process in partnering. Throughout their study, they found virtually no mention of this vital component of the partnering process. All organizations that choose to partner projects should consider the importance of gathering and disseminating lessons learned and celebrating success. Both tools are great investments for future partnering endeavors.

Outputs

Upon administrative closure, the team should have a well-organized collection of experiences, observations, and lessons learned from the partnering process. These valuable assets will form the institutional knowledge base from which will be drawn the framework for future successes in partnering.

Conclusions

Partnering fits well into the project management body of knowledge communications management process. In order to implement partnering, project managers should utilize the five tools and techniques discussed previously:
- Stakeholders' analysis
- Internal partnering
- Follow-up sessions
- Close-out sessions
- Team celebration.

Although the authors tailored their study to the Corps of Engineers, they gleaned many partnering-related lessons that are generic and can be applied to virtually any project regardless of the industry. These lessons include:
- Always consider using the partnering process as a means of improving overall project performance, especially project communication.
- Consider employing a professional facilitator. (They cost considerably less than the attorneys who will be paid to litigate the claims that partnering can help preclude.)
- If a project is formally partnered, conduct meetings at a neutral site, and limit attendance at the meetings.

- Senior-level management of all project team organizations must commit to the partnership and be personally involved in order to maximize its success.
- Use follow-up sessions to keep the partnership healthy and on track.
- Keep your organization in the partnering spirit on a day-to-day basis by using periodic internal partnering sessions.
- Make sure that "field" employees are operating in the spirit of partnering. Partnering agreements are made by executives but executed in the field.
- Celebrate success!

The Corps continues to place great emphasis on the partnering process and reap superb results. In recognition of its efforts in partnering and alternative dispute resolution techniques, Secretary of Defense William Perry presented the United States Army Corps of Engineers with the "Golden Hammer" Award in May 1995. The "Golden Hammer" is awarded to federal agencies that make significant strides in "redefining government."

Project management professionals cannot afford to ignore partnering as an inexpensive means of more effectively managing communications on projects in which they participate.

References

1. Project Management Institute. 1994. *Project Management Body of Knowledge (PMBOK Exposure Draft)*. Upper Darby, PA: Project Management Institute.

2. Partnering Task Force, Construction Industry Institute. 1991. "In Search of Partnering Excellence." *Special Publication 17-1* (July). Austin, Texas.

3. Albanese, R. 1993. "Teambuilding: Implications for the Design/Construction Industry." *Source Document 97*. Austin, Texas: Project Teambuilding Task Force, Construction Industry Institute (February).

4. Mosley, D., C. Moore, M. Slagle, and D. Burns. 1991. "Partnering in the Construction Industry: Win-Win Strategic Management in Action." *National Productivity Review* (Summer).

5. Jones, J. 1994. Presentation. Construction Project Improvement Conference, Austin, Texas (September).

6. Weston, D., and G. Gibson. 1993. "Partnering-Project Performance in U.S. Army Corps of Engineers." *Journal of Management in Engineering* (October).

7. Williams, A. 1993. *U.S. Army Corps of Engineers Policy Memorandum #14*. Washington, D.C. (March 31).

Paperwork by Project Managers

Quite often a "project manager" will do an outstanding job of planning the project but fail to plan for the administration of the project's paperwork, the paperwork generated by control systems, purchasing, subcontracts, safety requirements, quality control, general correspondence, inter-company correspondence, and all other written material relative to the project. Failure to plan for administration of project paperwork can cause a breakdown in an important part of the information system, the coordination of written communications. Proper administration of the paperwork helps the project by:

1. Keeping all key personnel informed and aware of the project's progress.
2. Filing pertinent information in such a way that it can be easily and readily retrieved.
3. Minimizing the duplicate and triplicate handling and filing of information.
4. Keeping an ongoing historical development of the project for use in claims and disputes.
5. Maintaining the submittal log, keeping it up-to-date.
6. Daily recording critical path method activities and using the critical path method schedule updates.

Developing Policies and Procedures for Handling Paperwork

Policies and procedures for handling project paperwork should fit the requirements of the project and be compatible with policies and procedures of the company. The project manager can accomplish developing such policies and procedures in six steps:

Step I. Determine the need for the development of a system of policies and procedures for paperwork. If an existing system can handle the job requirements, there is no need to develop a new one.

Step II. Identify the scope of the system. What will the system do? What will it not do? Who will be involved? When will it be done? How will it relate to the rest of the project's information system? In defining the scope, the project manager should prepare a format for the system that includes a list of the basic policies or procedures that will be developed.

Step III. Review, evaluate, and analyze all current policies and procedures. This should be done openly and candidly to allow all personnel a chance to suggest changes.

Step IV. Draft the new policies and procedures. Each policy or procedure should be clearly defined as to scope and purpose. All personnel involved with each policy or procedure should be identified. Each procedure should have a step-by-step "cookbook" type description that leaves no doubt as to how to perform it. All statements should be clear and concise so they are readily understood.

Step V. Train all personnel in how to use the system and to implement it. Explain the benefits of the system to everyone.

Step VI. Review and critique the system periodically to ensure that it is meeting the need for which it was designed.

Conclusion

Remember that administration of project paperwork is a work activity as important as any field activity. Due to the large amount of paperwork generated on most projects, the administration of paperwork can not be left to chance or to piecemeal development. One lost or incorrectly filed piece of paper, or one detail not followed up on, can cause lengthy delays to the overall project. Administration of project paperwork must be planned, and policies and procedures should be developed to ensure an efficient process.

Paperwork Game Plan

Any good paperwork game plan includes methodical documentation of any out-of-sequence critical path method schedule activities. The project manager must control any and all out-of-sequence critical path method schedule activity starts and follow true critical path method methodology. When you allow out-of-sequence starts, you risk rejection of your critical path method schedule.

Proper paperwork management requires keeping your critical path method schedule "current." Your approved critical path method schedule must be used daily and be posted at the project site. All contract parties are required to use this contract document requirement to coordinate the project activities. Regular monthly critical path method updates must be kept current each and every month in order to maintain the validity and authenticity of your critical path method schedule. Change orders (paperwork) should be added at each monthly critical path method update. Then, too, in order to control the risk, the project manager must make time impact analysis at the time of any delay or impact to your critical path method schedule. Study the project specifications as to proper notices of delays or impacts.

Job Documentation: A Project Manager's Responsibility

Today every construction project requires detailed "documentation" by the project manager or the contract administrator. Conscientious and orderly record keeping not only provides the information to effectively and efficiently "manage" a project, it is also essential preparation for contract disputes, delays, and litigation. Such preparation requires a comprehensive documentation system to define against or prove entitlement to an amount of damages resulting from a compensatory claim.

Adequate documentation may also satisfy a requirement for a logical and supportable demonstration of cause and effect. Documenting the many complicated problems that may develop during a construction project is burdensome. Nevertheless, since documentation is essential to the success of a delay claim, the importance of creating a paper trail cannot be overemphasized. Because disputes are not often settled until after a project is completed, which may be several years or more, management policy should recognize that committing anything to memory is only as good as the longevity of the people involved both physically and corporately. Documentation usually lasts longer than people and their jobs.

The following is a presentation of the guidelines of a comprehensive documentation system that could provide valuable "resources" to ensure success in most types of construction contract disputes.

Common Types of Claims

Claims by contractors fall into three common types: changes in the scope of work, changes in site conditions, and changes in the schedule.

Changes in the Scope of Work

Most construction contracts require a written change order, supplemental agreement, or other contract modification for changed or added work and its corresponding cost impact. A claim that the contract has been constructively changed by the owner may arise in absence of a written order.

The owner is normally responsible for issuing and final approval of change orders. Problems are often encountered when the owner relies on the architect/engineer to review and recommend approval and rejection of change orders based on unanticipated conditions or some area not adequately covered in the plans and specifications. This may cause a conflict of interest for the architect/engineer who, by approving such change orders in a timely manner, may be inappropriately admitting his own negligence of faulty omissions.

To prove entitlement to additional compensation for a change in the scope of the work, a contractor must:
- Show the original scope of work contained in the bid documents and confirmed in his bid estimate
- Show that the owner actually ordered a change or took action that resulted in a change
- Support the claim by reference to detailed records; the actual costs of changed or extra work should be separately recorded on a daily basis.

Changes in Site Conditions

Many construction contracts contain a differing site conditions clause that allows an equitable contract price adjustment if physical site or subsurface conditions are either different from those represented in the contract or materially different from conditions that are normally inherent in the type of work performed. Prompt notice to the owner is required if these differing conditions are found. Proof of anticipated conditions may be established by the following:
- Bid specifications and plans
- Bid estimate worksheets
- Owner's boring logs or soil reports
- Pre-bid site investigation report
- Pre-bid or pre-construction conference minutes.

Changes in the Schedule

Delays, out-of-sequence, disruptions, suspensions, or acceleration of work are changes in the project schedule. These changes may affect either planned work sequences or planned duration times. The contract usually contains the overall project starting date, planned project duration time, and anticipated completion date. Milestones or work sequences are normally found in accompanying special conditions or in schedules that accompany the bid documents.

Confirmation of the contractor's as-planned schedule may be obtained from bid worksheets showing durations of equipment usage or expected overhead requirements. Proof of the cause, nature, and extent of a schedule change often depends upon circumstantial evidence.

Documentation Requirements

Adequate documentation is vitally important to the contractor interested in survival. First, it provides the information needed to effectively bid, plan, and construct the work. Second, it provides the hard data needed to analyze and successfully resolve the construction claim. Contractors and owners who are able to monitor and manage the project in such a way as to anticipate potential claims as they occur will be in the best position to prove these claims successfully after litigation begins. More importantly, fair settlement of the claim outside the courtroom is often possible because of specific data provided by documentation management, cost accounting, and astute monitoring procedures that support a detailed damage analysis.

In the courtroom, a presumption of reasonableness arises in favor of such records, which satisfies the claimant's burden and shifts it to the other party who must then prove that the records are unreasonable or inaccurate. Project records should, at a minimum, be made contemporaneously with the event. They should be made by, or be based upon information from, a person with knowledge of the event, kept as a regular practice of the company, and sufficiently detailed to permit a third person to reconstruct project activities solely from the files.

It is also imperative for owners, contractors, architects/engineers, and subcontractors to be problem-oriented while maintaining documentation during construction to be able to identify and react to those problems that may "impact" the contract price or performance time:

- Lack of meticulous critical path method planning
- Out of sequence activities
- Lackadaisical attitudes as to critical path method updates
- No project management communications
- Very little "team" esprit de corps
- Changes to specifications and plans
- Delayed approval of shop drawings
- Suspension or stop orders
- No timely and adequate input to critical path method update
- Untimely response to information requested
- Interference by other contractors or owner
- Differing site conditions
- Abnormal weather and climatologic data
- Transportation or material delivery delays
- Unusually severe inspection
- Material shortage
- Labor shortage
- Defective or deficient plans and specifications
- Defective owner furnished materials
- No enigma management

- Lack of parameters as to "game plan"
- No field orientation as to critical path method methodology
- Poorly defined management critical path method philosophy
- People with whimsical and procrastination positions as to "critical path method schedules" and documentation.

There are many types of records that should be maintained during a construction contract. The following "guidelines" are intended to serve as a checklist of the types of construction project information that will help establish both entitlement and damages due.

Pre-Contract Documents

Documents included in the owner's bid package, which typically are drawings, specifications, soil data, special conditions, and specific instructions, as well as the contractor's calculations and bid preparation documents, are generally admissible evidence as to what was intended by a construction contract.

A reasonable contractor prepares his bid or proposal to provide what the contract requires—no more and no less. A prudent contractor will seek clarification to ambiguities in the bid documents, particularly if they have a cost impact. However, when disputes develop over such ambiguities or alleged changes in the contract requirements, an examination of the bid documents and the contractor's backup information may be the only way to resolve these issues. A comparison of the as-bid drawings with the as-built drawings should disclose any changes, variances, or dissimilarities. Investigation into the reason for these differences may reveal some owner action or inaction (e.g., a defective design) for which a contractor may be entitled to recover any related additional cost.

A contractor's bid estimate will indicate how he viewed the project and how he intended to accomplish the work. Bid estimates are often sensitive in that they may disclose errors, miscalculations, or omissions. Bid estimates will also include any subcontractor or vendor quotes indicating expected markups or material prices. Delays often prevent a contractor from obtaining these prices, and, if the basis for the items is documented, a claim may be supported and justified. As-bid schedules and manpower curves show the duration and crew sizes that the contractor intended or planned to use for the performance of work. Delays, acceleration, or changes in work will impact the as-bid schedule and labor requirements and ultimately the cost of the project. However, proof of the basis of bid is often necessary to support these claims.

Soil data supplied by the owner, in the owner's possession, or obtained by the contractor during a site investigation visit prior to contract are important evidence in decisions regarding differing site conditions. Reliance of this data by a contractor when such data is found to be in error is critical to determining entitlement for this type of claim.

In summary, the important pre-contract documents are:
- Request for bid issued by the owner
- Bid package drawings and specifications
- Pre-bid meeting minutes
- Logs of telephone conversations
- Owner's proposed schedule showing work by other contractors
- As-bid schedules and manpower curves
- Bid estimate worksheets, calculations, and quantity takeoffs
- Subcontractors' bids
- Vendors' quotes
- Site investigation report and photographs
- Contractor's bid submittal.

Contract Documents

Only those documents in existence at the time the contract is awarded are part of the contract. There is, however, one exception. Special conditions may state that the critical path method schedule prepared and approved after the issuance of the contract will be an integral part of the contract documents. Anything else prepared at a later date, except for formal change orders, is not part of the contract. It is essential that a clean, unchanged set of original contract drawings and specifications be kept for future reference to prove any changes that may occur during the project. It is also important to note that drawings or specifications issued at contract award may be different from those in the bid, and the contractor should verify such changes before accepting the work. The notice to proceed is also a significant contract-related item in that its date may unexpectedly follow contract award by several weeks or more and could delay the project from the beginning.

Therefore, the contract documents file should include:
- Original contract
- Approved critical path method schedule
- Minutes of contract negotiation meetings
- Drawings and specifications issued for construction
- Notice to proceed.

Correspondence

All correspondence on a project should be preserved in a chronological master file with each letter numbered and cataloged for convenient reference. Coordination meetings should cover such items as:
- Progress (reference critical path method activities by node numbers)
- Contractor's plans for coming weeks
- Delays (weather, strikes)

- Material deliveries status report
- Status of all change orders
- Status of submittal log, as to submittals to date and approvals
- Information requirements and the need for clarification of plans and specifications
- Distribution of coordination meeting minutes.

However, these minutes may often be prepared to represent just the preparer's particular outlook with little attempt for impartiality or accuracy. All participants may not always express objections to wording or representations in writing. Therefore, caution should be exercised, and minutes should be compared with information in other documents.

Memos of conferences and conversations with anyone involved with a project can be valuable months or years later in reconstructing the substance of those meetings. Request for approval or information on critical equipment, materials, design, or procedures are important documents to maintain. A log of such requests, as well as corresponding responses, may provide evidence regarding delays on a project.

Actions in approving a contractor's inspection system or quality control program, or actions in accepting or rejecting contract work, frequently go beyond contract requirements and give rise to valid claims. Punch lists prepared by the owner or architect/engineer can provide documentation as to the extent of unnecessary rework or extra work requirements being requested by the owner in form of inspection and acceptance of work.

Success of construction contract claims often depends on proving that notice of changes was given. All records of such facts, even notes and memos, should be retained. The contractor usually keeps a "shop drawing log" to record dates of when drawings were requested from the supplier or subcontractor, drawings or samples were received to be checked, drawings or samples were sent to the architect/engineer, drawings or samples were returned from the architect/engineer, and second submittals were made, if revisions were required and the date of final approval.

As-built drawings should be kept up to date. Seemingly minor field changes might prove to be particularly important in a "claims" situation that involves changed conditions, increased quantities, or a failure. The certification of final completion, issued by the owner, documents that the contractor has completed all work. However, the contractor should beware of signing such documents if they include acceptance of final payment, which releases the owner's liability for any unresolved liens or claims.

In summary, items of correspondence that should be maintained in project files include:
- Meeting minutes
- Conversation memos
- Internal office correspondence
- Request for information

- Inspection and testing reports
- Notices to owner and to owner's project site representative of any changes
- Drawings and specification revisions
- Shop drawing log
- Critical path method schedule and updates, plus all input
- Punch lists
- Certificate of final completion.

Contemporaneous Records

Contemporaneous written expressions of work progress, critical path method schedule updates, site conditions, and damages entered into a job log or diary can provide a valuable and factual evidentiary foundation, particularly if it is done in the form of a regular business record. Providing job foreman or superintendents with dictating machines makes it convenient to fully record notes and observations; tapes can be transcribed later to provide a written record.

Daily labor reports and equipment utilization reports filled out by the project manager, superintendent, or foreman are also common records to document resources used on a project. The report normally records the amount of labor present, the number of equipment items operating, the names and manpower of subcontractors working, and a description of critical path method activities in progress with reference to critical path method nodes.

Personnel should be encouraged to take photographs of site conditions on a routine and systematic basis, concentrating on problem areas critical to procedures and scheduling. A picture is worth a thousand words, or a thousand dollars, especially in matters involving delays on construction projects. Changes and additions to the work often cause delays. Although the reason for the change or addition usually cannot be photographed, the resulting delay, such as idle equipment or lack of daily progress, can be photographed.

Daily weather data observed at the project site or obtained regularly from local weather bureaus may be useful in cases where work was delayed until a different season requiring, for example, costs for winterization when none would have been required except for the delay.

Therefore, examples of contemporaneous documents include:
- Input to critical path method schedules
- Time and adequate input to critical path method schedule updates
- Diaries
- Daily reports by all persons
- Equipment utilization reports
- Progress photographs, particularly of problem activities, including date and name of the photographer
- Weather data.

Schedule Information—Critical Path Method

Schedule information is vital for proving delay or acceleration claims. Any out-of-sequence activities should be documented, as well. Depending on contract requirements or the complexity of a construction project, various types or combinations of "schedules" may be utilized not only to plan the work but also to graphically illustrate with great effectiveness at a trial the "impact" of delays, out-of-sequence work, and disruptions on a project.

Critical path method schedules are not only useful in managing a complex project but are also valuable tools in analyzing the "impact" of concurrent or unrelated changes, delays, or acceleration on the project schedule. Fragnets. histograms, bar charts, and short interval schedules are also useful evidence to demonstrate "impacts" on a project, as well as the prudence of management planning.

Any meeting minutes with schedule-related discussions should be indexed as such for future reference. Manpower-loading distributions directly related to schedules are important documents to show impacts of out-of-sequence activities, changes, delays, or acceleration claims. Management must require monthly critical path method updates with adequate and timely input by all team members in order to manage and document the actual start and completion dates of each and every activity in a given time period.

The critical path method schedule monthly narrative report should be used to document the exact status of the project progress, define the critical path, list parameters of any delays, outline any problem areas, and forecast the completion date.

In summary, the important schedule-related documents are:
- Input to the critical path method schedule
- Input to the monthly critical path method updates
- The original approved critical path method schedule
- All monthly critical path method schedule updates
- Fragnets and time impact analysis
- Manpower loading data
- Scheduling meeting minutes.

Cost Data

Providing the actual dollars lost is critical to a construction claim. Use and maintenance of effective accounting methods can provide the proof of damages necessary to support additional compensation.

Since "delay," acceleration, and impact claims frequently involve inefficiency claims and loss of productivity factors, which are difficult to segregate under traditional accounting systems, a method of isolating cost not covered by the contract is especially needed. A system that allows for concurrent segregation of unanticipated costs is not only easier and less expensive than the after-the-fact breakdown, it is also more convincing in the courtroom.

Cost reports are often prepared to study costs or production units as the project progresses. Analysis of such cost reports may show where the contractor's estimating department was incorrect or when inefficiencies were caused by the contractor's own mismanagement.

Although cost records on each project and between contractors will vary, the following list is a typical spectrum of cost data that should be preserved for potential use in providing damages:
- Control budget
- Weekly labor distribution
- Labor timecards coded to critical path method work activities
- Overtime labor records
- Labor fringe agreements
- Certified payroll reports
- Cancelled payroll checks
- Daily equipment cost records, including hours operated, hours idle, work performed by critical path method activity, and repairs made
- Purchase orders
- Bid analysis
- Paid invoices
- Material receiving tickets
- Cancelled accounts payable checks
- Job cost reports
- Subcontractor cost reports
- Revenue records
- Progress payment reports
- "S" curve of projected collections and actual collections of work in place
- Record of stored materials billed monthly
- Change orders
- Bank loans
- Cost assigned to delays.

Early Involvement of Experts and Attorneys

Construction disputes generally require the involvement of experts to help solve problems and provide litigation support. Experts or consultants may also be necessary at trial to give opinions based on assumed hypothetical facts or actual knowledge of the circumstances of the case.

Contract provisions and applicable law can generally be found, within certain limitations, to support the position of both parties. Ultimately, the facts most often determine the success of the claim. Therefore, the key to successful analysis and resolution of a claim is the contract disputes expert who excels in the persuasive presentation of facts obtained through a comprehensive documentation process.

It is prudent to involve experts during actual construction when a claim is probable. The expert may be able to recommend ways to mitigate damages or reduce the impact of a problem. He may also be able to suggest methods of preserving evidence or creation of demonstrative evidence through graphs for use during negotiation, arbitration, or trial. Most importantly, involvement by the expert during actual construction allows his testimony to be based on first-hand data and knowledge rather than on facts learned from others.

Involvement of the construction attorney is also desirable when problems develop. Her knowledge of the legal aspects of contract compliance and claim preparation provides reassurance to proceed on a sound legal basis. There is no method for management of a construction project that will guarantee the absence of claims.

Both legal counsel and an experienced claims consultant should be involved both in the structuring of the project documentation requirements as well as in the preparation, negotiation, and settlement of a claim. Documentation could mean the survival of your company.

Project Management Control, Computers, and Software

You cannot establish an effective planning and control system by simply buying project management or scheduling software and putting it on your computer. People manage projects!

Elements of Project Planning and Control

The objective of applying concepts is to obtain better control and use of existing company resources. Application of the project management concepts requires identifying unique, complex efforts that involve several function skills with scheduled completion dates and limited budgets. The project planning and control aspect of project management is comprised of three elements: management information systems; management processes, and people. To successfully establish a project planning and control capability, it is necessary to address all three elements. Many companies incorrectly assume that, if they have a management information system that reports information regarding the project, they have both the project planning and control system and capability.

Often, this could not be further from reality. If a company has not looked at the social issues and identified solutions for those issues, it reduces the likelihood of achieving a successful project planning and control program. Furthermore, if the management processes have not been identified, evaluated, analyzed, designed, and thoroughly documented, a company will have problems in planning and controlling its projects.

Management Information Systems

At the risk of alienating everyone in the management information system community, it is a known position in construction that an automated management information system—no matter how sophisticated or how well designed—performs only four functions for the project manager: the abilities to collect, store, manipulate, and report data. Thus, if the data that are input to the manager are not timely, accurate, and adequate reflections of the game plan and status (updates) of the project, the data that are reported by the system are useless.

Therefore, just because you have acquired an automated scheduling system, you do not automatically have a high-quality schedule of project activities and an accurate status of accomplishments thus far. It takes people to identify the detailed elements of work, establish the logical sequences of performance of that work, identify appropriate durations and resources, and monitor and control the project. In order to assure that what the people do is consistent with the project game plan and company practices, it is necessary to have clearly defined management processes that the people employ in a consistent, disciplined fashion.

Management Processes

Management processes are really the management functions that are employed in the management of any endeavor. Everyone has his own particular outline for these processes of functions, but, in general, they are pretty much consistent with the six management processes: organize, plan, authorize, execute, monitor, and control. In the planning and control of any project, all of these management processes have to be performed in a consistent and disciplined fashion.

Project organization is the first, and one of the most important, functions of project management. Its purpose is to assure adequate definition of project work, identification of organizations responsible for performance of that work, and the assignment of responsibility for work execution to the appropriate people.

The first step in the organizing process is to define the project work (activities). This is accomplished by subdividing the project into manageable segments and then describing the scope of work within each of these segments. One of the most effective ways for accomplishing this subdivision of project work is by means of a work breakdown structure. The second step in the organizing process is to identify the participants. To accomplish this, the project definition is examined, and a determination of the skills required to accomplish the work scope is made. Having done this, the project participants are selected based on skill mix requirements, and an organization structure is prepared consistent with the project participants.

The final step in the organizing process is to assign responsibilities. This is accomplished by assigning responsibilities for the execution of the individual segments of project work to the performing organizations. Each segment of project work is ultimately assigned to a single organization that is responsible for the accomplishment of that work; this prevents gaps or redundancies in work assignments. Organizing the project answers the questions of what is to be done and who will do it.

Planning tells us how and when the work will be performed and how much it will cost. The first step in the planning process is to have timely and adequate schedule input data to schedule the project. This is accomplished through a hierarchical system of schedules, starting with the project master schedule, down through detailed activity schedules and fragnets of critical areas. The process of doing this is imperative to maintain strict traceability between all tiers of schedules and account for all significant interfaces between performing organizations.

The next step is to budget the recourses required to perform the project scope. All resources that would be applied to the project (i.e., labor, materials, equipment, computer, and so forth) should be individually budgeted within each of the detailed activities that have been assigned to specific performing organizations. These budgets are then time phased to be consistent with how the work will be performed in a logical sequence, in order to support the schedule game plan of the project. An integrated baseline for the entire project is then developed by summarizing these time-phased budgets.

Finally, project performance is measured using this baseline as the "standard" for expected performance. Plan now for accurate daily records and documentation of start and completion dates of each activity to give timely and adequate input to the schedule update.

Once the work has been organized and planned, it is necessary to go through one more format management function before the work is actually performed: the authorization process. It is one of the keys to the ultimate success of a project. Project authorization entails the job of examining project definition and planning in light of project objectives and assuring that they are mutually supported.

The first step is to review the internal planning. Once the completeness and quality of the project definition and plans have been found to be satisfactory, the plans are approved. Now the actual formal authorization to perform the work is accomplished by means of contracts, directives, and other work authorization documents.

The next management process or step is actual execution or performance of the work. Once the work has begun, the project manager must begin asking the question, "Are we progressing in accordance with the game plan?" The project monitoring process provides information necessary to determine the answer. The first step in the monitoring process is to measure progress. This is accomplished by collecting progress and cost data for the completed work, using the same techniques as those employed for project planning, and at the same level of detail as was used in developing the integrated project baseline.

Next, the data must be analyzed to determine the project schedule, cost, and status. When there are significant deviations from the plan, the reasons for those deviations must be determined, and corrective actions must be planned to get back on course. The monthly narrative of the schedule update should detail the project status.

As a part of the formal variance analysis, periodic forecasts at completion of schedule and cost performance should be performed. Finally, the results of this performance analysis should be summarized and reported at various levels of the company management structure.

Because of changes both within the project and its environment, the work often will not progress in accordance with the original game plan. Thus, the final management process or function is control. The purpose of project control is to assure that work continues to be performed and measured in accordance with a formal plan that is complete and consistent with the current project objectives.

The first step in the controlling process is to evaluate and compare the results with project goals and the game plan. Also, you need documentation of actual start and completion dates of each activity at the monthly update of the schedule. If the results are not acceptable, alternatives are reviewed and appropriate actions selected; then improvements can be direct. This process entails re-planning the execution of project work to assure that project objectives are achieved in the best way possible. It also involves a disciplined, controlled revision to baseline plans and objectives. To achieve this disciplined control requires sound record keeping and focusing of the execution of this control on a select few designated project personnel.

Appropriate definition and application of these management processes from a closed loop environment in which the project can be planned and controlled in a consistent disciplined fashion is important.

People

What about the most important element—the people who perform the management processes and operate the system? There are two principal issues regarding the people element of project planning and control. These are the selection of individuals who will perform as the responsible managers of the various elements of project work and the training of these people.

There's seldom a problem in identifying the total body of players involved in a given project. The difficulty is in selecting the right individuals in whom to vest the responsibilities associated with project planning and control. The right players are those who are actually managing the performance of the detailed elements of project work. These are people who are critical to the execution of the six management processes for functions described above. Yes, all of the people in the organization are important to the successful accomplishment of the project, but the people I have in mind are the individuals who have the greatest impact on the degree of success that is achieved by the project.

The identification of these individuals is accomplished by identifying management control points. This is conceptually accomplished by integrating the organization structure with the work breakdown structure elements. That manager is responsible for the planning, performance, and control of the work.

This makes the selection of the control point manager seem reasonably simple. However, caution must be exercised in the selection of that individual, because you don't want to assign this kind of responsibility to someone who does not have the commensurate authority to fulfill the responsibility. You do not assign someone responsibility for an effort and then assume that she will automatically be able to control that effort, regardless of whether she has authority. The solution to this is to select the project manager who is responsible for the organization that is performing the principal portion of the work represented within the management control point. Then you establish a mini-contract between that project manager and the home office and give him the authority to execute that contract. If, after you have identified your control points and managers for those control points, you don't feel you can give them this kind of authority, you have most likely picked the wrong people.

Once you have identified all of the players and their specific roles, you have to provide them with the training that will give them an understanding of the new or modified management processes and the general care and feeding of the management information system. This training should be broad enough that it allows the people not only to understand their roles but also how their roles fit into the larger scheme of the overall project planning, scheduling, and control process. Finally, there is no such thing as a one-shot training program. It is necessary to establish a continuing training program because of the normal dynamics of any project and contractor organization.

Developing the Project Planning and Control System Capability

Okay, let's say that you are convinced that there really are three elements that have to be considered in developing a project planning and control capability. The next obvious question is: "How do I go about developing that capability?"

The first part of the answer to that question is to use the KISS (keep it simple, stupid) approach. In this day and age when there is so much technology available to us, temptation in designing and implementing any systematic approach to become embroiled is technological exhibitionism. Having just made a strong pitch for simplicity in the design of the system capability, the task itself is very complex. Thus, the challenge is to identify a simple, easy-to-use solution to a very complex set of issues. To successfully accomplish this, I recommend that the task be approached similarly to the way in which a sophisticated hardware or software design is developed.

The first step is to define your system specification or game plan. This is exactly what you do before using a hardware or software system. In this instance, a very basic system specification issue is: "Are we designing a project planning and control system capability for this project alone or for all future projects?" Next, before doing anything else, determine what it is you have available to you that might be useful in the design. In the case of the project planning and control system capability, you need to inventory your existing practices for each of the management processes. Then, develop flowcharts or narratives for each management process to describe how you are currently doing business.

Next, just as you would identify those aspects of any existing product design that are not consistent with your system specification, you would identify when your current practices do not fulfill the objectives of your project planning and control system capability specification. Then, you develop new practices or modification to the existing practices, which will allow you to accomplish the objectives outlined by our specifications. These are reviewed in the equivalent of a design review, and once the specific approaches have been identified, you develop revised flow charts and narratives that depict the system capability as it will exist.

Having done this, you then develop detailed project planning and control system documentation that can be used for reference and training purposes. Before publishing that documentation, however, one final review—analogous to the final design review—is conducted to assure full correlation between the system capability, as documented, and the specifications that were established at the outset of the effort.

Summary

You cannot establish an effective project planning and control capability by simply buying a project management software product and implementing it on your computer. There are three elements to the project planning and control capability that include not only the management information system but also your management processes and the people in your project organization. If you have a boss who doesn't understand this, it most certainly will be difficult to be the equivalent of that little child in Hans Christian Andersen's story; someone has to say: "But he has nothing on."

The design and implementation of a project planning and control capability is definitely a complex endeavor, but the product of that design effort should be as straightforward and simple as possible.

Project Planning and Control System Design Methodology

1. Define system specification.
2. Inventory existing practices for each management function.
3. Develop flow charts and narratives for each functional area.
4. Identify when current practices do not comply with specifications.
5. Define new practices and modifications needed to satisfy specifications.
6. Develop revised flow charts and narratives incorporating design decisions.
7. Using final flow charts and narratives, develop systems documentation.
8. Correlate system documentation to specifications.
9. Update game plan.

Pre-Project Planning for Capital Facilities

Project Management Institute 25th Annual Seminar/Symposium (October 1994)

Abstract

Pre-project planning of capital facilities is a critically important leadership activity with the potential for significant influence on project success. Results of a recently completed research investigation are presented in this paper, including discussion of the definition, process, benefits, and principles of pre-project planning.

Introduction

Pre-project planning has a significant impact on the outcome of the construction of a capital facility. The 1990 PMI Seminar Symposium in Calgary focused on front end planning of projects. To date, however, very little information exists in the public domain relating to research in the area of pre-project planning.

In 1990, the Construction Industry Institute (CII) identified pre-project planning as an important area for research. CII is a consortium of large owner and engineering firms founded in 1983 to conduct research in the engineering and construction arena. It currently has eighty-five members and is considered one of the premier research organizations in the world dealing with project management issues. Its approach to performing research is to charter a task force consisting of approximately fourteen industry personnel, split equally among owner and contractor personnel, along with an academic researcher, and then fund their research investigation. An ongoing, CII-sponsored task force is studying pre-project planning and its relationship to the construction of capital facilities. This paper will summarize some of the results that have been obtained thus far by this task force.

Current wisdom within the construction industry says that early stages in the project life cycle, such as business planning and pre-project planning, can have a much greater influence on a project's outcome than later stages. This relationship is conceptually shown in Figure 1. The curve labeled "influence" in Figure 1 reflects a company's ability to affect the outcome of a project during the various

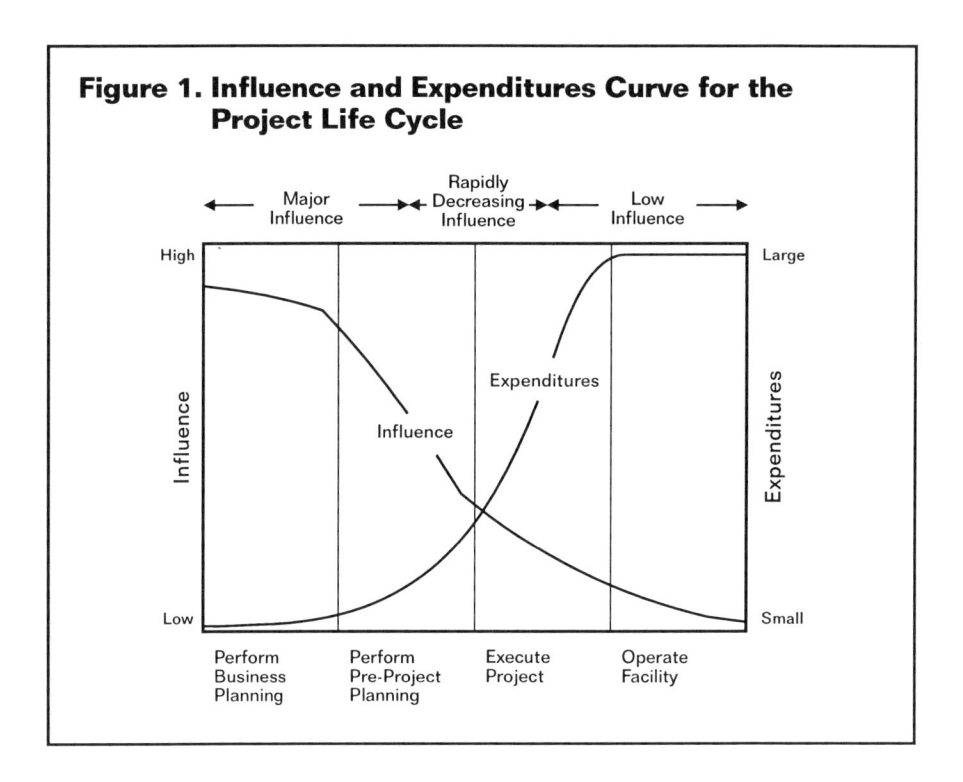

Figure 1. Influence and Expenditures Curve for the Project Life Cycle

←—— Major Influence ——→←— Rapidly Decreasing Influence —→←—— Low Influence ——→

Y-axis (left): Influence (Low to High)
Y-axis (right): Expenditures (Small to Large)
X-axis: Perform Business Planning | Perform Pre-Project Planning | Execute Project | Operate Facility

Curves: Influence (decreasing), Expenditures (increasing)

stages of a project. As the diagram illustrates, it is much easier to influence a project's outcome during the project planning stage when expenditures are relatively minimal than it is to affect the outcome during project execution or operation of the facility when expenditures may be significant.

In order to meet the charge set forth by the Construction Industry Institute, which was to find the most effective methods of project definition and cost estimating for appropriation approval, the task force conducted an extensive research investigation. The following five sections will outline some of the task force's findings in regard to this charge.

What Is Pre-Project Planning?

The task force has defined pre-project planning as the process of developing sufficient strategic information with which owners can address risk and decide to commit resources to maximize the chance for a successful project. Pre-project planning has many aliases such as front-end loading, front-end planning, feasibility analysis, conceptual planning, and so on.

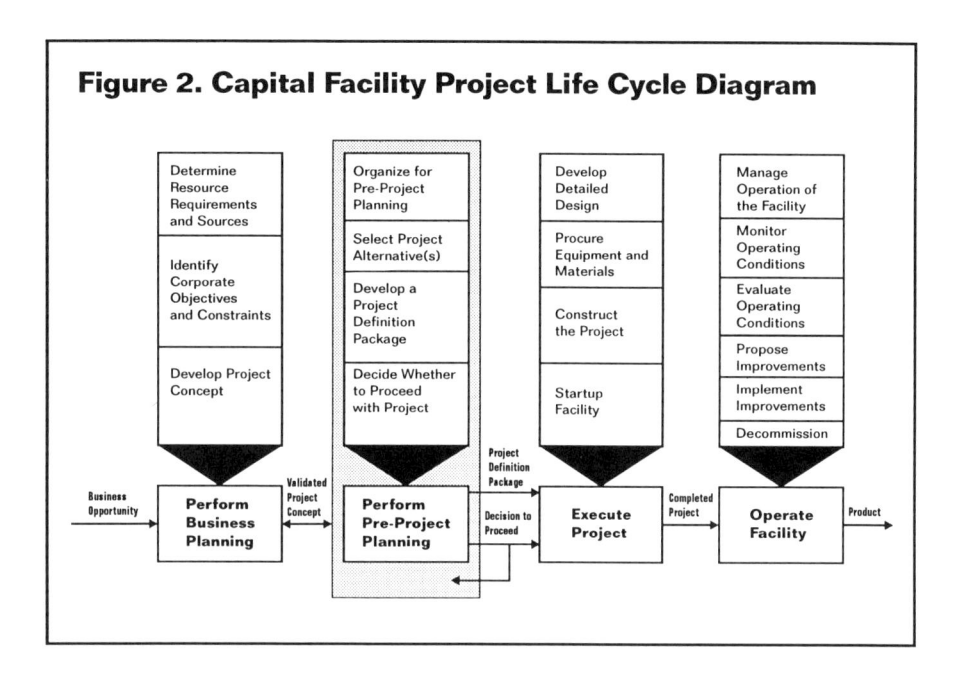

Figure 2. Capital Facility Project Life Cycle Diagram

Perform Business Planning	Perform Pre-Project Planning	Execute Project	Operate Facility
Determine Resource Requirements and Sources	Organize for Pre-Project Planning	Develop Detailed Design	Manage Operation of the Facility
Identify Corporate Objectives and Constraints	Select Project Alternative(s)	Procure Equipment and Materials	Monitor Operating Conditions
	Develop a Project Definition Package	Construct the Project	Evaluate Operating Conditions
Develop Project Concept	Decide Whether to Proceed with Project	Startup Facility	Propose Improvements
			Implement Improvements
			Decommission

Flow: Business Opportunity → Perform Business Planning → Validated Project Concept → Perform Pre-Project Planning → Project Definition Package / Decision to Proceed → Execute Project → Completed Project → Operate Facility → Product

Graphically, this process is shown in Figure 2 and includes a description of the major sub-processes required during each step of the project's life. Performing pre-project planning, the focus of this paper, is enclosed in the shaded box.

Using this definition, pre-project planning encompasses those sub-processes that occur after the project idea has been developed and validated in the business planning function and before the project is finally authorized for detailed design and construction. It is important to note that pre-project planning is at the interface between business planning and engineering.

The Pre-Project Planning Process

The Construction Industry Institute task force developed a generic model that shows the major sub-processes, along with their various functions, of the pre-project planning process. A summary level representation of this model is shown in Figure 3.

It should be noted that this process is not linear. Functions can be occurring concurrently; interaction, feedback, and iteration are inherent within the process.

The complete model is complex and involves several levels of detail. It is beyond the scope and intent of this paper to present a detailed explanation of the model and the modeling techniques. In any case, an understanding of the model is not a necessary prerequisite to understanding the process itself. A brief discussion of the pre-project planning process follows.

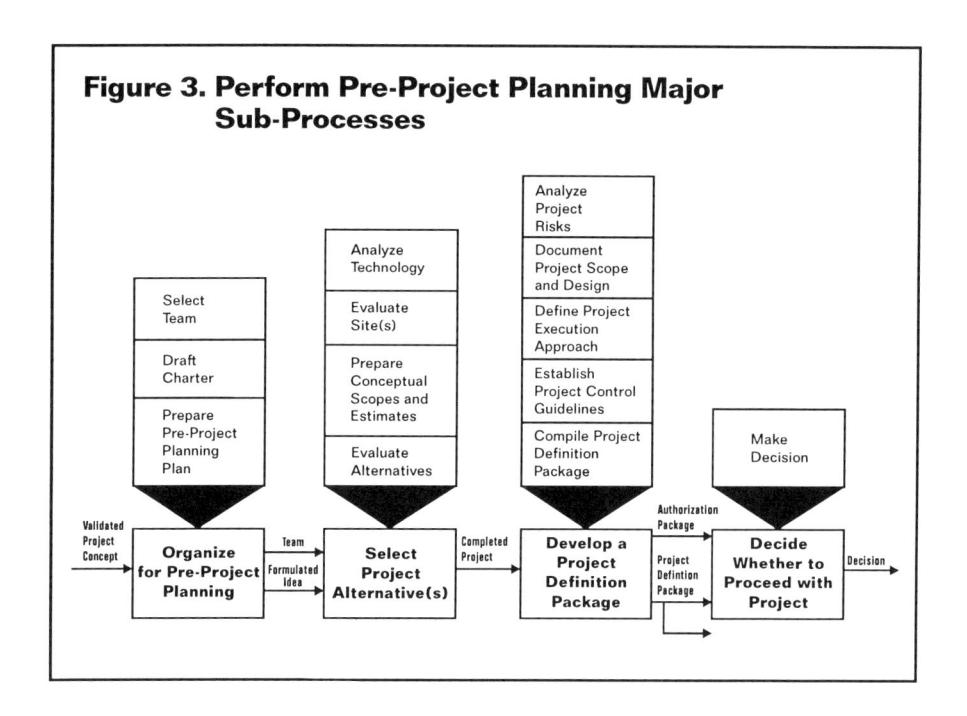

Figure 3. Perform Pre-Project Planning Major Sub-Processes

```
                                          Analyze
                                          Project
                                          Risks
                        Analyze            Document
                        Technology         Project Scope
                                           and Design
        Select          Evaluate           Define Project
        Team            Site(s)            Execution
                                           Approach
        Draft           Prepare            Establish
        Charter         Conceptual         Project Control
                        Scopes and         Guidelines
        Prepare         Estimates
        Pre-Project                        Compile Project      Make
        Planning        Evaluate           Definition           Decision
        Plan            Alternatives       Package

                                                        Authorization
 Validated                                               Package
 Project    Organize         Team      Select    Completed  Develop a      Project    Decide       Decision
 Concept    for Pre-Project  Formulated Project  Project    Project        Definition Whether to
            Planning         Idea      Alternative(s)       Definition     Package    Proceed with
                                                            Package                   Project
```

Organizing for pre-project planning is the first major pre-project planning sub-process and consists of the following three major functions:

Select Team: In this function, the team that is responsible for ensuring that pre-project planning is carried out properly is selected and developed. The team should be comprised of skilled and experienced members who can respond to the business and project objectives. The team may be dynamic in its membership but should in any case provide critical inputs from business, project management/technical, and operations.

Draft Charter: The charter defines the pre-project planning team's mission and responsibilities and further refines the original corporate-sponsored guidelines and concept for the project into a workable, project-based approach.

Prepare Pre-Project Planning Plan: Based on the charter and available resources, a plan is prepared, documenting the methods and time schedule for completing the pre-project planning activities to be performed by the team.

It should be noted here that the amount of effort and documentation would vary, depending on the size and complexity of the project. Team selection, charter, and plan may be defined in a memo or may require a relatively extensive effort along with substantial supporting documentation and instruction. The critical point here is that there must be a plan, and it must be clearly understood by all parties who will participate in the process.

Select alternative(s) is the second major sub-process and consists of the following four major functions:

Figure 4. Sample Project Types

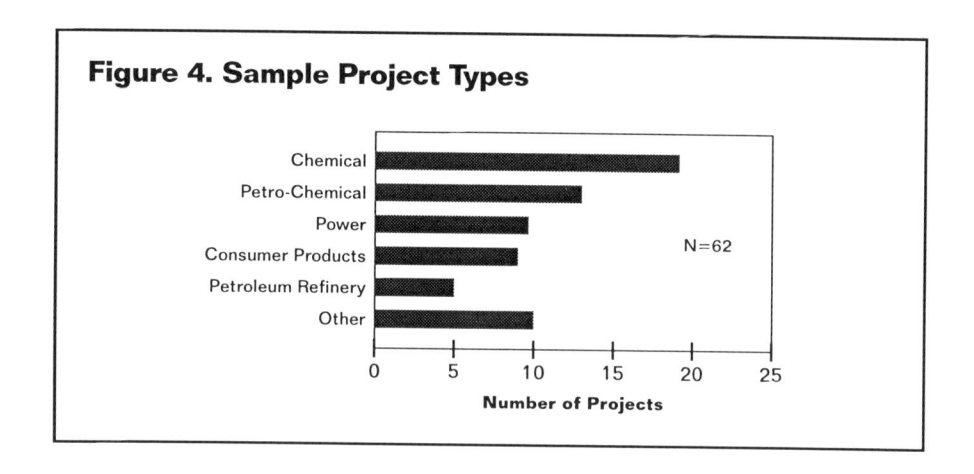

Project Type	Number of Projects
Chemical	~19
Petro-Chemical	~13
Power	~10
Consumer Products	~9
Petroleum Refinery	~5
Other	~10

N=62

- *Analyze Technology:* Existing and emerging technologies are evaluated for feasibility and compatibility with corporate business and operations objectives for usage within the project.
- *Evaluate Site(s):* Alternative site locations are evaluated to meet the client's needs in terms of relative strengths and weaknesses. Note that "analyze technology" and "evaluate site" are typically performed in conjunction with one another. Site alternatives can be global, local, or even inside an exiting building.
- *Prepare Conceptual Scopes and Estimates:* The team develops and assembles the required information on the various combinations of alternatives in a format that permits valid comparisons based on corporate and project objectives and constraints.
- *Evaluate Alternatives:* The team and decision-maker compare viable project options and choose the option(s) that is most advantageous to the business for further development.

Ideally, one alternative or combination of alternatives can be selected that will define the basic project. However, in some cases it may be necessary or desirable to move forward with more than one option. If this is the case, the project team must recognize that multiple options still exist and allow sufficient time and resources to deal with this more complex scenario. Too often, a project team will proceed with what it believes to be the selected alternative, only to be derailed when they discover that they have to go back and consider other alternatives.

Develop project definition package is the third major sub-process of the pre-project planning process and its five functions are given below:

- *Analyze Project Risks:* The team identies and analyzes risks associated with the selected project alternative. These analyses should include financial/business, regulatory, project, and operational risk categories in order to proactively seek to minimize the risk's impact on project success.

- *Document Project Scope and Design:* The team clearly identifies the commercial and technical intent of the project and brings the project design to that stage of completion that is necessary to reasonably minimize the risks associated with execution and operation of the facility.
- *Define Project Execution Approach:* This function involves addressing and documenting the methods to be used to perform the detailed design, procurement, validation, construction, startup, and so forth of the project.
- *Establish Project Control Guidelines:* The team develops detailed procedures to manage execution of the project, including control guidelines such as milestone critical path method schedules, procurement schedules, safety guidelines, validation master plan, and a control plan that addresses such issues as planning, scheduling, change management, and management information systems.
- *Compile Project Definition Package:* The team compiles the information developed in the four functions listed above into an authorization package that allows the decision-maker to decide on the viability of the overall project. A more detailed project definition package is also compiled and provides the basis for project execution if the project is authorized.

This formal planning process will greatly enhance all participants' comprehension of the project, its requirements and objectives. It will also enable clear communication of plans and objectives to the decision-maker(s), which will minimize the possibility of frustrated expectations because of miscommunication. Finally, and perhaps most importantly, clearly defined plans and objectives will ensure good transfer of information to downstream participants who must execute the project plan.

Make a decision is the final major sub-process of pre-project planning. In this sub-process, the decision-maker must weigh the business objectives of the project and determine through evaluation of the authorization package if the project will meet the company's needs. The decision must be made with a thorough understanding of the project's risks and objectives in mind. At this point, the decision-maker can either approve the project for further execution, kill the project, or send it back for further pre-project planning study.

Presentation of Research Results

Just what is a company's stake in performing pre-project planning? One of the initial task force objectives was to prove the need for pre-project planning. The following paragraphs describe the methodology used to meet this objective and some of the results obtained.

The task force and researchers first identified the variables that define success and pre-project planning efforts. Using these variables, data collection instruments were developed for their measurement. Construction Industry Institute owner members nominated projects for participation in the study. A study sample was then selected from the nominated projects, data were

Figure 5. Sample Project Sizes

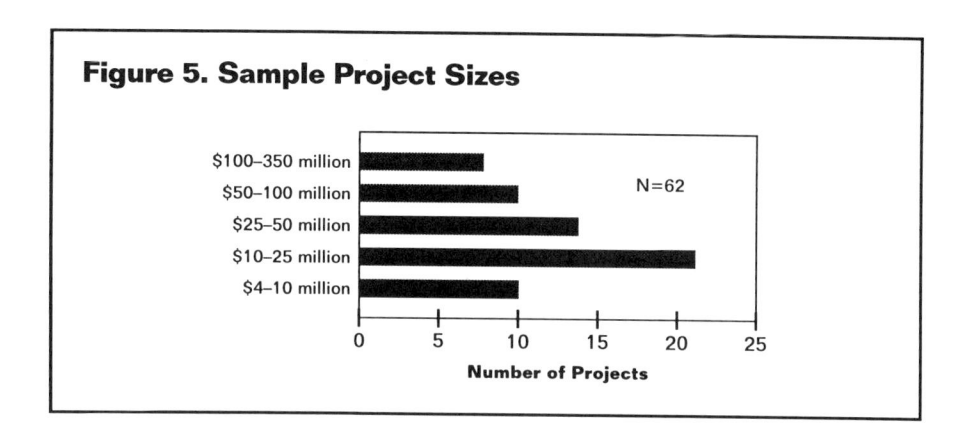

Project Size	Number of Projects
$100–350 million	~7
$50–100 million	~10
$25–50 million	~13
$10–25 million	~21
$4–10 million	~10

N=62

collected, and finally, various data analysis methods were employed to analyze the data. Data from sixty-two projects were submitted in this study. These projects included several types of facilities, as shown below in Figure 4. The authorized capital cost of the sample projects ranged from $4 million to $350 million, as shown in Figure 5. The projects had a median authorized cost of $26 million, and total constructed cost of these projects was approximately $3.4 billion.

The project questionnaire provided historical data on pre-project planning efforts expended and level of success the project attained. Of the sixty-two submitted, forty-four contained sufficient information for statistical analysis. Seven variables form a reliable index for measurement of pre-project planning effort. They are:
- Groups represented on the pre-project planning team
- Pre-project planning written charter
- Pre-project planning execution plan
- Duration of the pre-project planning effort
- Percent design complete at authorization
- Control guidelines developed
- Execution plan developed for engineering, procurement, construction, and start-up success.

The success index is derived by evaluating the following:
- Cost performance
- Schedule performance
- Percent design capacity attained
- Plant utilization.

Regression analysis performed on the two indexed variables revealed the relationship shown in Figure 6. The correlation coefficient (R) between the two indices is 0.61.

Further analysis of the data was accomplished by dividing the projects into subgroups of high, medium, and low pre-project planning efforts. Table 1 exhibits the level of success within each subgroup by displaying the range and

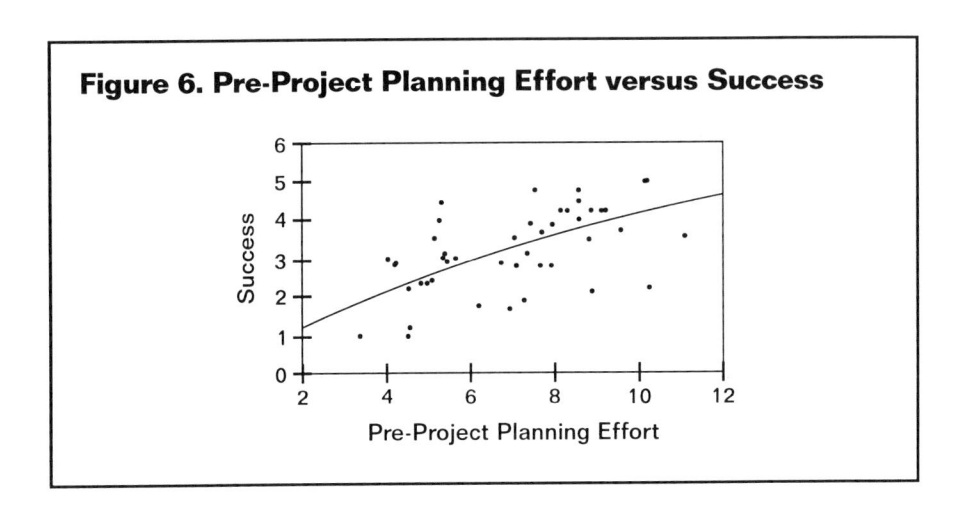

Figure 6. Pre-Project Planning Effort versus Success

mean values for each variable measured. Cost and schedule performance is measured in terms of percent deviation from authorization. Unit of measure for design capacity and plant utilization attained is percent of planned achieved at six months of operation.

The table demonstrates that, as the level of pre-project planning increases, cost and schedule performance improve, and variation is decreased. Additionally, higher percentages of attainment and utilization are found with higher levels of pre-project planning.

In summary, analysis of the questionnaire data exposed two important relationships. First, seven pre-project planning functions were found to produce a reliable measure of pre-project planning effort. Second, pre-project planning effort is positively correlated with project success.

As another part of the research investigation, a total of 131 telephone interviews were conducted with forty-nine project managers, forty business managers, and forty-two operations managers from fifty-five of the sixty-two construction projects submitted for study. Interviewees were asked a series of closed and open-ended questions to obtain their perceptions relating to success and effort. Using qualitative analysis techniques, the factors cited by respondents concerning project success and pre project planning effort were categorized, and the results are shown below.

Two open-ended questions asked of each respondent were:

1. What are your main reasons for your assessment of the project's level of success?

2. What are your main reasons for your assessment of the level of effort expended on pre-project planning?

Figures 7 and 8 give the results of the analysis of responses. Note that the responses are normalized as a percentage of all respondents within each group, and also that in some cases respondents gave multiple responses to the questions.

Table 1. Pre-Project Planning Subgroups

Indexed Subgroup	Variable	Range	Mean
High: Limits 8.1 to 11.1	Cost Schedule % Attainment % Utilization	–14% to +13 % –57% to 0% 50% to 125% 52% to 125%	–4% –20% 96% 100%
Medium: Limits 5.1 to 8.0	Cost Schedule % Attainment % Utilization	–28% to +86% –14% to +45% 42% to 140% 42% to 140%	0% +11% 98% 97%
Low: Limits 3.4 to 5.4	Cost Schedule % Attainment % Utilization	–34% to +142% –55% to 125% 20% to 100% 46% to 107%	+12% +24% 85% 85%

According to project representatives as a combined group, project control factors were most determinate of project success. The two project control factors considered most important were cost and schedule achievement. Operational characteristics, especially ease of operation and production quality, were also identified as determinate of project success. Other areas are as indicated.

However, as can be seen in Figure 7, there is considerable disagreement between the groups concerning the relative importance of each success factor. The project managers were most concerned with the execution phase of the project including project control, operating characteristics, ease of engineering, procurement, and construction, the construction/operation transition, and so on. The operations managers were most concerned with the downstream results and with having more input into project planning, especially in the area of technology evaluation. The business managers appeared to be more concerned with the overall project on a "macro" level. Differences of this nature may contribute to disagreement among project participants over project objectives and lead to communications breakdowns.

Figure 8, summarizing responses on effort factors of pre-project planning, shows that project representatives, as a group, stressed the importance of teamwork and communication, time and resources, and an accurate project definition package as significant for successful pre-project planning. Other categories identified were evaluation of alternatives, customer involvement, and corporate guidance in developing project objectives.

Again, some disagreement between groups exists. Analysis of each group's concerns supports the trend identified earlier. The project managers and

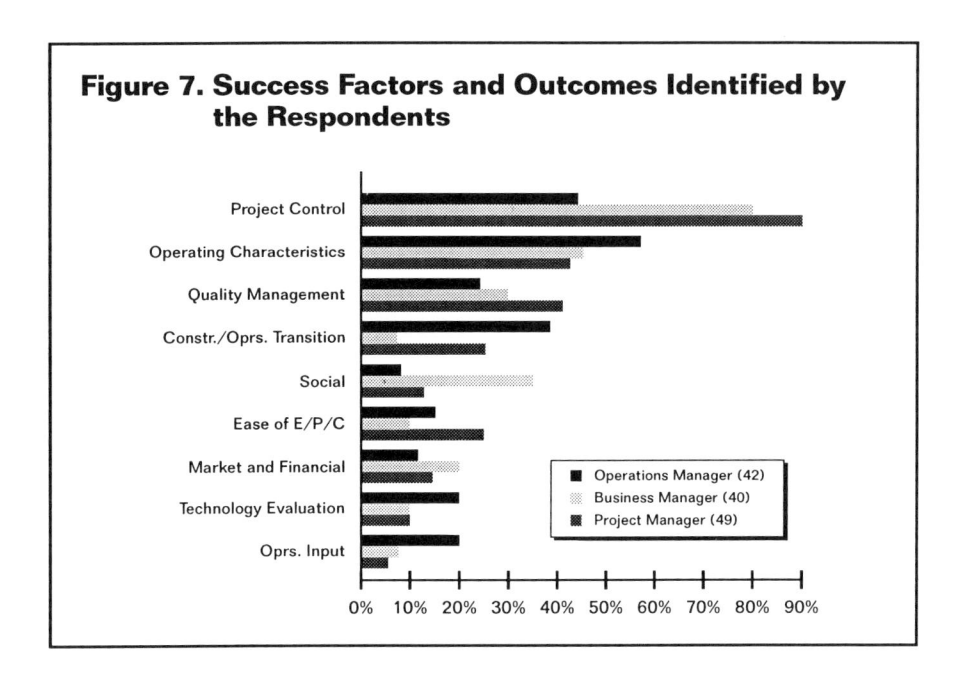

Figure 7. Success Factors and Outcomes Identified by the Respondents

operations managers focused more on specific pre-project planning effort factors that will have the most impact on the execution and operation of the project. However, the business managers seem to maintain a more global view.

There is meaningful convergence between the findings from the questionnaire and the interview data. The pre-project planning variables that form a reliable index for measurement of pre-project planning effort fall into three categories: teamwork, time and resources, and project definition package. Correspondingly, these are the three categories that are predominant responses from the interview representatives and that are essential elements of the model developed by the task force.

The success index derived from the questionnaire material is comprised of project control performance criteria and plant operating success. Interestingly, these are the two governing areas of responses of perceived project success from the interviewees.

Pre-Project Planning Principles

The Construction Industry Institute task force has identified several fundamental principles that are very important to the pre-project planning process. The probability of consistent success when planning and executing projects is greatly enhanced if these principles are recognized and embraced as a corporate philosophy.

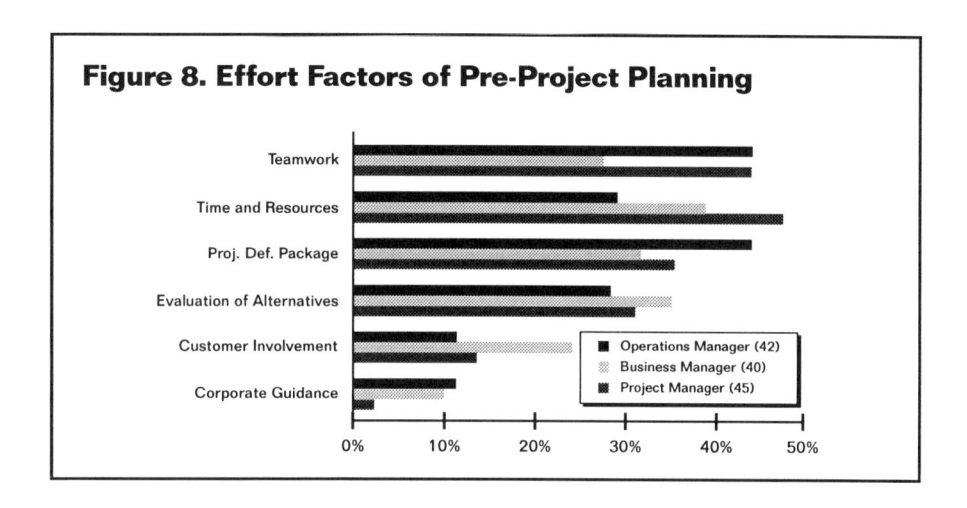

Figure 8. Effort Factors of Pre-Project Planning

[Bar chart showing effort factors by Operations Manager (42), Business Manager (40), and Project Manager (45) for: Teamwork, Time and Resources, Proj. Def. Package, Evaluation of Alternatives, Customer Involvement, Corporate Guidance; x-axis 0% to 50%.]

- Pre-project planning is a process that can be standardized. The concepts presented here need to be adapted to individual company needs and then tailored to each specific project. Nevertheless, the fundamentals remain the same and should be consistently applied to all projects.
- Pre-project planning is an owner-driven process that must be tied closely to business goals. Consultants and other contractors may play a major or predominant role in actual execution, but the owner must ensure that his business needs are being satisfied.
- Corporate goals and guidelines for pre-project planning must be well defined and clearly communicated to everyone involved in the process.
- Business, operational, regulatory, and social goals and requirements must be fully understood, clearly communicated, and effectively integrated into the pre-project planning process.

It is also important to recognize that there will be natural resistance to implementation of a formal pre-project planning process. The resistance will come from both business and technical personnel and will generally be based on two widely held perceptions: (1) "We cannot afford to spend money on conceptual planning for projects that may not be approved." (2) "This type of planning requires too much time and will delay the completion date."

The Construction Industry Institute task force research, together with substantial feedback from a number of owners who have a formal planning process, clearly indicates that quite the opposite is true. It has been demonstrated that good pre-project planning leads to:

- Improved cost performance
- Improved schedule predictability
- Better attainment of operational and production goals in the first six months of operation
- Better definition of risks.

In summary, pre-project planning represents a significant opportunity for owners to improve all aspects of project performance. Implementation is not without difficulty; however, the return on investment is definitely worthwhile. Statistics and feedback from companies who embrace these practices indicate that there is a very real opportunity to reduce project costs by at least 10 to 15 percent, while also achieving significant improvement based on other business and operations criteria. It must be stressed that the planning that is being advocated in this paper will take place at some point in the life cycle of every project—the most cost effective time for it to occur is during pre-project planning.

The Future

Major owner organizations are downsizing their corporate engineering and planning groups. This trend may tend to exacerbate old problems. However, there is an opportunity for North American business to increase competitiveness if the practice of pre-project planning, as described in this paper, becomes well recognized and utilized. Performance of adequate pre-project planning is owner driven; delegation of this work to consultants does not change this responsibility.

Pre-project planning provides one path to profitability. The model, Figure 2, shows business planning as the first function in the project life cycle. As globalization of our economy forces companies into increasingly severe competition, effective business planning is essential. The translation of business objectives and planning into a profitable project must pass through the pre-project planning function, for, as most project managers are aware, the activities and effort making up this process will occur sooner or later to a greater or lesser degree. Therefore, as project management professionals, we must focus our efforts on promoting the deployment of this "best practice."

Crisis management, due to a lack of planning, has become a way of life for many experienced project professionals. Changing this pattern through pre-project planning will involve some degree of behavior modification. It will also involve changing the attitudes of business managers who believe that time and money spent on these efforts is wasted. It is not wasted. It may, in fact, be the smartest investment that can be made to ensure project success.

References

1. Tortora, A.N. 1993. *Perceptions of Project Representatives Concerning Project Success and Pre-Project Planning Effort*. Masters Thesis presented to the University of Texas at Austin (December).

2. Gibson, G.E., J.H. Kaczmarowski, and H.E. Lore, Jr. 1993. "Modeling Pre-Project Planning for the Construction of Capital Facilities." A report to the Construction Industry Institute, The University of Texas at Austin. *Source Document 94* (July).

Communications for High Performing Project Teams

Project Management Institute 26th Annual Seminar/Symposium (October 1995)

Introduction

This paper will attempt to enhance *A Guide to the Project Management Body of Knowledge* (*PMBOK Guide*) on "Project Communications Management." In the *PMBOK Guide,* Chapter 10, the introduction says:

> Project Communications Management provides the critical links among people, ideas and information that are necessary for success. Everyone involved in the project must be prepared to send and receive communications in the project language and must understand how the communications they are involved in as individuals affect the project as a whole.

In this paper, the authors add to the *PMBOK Guide* by examining the subtleties of communication and prescribing specific approaches to ensure that project team members understand and practice these communications subtleties.

"Communications with Jazz"

> *Jazz! A special form of music without words, often without written music!*

When jazz formation, mood, or spirit is communicated through music, much is transmitted and much is absorbed. Experienced jazz musicians are comfortable with this subtle but effective method of "getting their message across."

Do you always get your message across? Effective communications in a project environment is, of course, critical. It always has been. We are today experiencing a revolution in the construction industry. There is a profound and irreversible move to dramatically reduce project timelines. The value of fast moving projects is clear. The direct cost savings are also frequently clear. But what about the subtleties? What about the impact of communications on these two parameters, time and cost? What about the inability to "listen to the jazz" caused by rapid schedules and fast-forwarded timelines.

For high performing project teams working in this environment, it is essential to pay attention to the communications subtleties. Clear and conscious planning to accommodate these subtleties is a critical success factor. Paying attention to communications processes, personalities, and attitudes will reap huge benefits in the high-pressure, fast-moving project environment. Projects cannot afford communications glitches—so much has to proceed without the opportunity to debate, discuss, and decide. Often "parallel paths" of design and construction planning are being pursued. The work is non-linear! One group needs to understand the other, often at levels well beyond the documents, well beyond the memo.

To fully comprehend these communications subtleties, and, more importantly, to benefit from all this "communications jazz," requires attention to three dimensions of communication:

- Communications processes
- Individual's personality
- Individual and team attitudes.

Each of these dimensions will be examined below and approaches will be described to ensure the practice of the subtleties of effective communications on the project team.

Processes

Much has been said and written about communication processes in a project environment. The clarity of contract communications is a requirement all have come to understand. Historically, "project meetings" have been a reliable process for insuring communications. Processes that physically locate the various representatives on a project in close proximity are also widely and effectively practiced.

Personality

Almost everyone has experienced the frustration of a different personality! Why can't they be like us? But they can't! Paying attention to these subtleties of personality difference in communications in a project team environment is critical. There is no time to communicate in ways to avoid the direct personality confrontations in a fast-moving project.

Attitudes

Even subtler than personalities may be attitudes. Attitudes are shaped by many factors that are not evident from the written biography of the team member; for that matter, they might not even be evident from a number of business-like encounters. But attitudes can profoundly impact effective communications.

So, what can be done to enhance communications, to positively affect the project team? What do we need to do about processes? What can we do about personalities? And how can we affect attitudes?

Processes—Approaches

It is insufficient to pay attention only to clearly documented contracts, plans, and procedures; thoroughly regular meetings with agendas; and clear written (and E-mail) communications. But all these are necessary. Without effective mechanisms and processes for team communications, the subtleties of personality differences and attitudes will likely wreak havoc on the project team and, of course, on the project.

The communications processes for high-performing project teams need to be designed and implemented to explore and explain the "unwritten" dimensions of the project and the project team. The creation of a project execution strategy document has proven to be an outstanding contribution, especially to fast track projects. In the project execution strategy, clarity and distinctions are provided to enable all to understand the philosophy of the various participants and their culture and the client's preferences in carrying out various aspects of the project. This project execution strategy articulates, as clearly as possible, the specific roles and responsibilities of all the players during the various phases of the project.

But the document itself is of only limited value. Maximum benefit is obtained by the process of having the project team members, themselves, in the very earliest days, create together the project execution strategy.

Personality—Approaches

So what to do about different personalities? A critical first step is an understanding by all team members that there are personality differences on the team. As trivial as this may sound, many often do not fully grasp that possibility and its implications. They are likely to interpret different responses and behaviors to reflect animosity, distrust, disrespect, and other interpersonal points of tension.

An excellent practice is to allow the team members to investigate together their personality differences, often adequately reflected in some standard personality instruments, such as the Myers-Briggs instrument. In addition to this simple reflection and discussion, it is sometimes useful to create some simulated (very close to real!) work situations to demonstrate how different personalities will show up in the midst of a project. This kind of group investigation enables all to see differences in behavior, conflicts, and the like as, most likely, only a difference in personalities. This personality difference can be explained, explored, understood, and, in almost all instances, adequately dealt with through a clear, conscious, verbal, and thoughtful process. And by having these conscious conversations, project team participants become comfortable with differences and able to deal with them quickly and in good spirit and humor in the heat of a fast track project.

Attitude—Approaches

The subtlest factor in effective communications is attitude. Just where do people get their bad attitudes? "The devil made me do it" is probably not a sufficient answer! Two people, alike in many ways, can face the same situation (like getting up in the morning) with very different attitudes.

It would be naive to even advance the possibility that the experience of a high-performing project team will fix one's attitude. In truth, attitudes almost always appear to be generated from somewhere inside the individual. So the project is not an "attitude adjustment" opportunity! But what can be done about the attitudes of the project participants?

An effective technique of dealing with "attitude problems" is to encourage (require?) that all members of the project team communicate their attitudes to each other! Team members can be instructed and encouraged to speak "how they feel." For example, faced with a missed critical deadline, a client could say to a contractor: *When you missed that deadline, I felt hurt, since we had talked together many times about how important that was to me.*

While that statement may seem not to contribute to any particular resolution of the current or possible future situation, it does do one thing clearly. It tells how the person feels. And if that person can be and has been honest, it will at least allow the other party to hear and hopefully understand that the person was feeling hurt. This would enable her to not misinterpret that the other person hated her, or be convinced that she was an idiot, or some other interpretation that might be made without an adequate explanation.

Now obviously this is relatively high-level effective communications! Sharing our feelings! It is exactly what is effectively practiced in marital therapy! It is difficult but powerful.

The Role of "Teambuilding"

A key success factor for fast track projects is for the team to be an effective, functioning, communicating set of people. A practice that enables this requirement, in the difficult and high-pressure situations of fast track projects, is the special focus on what has been called "teambuilding." This focus has proven to be highly valuable in many project situations. It usually consists of a very concerted upfront effort, often at an off-site location, to enable team members to really get to know each other. This "getting to know" includes an understanding of personality differences and an opportunity (in indirect ways) to examine "just what makes each other tick." Classic teambuilding outdoor exercises have often been used to enhance this understanding. In addition, these exercises enable people to develop a common bond. Since many of these activities are physical, "rough and tumble," and rarely leave everyone's clothes unsoiled, the participants have had the "foxhole experience" together.

But the upfront "teambuilding" is insufficient for project success. Periodically, probably in the range of every three months, the team members, or at least the senior leaders of the project team, should come together for some time period to simply examine and discuss how the team is doing. An effective focus for some of this can be some of the published evaluation instruments that have been developed to assess team performance. It is especially useful for a team to track its performance over time using these instruments to see how improvements and "slipping" is happening.

Summary

There is a timeless adage: *You get results from what you pay attention to.*

Paying attention to communications, especially the subtleties of communications, on a project team can reap high rewards. Project teams that use processes for effective communications, such as the project execution strategy development and project "teambuilding," have a significant payout for these investments. And people who participate in these projects perform at high levels and have a qualifying and rewarding personal project experience!

So, pay attention to the subtleties of project team communications! Appreciate the "jazz!"

Philosophy and Critical Path Method Communications

Communication is vital in project management. One of the project manager's critical responsibilities is to maintain communication links both within and outside of his project. This paper concentrates on one area, scheduling philosophy, and how it relates to project communications. It is an overview of a number of commonsense principles developed through experience rather than a scholarly approach based upon extensive research. The paper is intended to create interest and raise the level of consciousness in establishing and maintaining a positive scheduling philosophy within an organization.

The continued increase in the size and complexity of construction projects has placed an even greater emphasis on planning and scheduling. Most organizations involved in large projects have separate groups for the project planning, scheduling, and control functions. Personnel in these groups do not exercise actual control since that is vested with the project manager. However, the planning, scheduling, and control specialists must assimilate information from different sources and communicate and apply an array of techniques and methods aimed at helping the project manager understand a situation, diagnose it, and then take action.

Studies have shown that there is a mutual dependency between a trusting relationship and effective communication performance. A trusting organizational climate is generally required for effective communications, as well as daily use of critical path method schedules. The fact that a sound scheduling philosophy is an important ingredient in project communications will be developed throughout the paper. It is very easy to recognize that if the "scheduling philosophy" promotes a trusting and supportive climate, communication practice would generally be good in the area of project "time" control. Conversely, if the climate surrounding project scheduling is hostile and threatening, communication suffers.

A trusting and supportive scheduling climate is accomplished through day-to-day implementation of basic principles in the following four areas:
- Basic techniques used regardless of the scheduling system
- A project scheduling system
- Competent and motivated people

- Management (project, functional, and company executives) support of the system and recognition of its capabilities and limitations.

A review of the communication process is necessary before a complete understanding of the scheduling process can be detailed.

Project Communication

Project communication is not merely the transfer of information but, according to many investigators conducting research in this field, it can better be defined as the transfer of commonly meaningful information from one participant to another. This definition encompasses the fact that not only is information transferred, but the receiver has correctly interpreted the message.

This process involves more than the transmittal of facts. It also involves feelings that result when information is exchanged. Facts and feelings are the two essential ingredients of information flow. Since the project management concept is based on single-point authority, the project manager is charged with maintaining all communication links both within and outside his project. These communication links encompass the three systems of communication: the downward system, the upward system, and the horizontal system.

All of these communication links are vital in successfully executing the project. The project manager can personally expedite most of the communication links outside of his project. However, internal communications within the project team must function continuously with or without the project manager's involvement. This internal communication is the information flow required within the project organization to accomplish the "objectives" of the project. In the communication process between any two individuals or organizations, there may be barriers to the flow of information. Some major communication barriers with construction schedules are:

- Differing perceptions: What, why, when, how, who, and where of the project objectives may not be clearly stated. The objectives may also be perceived differently by the various members of the project team.
- Personality conflicts or interpersonal hostility barriers: Differing personalities, management styles, and a myriad of reasons that create hostility between individuals will disrupt the flow of information.
- Resistance to change barrier: The failure to obtain input from those involved, and the "not invented here" attitude may also hinder communication between organizational groups. The same barriers apply to critical path method schedules.
- Organizational barriers: Transmittal of incomplete or simplified information or omitting someone from the information process breaks communication links.

- Resource competition barrier: Competition for personnel and facilities allocated to various projects often interrupts communication and results in conflicts.
- Information distribution barriers: Rules and methods of communicating and a very restrictive application of the "need to know" principle may also be a barrier.
- Human barriers: Preoccupation with one's own situation, emotional blocks, past experiences, inarticulateness, mind wandering, defensiveness, and fears involving individual's status may interfere with the communication process.

The means of alleviating these conditions are as varied as the individuals and organizations that must deal with them. However, knowing that these barriers to communication exist should lessen their effects on project schedule execution.

Scheduling Philosophy

One of the dictionary definitions for philosophy is that it is the body of principles underlying a given human activity. Thus, "scheduling philosophy" may be defined as the principles, both technical and interpersonal, that comprise the concepts and techniques regarding time control of an endeavor.

The importance of scheduling philosophy in project communications can be drawn from the following:

- To accomplish any complex project, it must be divided into manageable tasks. These are then performed by specialized functional or discipline-oriented organizations. The complicated matrix organization that results gives the project manager many project and organizational interfaces to manage.
- Two different types of decisions affecting a project are made by management: first, the design of the management system (tools and procedures) and second, a large and indefinite number of daily operation decisions.
- One of the most difficult tasks involved in managing the project and organizational interfaces is that of maintaining communication links. Communication must transfer commonly meaningful information, and to accomplish this, both facts and feelings are involved.

A scheduling philosophy should be present, which helps develop and support a positive working environment that enables control to be exercised. This means that not only are effective systems and procedures in place but that the interpersonal relationships are equally effective in developing and maintaining a unified team for executing the project.

The first area for building a trusting and supportive scheduling climate is in the implementation of certain basic techniques related to the network-based system. The basic techniques employed in a scheduling system provide not only a methodology for using the system, but they also provide a means of alleviating several of the barriers of communications. Obtaining "input" from those involved in the project reduces the resistance to change barriers. Implementing the simple concept that follows can bridge organizational barriers that cause transmittal of incomplete or over-simplified information.

Scheduling work same as it is to be performed and reporting requirements to management, parent companies, government agencies, owners, and architect/engineers may place demands that tend to force the breakdown of the schedule into something other than the way the work will be performed. Careful consideration must be given to the subdivision of work into manageable activities.

To be a useful tool, the logic networks and durations must reflect reality as closely as possible. The critical path method must help you control the project you are building, not the one you thought you were going to build.

Failure to schedule work in the manner it is to be done will result in the documents being ignored by those responsible for doing the work. The critical path method schedule documents have no practical meaning to them and thus cannot be used as working tools for planning, scheduling, and control. The schedule has then become essentially a reporting document for someone else.

A barrier to communication has been established due to an organizational requirement that the "schedule" be prepared in a format inconsistent with the way the work will be performed. Conversely, if the schedule is developed properly, it can be a useful tool for transmitting information across disciplinary lines.

Schedule Monitoring

Closely related to the principle of scheduling the project in the same manner as it is performed is the follow-up involved in updating and monitoring the project. The many barriers to communication necessitate a close follow-up. Is the project "plan" of execution actually being implemented? This question needs to be answered at the same time that information is gathered for determining where we are and where we are going. Early detection of any divergence from the project plan of execution is important to the success of the project.

Some of the more common communication barriers that have resulted in the project plan not being implemented are:

1. Differing perceptions: What is required to accomplish an objective in scheduling may be perceived differently by certain members of the project team and the project manager.

2. Personality conflicts: A project manager's personality or management style of scheduling that is much different than those previously experienced by the project team members may initially create problems.

3. Resistance to change: "We didn't do it that way on the last project" or "That isn't our standard way" are examples of frequent communication barriers affecting the desired implementation of the project schedule.

4. Human barriers: Preoccupation with maximizing one's own performance based upon past experience often results in certain portions of a project being started contrary to that outlined in the project schedule.

Most of these communication barriers occur even though everyone involved is proceeding with good intentions.

The follow-up involved in updating and monitoring the project is done most effectively in an open and trusting scheduling relationship regardless of the scheduling techniques. This permits the situations resulting from the communication barriers to be understood and corrective action taken in an efficient and timely manner.

Schedules and Level of Detail

The amount of detail that is included in the master project schedule is a question that seems to arise frequently. The planning, scheduling, and control of the day-to-day operations should be developed within the framework of the master schedule. Summarization should be utilized for higher-level management reports.

Management Support and Critical Path Method Schedules

The final area in which the day-to-day implementation of basic principles promotes a sound scheduling climate is management support. All organizations must be time conscious as time is a money-consuming commodity. Thus, most organizations are acutely aware of the importance of the schedule for a project. Many organizations search for the "perfect" scheduling system to ensure that sound scheduling practices are maintained. Consistent management support is required to implement and maintain a sound scheduling function.

Surveys indicate that management support is one of the prime reasons for the successful use of critical path method schedules. The project manager must create an environment that will enable control to be exercised. This does not mean that she actually does all the work involved. Her responsibility, which is nontransferable, is to see that the work is accomplished and that its execution is monitored. The project manager should seek and accept sound advice and fully use the capabilities of control personnel.

One of the basic criteria of any effective scheduling system is that is should prevent irritations, embarrassment, and fights over real or imagined problems. The success of the scheduling system in accomplishing this requirement is dependent more upon people and their interpersonal skills than the mechanistic aspect of the system. The most important individuals are the project managers and other managers who direct how projects are executed.

Summary of Scheduling Philosophy

The scheduling philosophy that is developed and maintained in an organization becomes part of the climate that exists on a project. Communication practice is generally good in a trusting and supportive climate. Thus, those principles involved in developing a sound "scheduling philosophy" also improve project communications when they help establish a good environment to exercise control. The communication process involves the transfer of commonly meaningful information and also feelings. The project manager must maintain communication links both within and outside of his project. Communication with company management, clients, architects/engineers, and the project team are the project manager's four important links.

Internal communication is the information flow required by the project team to accomplish the objectives of the project. There may be barriers, however, to the flow of information in the communication process between individuals. Some of the major reasons for communication disruptions are differing perceptions, personality conflicts, resistance to change, organizational, information distribution, and human barriers.

The day-to-day implementing of basic principles in establishing a sound scheduling philosophy also helps to alleviate the conditions that create barriers to communication.

Critical Path Method Updates and Control

Daily record *actual* start and completion dates of each and every activity to provide timely and adequate input to the critical path method schedule update. Use *snode* and *enode* on daily reports. At the very heart of integrated cost and schedule control and its primary justification is the ability to influence the outcome of adverse cost and schedule trends.

Resolve the enigma of updates and control by a critique of some factors of schedule control. The *first* of these factors is completion of prerequisite activities. Activities that are precedent by management, physical, manpower, no starts, and out of sequence starts constraints must be completed before an activity may be commenced. The game plan requires equal and diligent attention to all constraints. The completion of prerequisite activities or, more technically correct, precedent activities, is the first of major issues involved in field production control. The informational processes must routinely confirm that prerequisite activities are being completed as expected.

The *second* prerequisite is having the necessary materials at the actual site of work for placement by the workforce. Manage the submittals and delivery schedules. Bricklayers cannot build walls with bricks or blocks that don't exist; carpenters cannot construct woodwork without the necessary lumber and connecting devices; and ironworkers cannot erect steel that has not yet been delivered. This informational and administrative process by the project manager must confirm that materials have been submitted, approved, and delivered to the work site. In fact, the project manager's check-off list should include all materials, tools, and equipment. Note that your critical path method schedule requires timely and adequate input to the submittal schedule and the delivery schedule.

The *third* major consideration in production control is workforce availability. The consideration with respect to workforce includes the proper crew mix, related to the estimated quantities and activities duration. It also includes the physical limitations of the work.

Project Manager's and Critical Path Method Planning

The foregoing three considerations are all part of the planning detail, which should go into the job, and are customarily implemented at the field level. Some project managers have a major false perception—which developed early with the critical path method, leading to its early disfavor for construction planning and scheduling—that must be addressed. The false perception is that detailed planning and scheduling of the kind available through the critical path method will automatically result in proper schedule control. This is, of course, not true. The early discovery of this fact led to some disenchantment with the critical path method. The problem, however, is not the method itself. The problem is the expectation that the project "game plan" and schedule can simply be wound up, turned loose, and left to run its course, resulting in proper schedule control. Project managers beware!

Project Manager's and Critical Path Method Control

Implementation plus monitoring plus control equals what is required in support of the extraordinary analytical and informational capability of the critical path method. A system of monitoring and controlling performance is also required. Updated schedules must be re-implemented whenever significant variances occur related to job conditions.

Proper planning and scheduling are critical to a well-controlled project; it is equally true that proper implementation, updating, monitoring, and re-implementation are also required. This process is cyclical and should be continued throughout the construction of a project.

The Realities of Project Management and Field Construction

As noted, not all of the logic relationships shown are the result of physical constraints. As a consequence, the actual conditions in the field environment may require adjustments from time to time in either sequencing or the phasing of the work to be accomplished. This of itself should cause no great discomfort either in the field environment, among the planning and scheduling resource, or with project management.

The major focuses in field construction should continue to be high production, productivity, and schedule control. Cost and schedule, information-wise, bear a very close relationship.

Controlling the schedule, for example, will go a long way toward controlling the cost of time-related activities. What is required is the control of cost and schedule together, but with schedule being the primary focus in the field environment, there is little opportunity to directly affect cost outside of the schedule.

Schedule Flexibility

Maintaining effective cost and schedule control involves two principal requirements. The first is to have a valid game plan and schedule for the project. The second is a dynamic response capability that allows for field variances without upsetting or disrupting the production control processes and the downstream elements involved in integrated cost and schedule control.

The Schedule as a Time Budget

The most effective way to view the original schedule is to consider it as a "time" budget for individual activities, groupings of activities by trades, and the entire project. The original schedule should be maintained with the same degree of integrity as an historical document, as in the cost budget. The original schedule will be used for generating time performance ratios and is a significant component in production performance ratios as well.

The Planned and Actual Schedules

As the job progresses, a schedule recording actual performance (a daily record of actual starts and completions of each activity) is generated. The actual schedule is similar to job costs in some respect. It is different from job costing in that the actual becomes the basis for planning the remaining work carrying the project through to completion.

The primary record is an actual start and actual completion. Where appropriate, a percentage completion may also be reported at the update. With variances between the planned and actual start dates and the planned and actual completion dates on each activity noted, the historic performance data need to be inserted into the actual logic network diagram in place of the planned performance data, and the actual schedule needs to be recalculated and updated.

Schedule Updates and the Turnaround Document

A major benefit of frequent schedule updates is the dynamic and interactive nature of the turnaround document for each planning horizon. Take, for example, a project in work for which the planning horizon is a calendar week. The turnaround document provides information on actual performance for the calendar week. The updated schedule then becomes the basis for generating the turnaround document for the next planning horizon. When this process is meticulously followed, the turnaround document prepared by the project manager for production management and control over the next planning horizon is based on what actually has taken place through the end of the previous period, not on some (planned) schedule that may have been prepared months earlier.

Processes for Schedule Update

Receipt of timely and adequate input. It has been pointed out that the planned job schedule is maintained as a time budget. The actual schedule is the schedule that is updated (monthly) for each planning horizon. The schedule updating includes the data capture processes involved with the utilization of the turnaround document (daily records of actual dates).

The data on the turnaround document reflects the current state for each activity, which has been either started, worked on, completed or percentage of completion, or started in some earlier planning horizon but not completed.

Initially, the assumption is made that the durations and logic relationships of activities yet to be addressed will remain unchanged. The schedule is then recalculated using the actual data for the activities in the most recently planned horizon. The result is a complete new schedule from the end of the most recent planning horizon through the end of the project.

The updated schedule should be evaluated for validity. When significant changes or modifications have occurred in the game plan and schedule for the project, whether from some major delay or from some significant acceleration, it may be necessary to reconstruct the logic of the schedule from the end of the last planning horizon to completion. While there may be some reluctance to undertake a major revision, such should be undertaken at any time the validity of the historic schedule becomes suspect or major changes occur.

Scheduling Monitoring

Schedule monitoring occurs as a result of the data capture on actual performance through the updating process. Schedule monitoring provides a clear indication of schedule performance and will be reflected in the time performance ratio calculations at the update.

Schedule monitoring alone, however, is not sufficient. The schedule must be updated, analyzed, and evaluated at frequent intervals to maintain validity and a realistic relationship to what is taking place in the field. Each schedule update carries with it, to some degree, a re-implementation of the schedule, especially when significant changes are occurring as a result of job performance.

Any activity falling outside the expected (planned) time performance must be examined in detail and the reasons for delays clearly identified. With the reasons for the delays identified, corrective action must be taken immediately. The reasons for delay may be many. The most likely problem may be poor planning or an inadequate workforce. Closely associated with workforce may be inadequate project management. Immediately behind in importance would be having adequate materials, equipment, and technical information. Also change orders may cause delays, plus strikes and weather.

The Implementation of Corrective Action

Corrective or recovery action must be based on current (updated) valid information on performance. No single process or procedure can provide the overall control cycle. It rather results from the effective use and knowledge of schedule methodology, schedule monitoring and updating, and the weekly progress meeting held by the project manager. Also important are the project action checklist resulting from the weekly progress meeting and the continued cooperation and good communications from all of the team members for the project.

The potential for causing schedule problems is not related to the value of the activity. A relatively small item can cause schedule and related cost problems many times its own cost. It is therefore necessary to have the informational systems working to determine which ninety-five items are performing as expected so that project management can identify the five that are not performing satisfactorily. Once a clear focus on the problem is available, there is time for action.

Summary—Update and Control

Schedule monitoring and control, as it turns out, is a matter of careful planning and scheduling, as well as implementation and monitoring of the schedule. Schedule monitoring and control assumes a properly planned and scheduled project. It also assumes a projection team ready, willing, and able to address the project for maximum productivity and production.

The critical path method, with its extraordinary analytical capabilities, is an effective tool for schedule monitoring and control. Its weakness needs to be recognized along with its most useful capabilities in the measure of schedule performance. The planned schedule serves as the benchmark of "time" performance in much the same way that the budget provides the basis for job cost performance measurements.

The actual schedule is maintained independently of the planned schedule and "updated" frequently, based on actual performance data. There are three cycles within the planning and scheduling process, which are repetitive in nature and essential to integrated cost and schedule control.

First of these is the planning and scheduling cycle of work that established the basic job strategy. Next is the production cycle of work that involves an implementation of the game plan and schedule. The third, and perhaps the most critical in schedule control, is the monitoring and control cycle of work. This cycle captures data on actual performance and through performance ratios compares actual performance to planned performance. When an exception of status occurs—that is, an activity is performing outside acceptable limits—corrective strategies must be designed and implemented to maintain or regain full control of the schedule.

Analysis of Out-of-Sequence Activity Starts

Document any out-of-sequence starts. Vigilance by the project manager includes evaluation of any out-of-sequence critical path method activity starts. Scrutinize all activity—leads and lags—at each update. Know the true critical path method methodology as to restraints to logic and sequence of critical path method activities.

Current Critical Path Method Schedules versus Abandonment

The approved critical path method schedule must be used daily and be posted at the project site. All contract parties are required to use this contract document requirement to coordinate the project activities. Regular monthly critical path method updates must be kept "current" each and every month in order to maintain the felicity and authenticity of the critical path method schedule. Change orders should be added at each monthly critical path method schedule. In order to control the risk, the project manager must make a time impact analysis at the time of any delay or impact to the critical path method schedule. Study the specifications as to possible abandonment in the event your critical path method schedule is not current.

Today's Needs in Project Management:

The Project Management Technique: Manage, Schedule, and Cost

Critical Path Method Planning and Problem Avoidance

Project management is a modern methodology characterized by new approaches to management restructuring and adaptation of special management techniques in order to more efficiently and effectively utilize resources and time. Resources of manpower, equipment, facilities, materials, money, and information and technology are managed efficiently and effectively, keeping projects on schedule and within planned cost at the desired standard.

Critical Path Method Planning Methodology

A construction project may be defined as a one-shot, time-limited, goal-directed, major undertaking requiring the commitment of varied skills and resources.

1. It has been described as a combination of human and non-human resources pulled together in a temporary organization to achieve a specified purpose.

2. A project has a single set of objectives, and when these objectives are reached, the project is completed.

3. A project has a finite and well-defined life span.

4. A project consists of sequential phases: concept, planning, construction, and project closeout.

The Construction Project Environment

1. Need for flexibility. No two projects are alike from a project management point of view. Differences in technology, geographic locations, the client

approach, contract terms and conditions, the schedule, the financial approach, and environmental factors contribute to the need for flexibility in all phases.

2. The task force concept is the most effective means of realizing project objectives.

3. Maximum authority, responsibility, and accountability rest with the project manager.

4. Basic project management principles do exist. There is, however, no single archetype construction project organization or project procedures yet devised that can be rigidly applied to more than one project.

5. Major projects often involve resources of a large number of organizations. Each must be directed and coordinated toward a common set of project objectives of quality performance and cost and time of completion.

Critical Path Method and Resolving Enigma

As project management has grown and developed, several guiding factors have evolved, which form a basis for this management approach.

1. The establishment of the project manager as the focal point for the integrative responsibility. This has resulted in:
- Single person total responsibility
- Project rather than functional dedication
- A requirement for coordination across functional interfaces
- Proper utilization of integrated planning, scheduling, and control.

2. Establishment of an integrated planning and control system that effectively coordinates the horizontal and vertical units of a company toward better project identification and control. Requirements for the integrated planning and control system include complete activity definition, resource requirement definition, timetable establishment, and establishment of a basis for performance measurement by utilizing critical path method schedule updates.

3. These two factors, establishing the project manager and a planning and control system, if properly executed, result in assurance that functional units will understand their total responsibility toward achieving project needs and will ensure that problems resulting from scheduling and allocation of critical resources are known beforehand. These procedures also allow for early identification of problems that may jeopardize successful project completion so that effective action can be taken to prevent or resolve the problems.

4. These two factors are somewhat constrained by the fact that each project is normally of a finite time duration and exists as a separate entity within the company except for administration purposes, and the resources must be scheduled and fitted to satisfy the needs of the project, not vice versa.

5. In the project environment everything *seems* to revolve around the project manager. The project is a specialized, activity-oriented entity; however, it cannot exist apart from the traditional structure of the organization.

6. Project managers are responsible for day-to-day operations of the organization.

Predicting Project Success

Actions by the project manager and the project team that contribute to project success include:
- Insist upon the right to select key project team members
- Select key team members with proven track records in their fields
- Develop commitment and a sense of mission from the outset
- Seek sufficient authority and a projected organization form
- Coordinate and maintain good relationships with client and team
- Seek to enhance the public's image of the project
- Have key team members assist in decision-making and problem solving
- Develop realistic cost, schedule, and goals
- Have back-up strategies in anticipation of potential problems
- Employ a workable set of project planning and scheduling tools
- Stress the importance of meeting cost, schedule, and performance goals
- Keep changes under control.

Major Causes for Failure of Project Management

- Selecting a concept that was not applicable. Since each application is unique, selecting a project that does not have a sound basis, or forcing a change when the time is not appropriate, can lead to immediate failure.
- The wrong person selected as project manager. The individual selected must be a manager. He must place emphasis on all aspects of the work, not merely the technical ones.
- Upper management not supportive. Upper management must concur in the concept and must behave accordingly.
- Inadequately defined tasks. There must exist an adequate system for planning and control to ensure that a proper balance between costs, schedule, and technical performance can be maintained.
- Management techniques misused. There exists the inevitable tendency in technical communities to attempt to do more than is initially required by contract. Technology must be watched, and individuals must buy only what is needed.
- Project termination not planned. By definition, each project must stop. Termination must be planned so that the impact can be identified.
  Lessons to Be Learned from Project Failures
- When starting off in project management, plan to go all the way.
- Do not skimp on the project manager's qualifications.
- Do not spare time and effort in laying out the project groundwork and defining work.
- Establish and use network-planning techniques, having the critical path method schedule as the focal point of project implementation.

- Be sure that the information flow related to the project management system is realistic.
- Be prepared to continually re-plan activities to accommodate frequent changes.
- Whenever possible, tie together responsibility, performance, and rewards.
- Long before a project ends, provide some means for accommodating the employee's personal goals.
- If mistakes in project implementation have been made, make a fresh try.

Using Project Finance to Help Manage Project Risks

Project Management Journal XXII:2 (June 1991)

Introduction

The past decade has seen increased use of innovative techniques for financing large construction projects internationally as well as in the United States. As a result of constraints on government spending and the rapid escalation of construction costs, both the public and private sectors have developed new and more efficient methods of financing projects that would otherwise be delayed or foregone.

Declines in oil and commodity prices have resulted in reduced funds available for construction spending in resource-producing countries. Resource-poor developing countries have faced tight international credit markets as debt levels have increased, and the availability of resource revenues for recycling through commercial bank lending have declined. Governments in developed countries, including the United States with its large deficits, have faced pressures for slower budget growth. Internationally, the value of new construction contracts awarded fell by 33 percent between 1981 and 1986.

Technological advances in many capital-intensive industries, including mining, petrochemicals, and utilities, have accelerated capital replacement costs faster than the rate of inflation. Innovative financing techniques have become increasingly important to the feasibility of projects, such as development of natural resources and construction of industrial and power plants. One such technique is referred to as project finance, a method under which revenues from a project are the sole source of debt repayment and return on equity. Unlike traditional methods of construction financing, project finance lenders typically have limited recourse to the assets of the project owner. "Pure" project finance provides no recourse; if project revenues are insufficient to cover debt service, lenders have no claim against the owner beyond the assets of the project. The project is, in effect, self-funding and self-liquidating, in terms of financing.

Project finance generally involves a consortium of sponsors, which, depending on the nature of the project, may include the owner of the resource being developed, users or customers of the resource (off-takers), engineering and construction/contractors, equipment vendors, and operations and maintenance contractors. As used in this article, "sponsor" refers to those participants who initiate a project and provide sufficient equity or recourse to make it attractive to passive investors. Sponsors usually work with financial intermediaries to arrange placement of debt and, if needed, additional equity.

The limited recourse, consortium of sponsors, and use of third-party—rather than in-house—funds, which are characteristic of project finance, can also assist project management. In the absence of a participant with the traditional owner's responsibility for assumption of residual risk and guarantee of debt repayment, it is necessary to more carefully identify risks that occur throughout the life of the project, from conception to operation. Then, allocate those risks to the participants who are best able to manage them.

The interest of individual sponsors in the success of the project should encourage them to manage the risks for which they are best qualified. Risk avoidance, which appears to be common on many construction projects, should represent less of a problem in project finance than in traditional methods of construction finance. This process should improve project efficiency. The fiscal discipline imposed by use of someone else's money should improve the effectiveness of management of project resources.

The concept of project finance is not new. It was used in the nineteenth century to fund construction of the Suez Canal and British railroads. More recently, project finance has been used to develop North Sea oil fields and to construct EuroTunnel, which is being built without the financial backing of the governments of France or the United Kingdom.

In the United States, project finance was used by wildcatters in the thirties to develop Texas oil fields, with oil in the ground used as security for loans to be repaid by development of the field. Typically, however, private sector construction projects have been financed with corporate funds, and federal grants or tax-exempt bond issues have funded public works. Project finance can provide a source of capital to entrepreneur and small, growing businesses.

The supply of public and private sector construction projects seeking finance and the demand for assets by investors such as banks, pension funds, and insurance companies represent the elements of a market for project finance. Following sections discuss market supply and demand and describe the role of financial intermediaries in arranging capital and allocating risk through the project finance process, in order to match supply and demand.

The Supply of Projects Seeking Finance

While approximately $250 billion in construction contracts were awarded for major projects in the United States in 1987, many potential public and private projects are deferred or delayed each year because of funding constraints. Use of project finance provides a means of increasing the availability of construction funds, particularly for firms or governmental bodies whose access to traditional sources of capital is constrained.

Public Sector Projects

Population growth, cutbacks in government spending, and a continually deteriorating infrastructure have generated a supply of socially beneficial projects that lack funding. In the United States, the availability of federal grants for public works projects has been constrained by budget deficits. Meanwhile, the ability of state and municipal governments to finance construction through bond issues has been affected by changes in tax laws and limits on debt capacity imposed by law, political considerations, or capital markets.

Provisions of the Tax Reform Act of 1986, including broadened application of the alternative minimum tax, reduced the attractiveness of municipal bonds to some investors and stimulated consideration of alternatives for financing public sector projects. Limitations on the preferential tax treatment of bonds for non-public purposes—i.e., "private activity bonds" for industrial development, airports, ports, and environmental facilities—have resulted in the use of project finance for infrastructure improvements aimed at stimulating economic development, including construction of transportation and environmental systems.

Advantages of using project finance to fund infrastructure improvements can extend beyond the ability to reduce governments' capital requirements; improvements in efficiency may also be attainable through reduced involvement of political considerations and less stringent legal and regulatory requirements for private sector construction projects. In addition, use of project finance in the public sector can facilitate the transfer of expertise and technology from the private to the public sector.

Privatization represents a public-private partnership for the provision of facilities or services typically considered the responsibility of government. Governments at all levels have recognized advantages in privatization, and the inventory of successful projects is extensive. Examples of privatization have included construction or operation of environmental source of revenues for future pay and transportation systems, correctional and medical facilities, and public office buildings and housing.

"Build, Own, Transfer" (BOT) Projects. A frequently proposed, but less frequently implemented, mechanism for funding infrastructure privatization with project finance is the "build, own, transfer" model, in which a private consortium finances construction, then transfers ownership to the public sector in return for a claim on future revenues generated by the project. The EuroTunnel, crossing the English Channel, is an example of a BOT project. A consortium of private lenders and investors has financed construction with five billion pounds sterling of debt and one billion pounds of equity without the financial backing of the governments of France or the United Kingdom. Revenues will be provided through fees paid by railroads using the tunnel. The operating concession for the sponsoring consortium runs for fifty-five years, with debt repayment in eighteen years.

Transportation Projects. Tunnels and bridges have also been constructed in Hong Kong and London using the build, own, transfer method of project finance and are under consideration in Canada and Turkey. Tolls, leases, or operating concessions provide the source of revenue for future payments to lenders and investors. In the Canadian example, selection of a developer for a bridge to Prince Edward Island will be based on the minimum subsidy required to build and operate the eight-mile-long structure. In the United States, project finance is planned for private toll roads in Colorado and Virginia and is being considered for bridge rehabilitation projects.

Environmental Projects. Environmental projects have been among the most common public sector applications of project finance in the United States, partly due to the relative certainty of future revenues. In addition, while federal law mandates sewage, water, and hazardous waste treatment, programs to fund construction of costly treatment facilities have been the targets of recent and proposed cutbacks, forcing many municipalities to consider privatization or other innovative financing techniques.

Energy Projects. Energy projects, including co-generation, biomass, and waste-to-energy plants, have also been developed using project finance. Like environmental projects, the relative certainty of future revenues from many energy projects makes them attractive public sector candidates for project finance. Project-financed power plants have been developed throughout the United States, as well as in Turkey, Northern Ireland, Indonesia, and Pakistan. In 1987, approximately $3.5 billion in energy projects were project-financed.

Private Sector Projects

The private sector origins of modern project finance lie in development of natural resources, including oil fields and mineral deposits. Due to the large capital requirements and associated risks, oil and mining companies have sought a means of financing exploration and development that would manage risk and avoid credit degradation resulting from a large increase in corporate debt.

Project finance provides a means for firms to keep debt off their balance sheets, allowing them to reflect more favorable financial leverage and maintain desirable credit ratings. Corporations with less than a majority ownership position in a limited partnership need not include debt of the partnership on their balance sheets. Use of project finance allows partnerships to fund construction projects without reflecting project debt on the books of the corporate partners.

The project finance process can also help to improve project efficiency by imposing greater fiscal discipline and necessitating more effective utilization of project resources. Shared risk of project failure among sponsors should encourage efforts that facilitate success.

Off-balance sheet financing remains a principal advantage of using project finance to fund private sector construction projects. This could change, however, as the Financial Accounting Standards Board is considering requiring partial consolidation, meaning that limited partners would have to include on their corporate balance sheets the percentage of partnership debt equal to their ownership position.

Natural Resource Projects. Natural resource development has continued to be a primary source of supply for private sector projects, particularly internationally, where ability to generate hard currency revenues is a key consideration in assessing suitability for project finance. Recent examples of the use of project finance to develop natural resources have included geothermal fields in California, the Red Dog zinc-lead-silver mine in Alaska, the Hibernia oil field off Canada's east coast, and coal mines in Australia, Venezuela, and Pakistan.

Hotels and Industrial Facilities. Hotels have also been a source of supply for private sector projects for project finance, partly, as with natural resource development, due to the ability to generate hard currency revenues. Several hotels in New York City and one in Mexico City were project financed. Industrial plants that have been developed using project finance include an automobile manufacturing facility in Illinois for a joint venture of Chrysler and Mitsubishi and a manufacturing facility for Pitman-Moore.

The Sources of Project Financing

Demand for project finance opportunities has arisen as a result of investors' desires for assets, marketing efforts of engineering and construction contractors and equipment suppliers, and efforts by financial intermediaries to develop fee-generating business. Project finance compares favorably, in terms of satisfying investors' goals, with other opportunities available to large investors. According to persons familiar with project finance in the United States, it is currently a buyer's market with "too much money chasing too few projects."

Institutional Investors

Recent increases in the funds held by such institutional investors as pension funds and insurance companies, shown in Table 1, have created a demand for large, long-term investments with stable returns. These investors are typically looking for assets with fixed rates of return and terms of up to twenty years, in

Table 1. Assets of Financial Institutions

Type of Institution	Assets in $ Billions 1978	1986	% Change
Savings Institutions	$1,400.4	$2,961.1	111
Commercial Banks	1,220.9	2,580.6	111
Insurance Companies	512.2	1,251.5	144
Pension Funds	424.9	1,104.5	160
Mutual Funds	56.8	705.6	1,142
Finance Companies	159.7	412.1	158
Credit Unions	58.4	166.1	184
Brokerages	27.9	77.9	179
Real Estate Investment Trusts	3.5	8.5	143
TOTAL	$3,864.7	$9,267.9	139

Source: Flow of Funds Accounts, Federal Reserve Bank

order to match the cash flow characteristics of their liabilities. Pension funds may also view public sector project finance opportunities as a means of community reinvestment. Since project finance is generally used for major projects, often costing several hundred million dollars, institutional investors can acquire a sizable asset with a single transaction. With all-in returns of up to 25 or 30 percent, project finance represents an attractive investment opportunity for institutions.

Corporations

Capital funds of large corporations also actively seek project finance opportunities in order to acquire high yield assets, involving debt as well as equity positions. In addition to relatively high yields, corporations with large appetites for tax shelters can benefit from the tax advantages of project finance, although these may diminish as the Tax Reform Act of 1986 is fully implemented. Currently, tax benefits resulting from depreciation, investment tax credits, and interest payments of unincorporated partnership arrangements can be passed to corporate partners. In addition, alternative energy projects enjoy special tax advantages under regulations established in response to the oil crisis of the seventies.

Commercial Banks

Commercial banks, while prohibited from taking equity positions, can act as project finance lenders in order to acquire assets for their own portfolios. Through the use of warrants or conversion features attached to debt, banks can sometimes obtain "equity-like" positions that yield higher returns than straight debt. Commercial banks also act as intermediaries in project finance in order to generate fees by providing financial advisory services or underwriting debt issues.

Investment Banks

Investment banks frequently seek project finance opportunities in order to generate fees from underwriting debt and equity and from acting as financial advisors to the consortium that is sponsoring a project. A financial advisor might also participate in project finance as an investor, but the potential exists for conflicts of interest. As project financial advisor, the intermediary is responsible for protecting the interests of the sponsoring consortium; the interests of investors may not coincide with those of project sponsors.

Niche Banks and Developers

Developers and "niche" banks that specialize in privatization and project finance have emerged in recent years as the use of these financing techniques has increased. They serve as financial advisors to a sponsoring consortium in order to generate fees and may, in some cases, provide equity investment. Developers and niche banks often maintain ongoing relationships with institutional and corporate investors, arranging capital for a series of project finance deals.

Utility Subsidiaries

Recently, unregulated subsidiaries of utilities have become increasingly important sources of demand for project finance opportunities, particularly in energy projects. Utilities are typically generators of stable cash flows, with minimal capital requirements other than the ones necessary and approved to meet demand. In addition, utilities generally have good access to capital markets and may wish to acquire assets with yields higher than those attainable on investments that are permitted by regulators.

Vendors and Contractors

Vendors and contractors participate in project finance as a means of selling goods and services. Investment by a vendor or contractor may be limited to the goods or services provided to a project, or a more extensive investment position may be taken. Lack of a secondary market for project finance instruments, however, k-nits investors' liquidity and the ability of vendors and contractors to participate in project finance. Often, vendors and contractors may invest in a project through provision of goods or services or with subordinated debt with the intent of unwinding the position in post-completion financial restructuring.

Risk Management

Allocating Risk and Arranging Capital
Effective management of risk is the essence of project finance. With limited recourse beyond the assets of the project, there is no participant with a traditional owner's responsibilities in terms of residual risk assumption and guarantee of debt repayment. Through the process of identifying and allocating risks, project finance can help to improve the efficiency of project management.

Financial intermediaries often play a crucial role in project finance, allocating risk and arranging capital to match the supply of investment opportunities seeking finance with demands by investors for such opportunities. Banks and developers are typical intermediaries in project finance, serving as advisors to a sponsoring consortium. Some firms frequently involved in project finance, including large engineering and construction contractors, equipment suppliers, and corporate investors, maintain in-house financial advisory capabilities or an ongoing relationship with a financial intermediary.

Allocating Risk
While little can be done to alter the underlying risk profile of a project, the project finance process can be used to improve risk management. Consortium ownership creates shared liability that should encourage efficient identification and allocation of project risks.

Involvement of off-takers, vendors, and contractors in a sponsoring consortium allows allocation of risk to those parties best able to manage it. For example, guarantees in off-take contracts can be used to transfer risk due to changes in market conditions from the project to customers. Take-or-pay contracts guarantee the project a future stream of revenues.

Lump-sum, turnkey construction contracts can be used to transfer completion and cost overrun risk to engineering and construction contractors. Performance guarantees and incentives in purchase agreements and overhead and maintenance contracts can be used to transfer operating risk to equipment suppliers and operators. Involvement of government can be used to manage political risk.

Types of Risk
Several types of risk associated with the developmental, construction, and operating phases of a project are discussed below.

Technology Risk. The possibility that a new technology will prove uneconomic or unfeasible or that regulatory changes will affect use of a technology. Involvement of the technology provider in the sponsoring consortium can help to manage this risk.

Credit Risk. The possibility that the credit worthiness of the project as a whole or of an individual sponsor will not be satisfactory to investors.

Obtaining letters of credit from banks may enhance credit worthiness and also imposes some level of bank oversight.

Completion Risk. The possibility that the project will not reach the operating stage, i.e., construction will not be completed within the projected schedule and design criteria. Typically, some form of completion guarantee is provided to investors by the sponsoring consortium with a specified completion date and minimum rate of operating efficiency. This risk can be allocated to engineering and construction contractors through the use of turnkey contracts and performance incentives. Engineering and construction contractors can manage some of the risk through contractual arrangements with equipment and material suppliers.

Cost Overrun Risk. The possibility that construction or operating costs will exceed projections. This risk can be allocated to engineering and construction contractors and equipment vendors through the use of fixed-price, lump-sum contracts.

Off-Take Risk. The possibility that project operations will not generate projected revenues because of changes in market prices or demand for the product. Guarantees in off-take contracts, including take-or-pay and take-and-pay clauses, can be used to transfer this risk from the project to customers.

Equity Resale Risk. The possibility that contractors and other sponsors may not be able to liquidate their equity positions upon successful completion of their participation in a project. Because of the limited secondary market for sponsor equity positions, sponsors may manage this risk by using subordinated loans, rather than equity investments, to provide capital to a project, with subordination of the loans limited to specific senior, third-party project lenders. As debts, the loans will eventually be repaid, and the advantages and upside potential of an equity position can be preserved through the use of warrants or conversion rights included in the subordinated loan agreement.

Interest Rate Risk. The possibility that interest rates will increase, forcing the project to bear additional financing costs. Coupon swaps—which involve the exchange of a coupon of one configuration (i.e., fixed or floating interest rates) for a coupon stream with a different configuration but with essentially the same principal amount—can be used to manage this risk. Investors and borrowers in project finance have access to a variety of fixed and floating rate debt markets and can use coupon swaps to arrange debt service income and cost in any desired configuration.

Currency Risk. The possibility that changes in foreign exchange rates will alter the home currency value of cash flows from the project. Exposure to currency risk can be hedged in the short-term through transactions in currency forward and futures markets. In the case of recurring cash flows, such as collection of revenues from an operating project, hedging can be accomplished with either a long-date-forward currency contract or a series or strip of short-date-forward currency contracts. Currency swaps, involving exchange of currencies at an agreed upon rate, can also be used to manage long-date currency risk.

Political Risk. The possibility that legislation or regulations affecting a project will change. Internationally, political risk includes the possibility that host governments will expropriate project assets without adequate compensation or will not allow repatriation of funds. Strong commitment to a project from local and national governments, or governmental involvement in a sponsoring consortium, can help to manage political risk. The Overseas Private Investment Corporation provides insurance to United States companies against the risk of expropriation of foreign assets.

Uncontrollable Circumstances or Force Majeure Risk. The possibility that events beyond the ability of project sponsors to foresee or control will affect construction or operation. Project sponsors and equity investors typically assume this risk, although there is growing pressure, with some success, for lenders to assume a portion of the risk. Some of this risk may be managed through standard insurance coverage.

In order to manage these various types of risk, the project financial advisor develops a matrix of project participants and risk components associated with the project. The body of the matrix identifies risk allocations. Cells in the matrix reflect the various contractual agreements that allocate risk. Based on agreement among project participants on recourse and allocation of risk, the financial advisor develops a term sheet. The term sheet defines the rights and obligations of borrowers and describes default conditions and remedies. The term sheet serves as the bid document for accessing capital markets.

Financing

Financial Arrangements

Capital for a project can be arranged in a variety of ways. In the traditional approach, a lead bank is designated to arrange placement of debt through other banks. The borrower is apprised of the response of capital markets to the financing offer by the lead bank. In contrast, project finance often utilizes a "club loan" approach, in which a financial advisor works with a "club of lenders" that bids on financing a project based on the term sheet. This should lead to increased competition and efficiency. Sponsors interface closely with capital markets through the financial advisor and, therefore, have a first-hand view of funding alternatives. Companies that are involved in project finance on a recurring basis often maintain an ongoing relationship with a cadre of lenders and may not utilize a financial advisor. Working relationships between sponsors, financial intermediaries, and corporate clients and investors facilitate private placement of debt and equity.

Financial Engineering

Sponsors or financial advisors often perform a function that can be characterized as "financial engineering" in order to enhance a project's attractiveness to potential investors. Financial engineering may involve altering the size, timing, quality, direction, or currency of cash flows to meet investors' needs. Mechanisms typically used in financial engineering include swaps, options, caps and floors, leases, limited partnerships, joint ventures, warrants, and conversions, as well as traditional forms of debt and equity. Financial "engineers" may also package several project finance deals together in order to enhance the credit of weaker projects and provide an investment sizable enough to be of interest to large investors.

Conclusions

The project finance market involves a supply of public and private sector projects seeking finance and a demand for such projects by investors, lenders, financial intermediaries, engineering and construction contractors, and equipment suppliers. On the supply side of the market, project finance provides a means of funding the construction of projects that might otherwise be delayed or foregone. On the demand side, project finance provides investment opportunities that meet the needs of a wide range of institutional and corporate investors and lenders and provides a source of fees for financial intermediaries. Contractors and vendors benefit from project finance because it allows them to provide goods and services for design, construction, operation, and maintenance.

The project finance process, characterized by limited recourse to the assets of the sponsor, use of third-party funds, and allocation of risks to those parties best able to manage them, can also assist project management. Limited recourse and use of external funds may impose greater fiscal and management discipline and facilitate effective use of project resources while risk management techniques can help to improve project efficiency. Domestic and international markets for project finance are growing and appear likely to continue to do so as investors seek large, high-yield assets with relatively long terms, and governments and corporations find that their abilities to finance increasingly expensive construction projects through traditional methods are constrained. More effective project management is an additional advantage of the project finance process that is likely to encourage its continued use.

Acknowledgment: Support of this work was provided by the National Science Foundation and Lehigh University's Engineering Research Center for Advanced Technology for Large Structural Systems.

Assuring Excellence in Execution in Construction Project Management

PM Network (October 1995)

Construction projects come in various sizes and complexities and cover such diverse fields as governmental and institutional, industrial, petrochemical, pulp and paper, power generation, civil, and so on. Yet all require a clear and concise set of controls to ensure the project's timely completion, budget control, and adherence to specifications and codes. Among the many difficulties facing any organization engaged in the management and control of all the various activities and information flows associated with construction projects is the establishment of a set of procedures and documents that can be universally applied to each type of project. This means that these documents and procedures must be, at the same time, both flexible enough to adapt to the differences in types of projects and yet strict enough to enable a project manager to come into a project, ascertain its true overall status, and exert just the right degree of control and direction to properly manage the project to a successful completion.

Quality Preparation

Like most things in life, quality preparation for a task is undoubtedly the single most important and overriding factor in ensuring quality outcome. But the real question is: preparation of what, specifically? All projects can be broken down into three separate and distinct time elements: pre-construction, construction, and post-construction.

For the purpose of this discussion, we will assume that the project has been designed, at least to the stage where it can be bid, and the bid package(s) has been prepared. Specifications and drawings are available, several bidders have picked up the packages, and the project manager has just been assigned. What's next? To some extent this depends on the size and complexity of the project and the size of the staff that will actually manage the contractors and the project. However, regardless of its complexity, number of packages, or the size of management's staff, certain documents need to be in place that will allow the staff members to fulfill their roles.

Bid Documents

A good set of bid review forms, a detailed submittal register, a work item listing, a schedule of values, and a file system are chief among these needed documents. At the stage described at the start of this discussion, the two most important documents to be prepared at this time would be the bid review forms and the submittal register. The reasons for this are simple. Contractors are currently preparing bid packages, and their arrival will be the next milestone event in the project. The project manager needs to be prepared to make an objective evaluation of the various proposals he will receive. A good set of review forms is indispensable for this. The review forms should cover such broadly defined topics as compliance with the RFP, support evaluation, technical evaluation, and financial evaluation. If price is the only criteria for evaluating a proposal, you will undoubtedly get what you pay for, and in some cases this may be appropriate.

Bid Review

Each of the sections in the bid review form should have a weighted value assigned to it and the contractor/bidder graded on how well she meets the requirements of each section. The total of all the sections' scores is then the bidder's overall grade. Minimum scores can be assigned to each section so that a bidder may not fail a section and still get the job. A comparison sheet in the form of a linear matrix can then be used to compare all the bidders' scores for each topic of review, as well as any preset minimums.

Bid Evaluation Procedure

1. Each member of the review committee will fill out a "payment schedule bid analysis" form (see Table 1). This form is used to compare each bidder's cost proposal for each element of the project with the project estimate, as well as with each of the bidder's proposals.

2. Each member of the review committee next fills out the "bid evaluation form" (see Table 2 for an example of a portion of section "C") for each section of each bidder's proposal.

3. An arithmetic mean for each section of each bidder's proposal is then compiled and entered on the "comparison of bid evaluations for sections" form (see Table 3) in order to compare elements of each bidder's proposal.

Table 1. Payment Schedule Bid Analysis

Project Name _____ Bid Package Number _____
Bid Evaluation Form _____ Date _____

Payment Schedule Bid Analysis	Bidder #1	Bidder #2	Bidder #3	Bidder #4	P.C.M. Estimate	Remarks
Bill #1 Site Drainage						
1. Storm Water Retention Pond					1,091,149	
2. Pond "A" and Lift Station "A"					1,177,607	
3. Underpass Pump Station					1,365,640	
4. Gener. and Elec. Equip. Structure					115,860	
5. Force Main "A" to Pond "B"					518,100	
6. Force Main Effluent Stor. to Pond "B"					216,460	
7. Pond "B" and Lift Station "B"					1,001,154	
8. Force Main "B" to MH #23					615,680	
9. Site Electrical					2,021,471	
Total Bill #1					**8,123,121**	
Bill #2 W.W.T.P. Module #3						
1. Package Treatment Unit [C & A]					1,145,370	
2. Effluent Storage Basin [C & A]					1,196,455	
3. Effluent Filters [C & A]					108,750	
4. Sludge Drying Beds [C & A]					363,515	
5. Site Works Misc.					38,815	
6. Package Treatment Unit [M & E]					4,225,000	
7. Effluent Storage Basin [M & E]					121,000	
8. Effluent Filters [M & E]					42,100	
9. Raw Sewage Pump [M & E]					156,600	
10. Blower B-104					149,750	
11. Sludge Drying Beds [M & E]					105,400	
12. Site Piping					217,700	
13. Site Electrical					525,000	
Total Bill #2					**8,395,455**	

4. The results of each bidder's section scores is next entered onto the "overall comparison of bid evaluations" (see Table 4) for an overall comparison of all sections for all bidders.

Compliance Evaluation

In the compliance section, the question is simple: "Did the bidder supply the documents and information requested?" Not "how well was it done," only "was it done?" If twenty items were requested, how many were submitted, and which ones were missing? This often indicates how well the bidder has read the documents and how well instructions will be followed. If requested information was not provided, did the bidder at least mention why not, or somehow acknowledge that it was supposed to have been provided?

Table 2. Section "C" – Technical Evaluation

Project Name _____ Bid Package Number _____
Bid Evaluation Form _____ Date _____
Bidder: _____ Evaluator: _____
Section "C" – Technical Evaluation _____ Total Relative Weight 25%

Item	Subject	Value	Score 0% 20% 40% 60% 80% 100%	Grade
1.	**Plan of Operations**	20%	— — — — — —	
	a. Covers All Aspects of the Work	.40	— — — — — —	
	b. Logic	.40	— — — — — —	
	c. Level of Detail Reviewed	.20	— — — — — —	
			Total: ___ x 20%= ___	= Score of Item #1
2.	**Schedule**	20%		
	a. Feasibility	.30	— — — — — —	
	b. Material Deliveries	.20	— — — — — —	
	c. Submittals Scheduled	.10	— — — — — —	
	d. Manpower Loaded	.20	— — — — — —	
	e. Critical Path Defined	.20	— — — — — —	
			Total: ___ x 20%= ___	= Score of Item #2
3.	**Manpower Forecast**	20%		
	a. Sufficiency of Numbers	.35	— — — — — —	
	b. Sufficiency of Crafts	.35	— — — — — —	
	c. Crew Size	.30	— — — — — —	
			Total: ___ x 20%= ___	= Score of Item #3

Support Evaluation

In the support evaluation section, questions about the contractor's ability to support the project need to be addressed. Questions such as these are typical: Are there adequate warehousing or fabrication facilities? What experience level is possessed on similar projects? Is the required professional staffing proposed? What are the qualifications of key personnel? Is there sufficient support equipment in the plan? Who are the proposed subcontractors?

Technical Evaluation

This section should cover the bidder's ability to conduct the operation and should address such areas as the overall plan of operations, schedule, labor forecast, site plan, quality control program, safety program, maintenance program, and so on.

Financial Evaluation

The financial evaluation should not only address the quoted price and its distribution of costs throughout the project but should look into the overall

Table 3. Comparison of Bid Evaluations for Section "C"

Project Name _____ Bid Package Number _____
Bid Evaluation Form _____ Date _____

Items	Relative Weight	Bidder #1	Bidder #2	Bidder #3	Bidder #4	Remarks
1. Plan of Operations	20%					
2. Schedule	20%					
3. Manpower Forecast	20%					
4. Site Plan	10%					
5. Q.C. Program	10%					
6. Safety Program	10%					
7. Maintenance Program	10%					
Totals	**100%**					

Grade x 25% = _____ Bidder #1 Score for Section "C"   Grade x 25% = _____ Bidder #3 Score for Section "C"
Grade x 25% = _____ Bidder #2 Score for Section "C"   Grade x 25% = _____ Bidder #4 Score for Section "C"

Table 4. Overall Comparison of Bid Evaluations

Project Name _____ Bid Package Number _____
Bid Evaluation Form _____ Date _____

Section	Relative Weight	Min. Acceptable	Bidder #1	Bidder #2	Bidder #3	Bidder #4	Remarks
A. Bid Request Compliance	25%	17.5%					
B. Support Evaluation	25%	17.5%					
C. Technical Evaluation	25%	17.5%					
D. Financial Evaluation	25%	17.5%					
Total	**100%**	**70%**					

financial stability of the contractor. This should include a look at the contractor's working capital, net profit to gross revenue, current assets to liabilities ratio, overall net worth, and remaining capacity of bond.

Submittal Register

The importance of a properly constructed and organized submittal register cannot be overstated. Its position of importance is equal to that of the construction master schedule, yet it is often either completely overlooked or totally misunderstood. Many projects have the contractor prepare a "submittal register," and the results of this often prove frustrating at best. There is only

Sample Submittal Register

Specification #	Submittal #	Name	Sched. Due Date[3]	Actual Date[4]	To Reviewer[5]	Sched. Return[6]	Actual Return	To Contr.	Grade[7]	Remarks
[1]IT 16.2	[2]A 001.0	Site Plan	15 Mar 92	22 Mar 92	22 Mar 92	5 Apr 92	25 Mar 92	25 Mar 92	A	_____
IT 16.2	A 002.0	Key Persnl.	15 Mar 92	22 Mar 92	22 Mar 92	5 Apr 92	1 Apr 92	1 Apr 92	A	_____
IT 16.7	A 001.0	Company Org.	15 Mar 92	22 Mar 92	22 Mar 92	5 Apr 92	1 Apr 92	1 Apr 92	A	_____
02441	A 001.0	Pipe and Tube	15 Apr 92	17 Apr 92	17 Apr 92	1 May 92	29 Apr 92	30 Apr 92	B	_____
02441	A 002.0	Values	15 Apr 92	17 Apr 92	17 Apr 92	1 May 92	29 Apr 92	30 Apr 92	B	_____
02441	A 003.0	Solenoid Valves	15 Apr 92	17 Apr 92	17 Apr 92	1 May 92	29 Apr 92	30 Apr 92	B	_____
02441	A 003.1[8]	Solenoid Valves	15 May 92[9]							
02484	A 001.0	Copolymer	20 Apr 92	27 Apr 92	29 Apr 92	13 May 92				
02441	B 001.0	Sledding Plan	15 May 92							
02441	B 002.0	Main Plan	15 May 92							
02441	C 001.0	Lateral Volume	10 Oct 92							

1. Specification Sources:
   IT   Instructions to Tenders   GC   General Conditions of the Contract
   SC   Special Conditions of the Contract   XXXXX   Technical Specifications

2. Submittal Types:
   A. Manufacturers/Contractors Data   E. Samples   J. Test and Commissioning
   B. Shop Drawings   F. O & M Manuals   K. As-Built Drawings
   C. Tests (field)   G. Training   L. Spare Parts List
   D. Factory Tests and Certification   H. Warrantees/Guarantees   M. Spares

3. This date is developed from the construction master schedule to allow for lead time.
4. The actual date the submittal is received.
5. The reviewer may be the owner, A&E, or an in-house technical services division.
6. The reviewer should have a set amount of time to review submittals, i.e., 10 working days.
7. Grades of A or B are acceptable; C or D require resubmission.
8. Second submission.
9. The scheduled resubmission date is a programmed number of days added on to the date the submittal was returned to the contractor.

Note: The submittal register should be separated by types, keeping each type of submittal together.

one way to properly prepare a submittal register: you must completely review each and every specification and every note on every drawing. There is no denying the fact that putting this document together is a chore, but if you wait until after the project is under way, it is nearly impossible to do because of the amount of time necessary to complete this effort. The project manager, not the contractor, needs to be the one who sets these priorities.

To begin with, the submittal register should be the one document where every submittal required of the contractor can be found and tracked. It should be:

- Organized into like groupings, such as manufacturer's data, shop drawings, samples, test data, and so on
- Be able to show the source of the requirement for the submittal, i.e., specification number, special conditions, bid instructions
- Provide a schedule of the submittals' submission
- Reflect the status of those submittals that have been submitted.

Two reports need to be generated from the submittal register. The first would be those submittals past due, for either their first submission or resubmission, from the contractor, and the second would be those submittals that are overdue from the reviewer. The failure to achieve a timely submission, as well as a review of the submittals, is a primary cause of construction delays and claims.

Conclusion

There are undoubtedly many other documents, forms, and procedures that need to be developed and promulgated during this time in order to organize and bring effective control and documentation to the project. The point to be stressed here is that to ensure excellence in the execution of construction project management, management must start at the very beginning of the project. If the controls that ultimately bring quality to the project are not in place before construction starts, it will be very difficult to implement them at a later stage.

The Residual Costs of Inferior Project Management

Project Management Institute Seminar/Symposium (October 1990)

Preface

This paper was developed to present an actual case study that highlights a transition during the eighties on mega-projects wherein the owner (public or private) finds himself in a defense position for major liability action. The real problem is that the onboard staffing of such owner is usually not prepared to provide adequate technical and management expertise for a courtroom defense. The project management consultant role becomes one of reconstruction of the management pattern while presenting a qualified expert witness.

Introduction

As participants of the panel, the authors prepared an abstract with cover letter to provide insight toward one of the downside areas growing daily on major projects. The downside area highlighted is the transition in the late eighties for mega-projects wherein the owner quite often finds herself in major liability actions or in local claims resolution. Quite often in these same cases the owner does not have an onboard technical staff with the depth to technically redevelop implementation scenarios and develop data banks for analysis; analyze the process as implemented, using techniques such as mass diagrams; nor to provide representation via deposition or in court as an expert witness. This is causing a shift in the transitional role of the project manager or engineer to that of reconstructing a project that is already completed via data reviews and structured interviews and using project management techniques to prove or disprove the completed work effort. The authors will attempt through this presentation to provide a report using a specific case study that demonstrates the depth of technical expertise necessary to provide the legal representatives with a choice; settle out of court, or take a chance on the judge and jury.

The Nature of the Case Study to be Presented
The case study involved a transportation construction project to build an urban highway connector fifty-two blocks in length, which consisted of the construction of a four-lane roadway, sidewalks, curb and gutter, storm drainage, three culvert crossings, traffic signals and lighting, pavement marking, and tree plantings. On or about November 9, 1984, all pertinent parties signed the written agreement for construction. A preconstruction meeting was held on January 22, 1985. The contractor breached the contract July 1, 1987; the owner (a county commission) issued a notice to proceed with a second contractor to complete the unfinished work left by the original contractor. The original contract in 1984 dollars was for $5,668,734.54; the second contract amount was for $2,155,753.27 in 1987 dollars. The original contractor, demanding judgment for damages, plus interest and costs, for approximately $3.5 million, initiated a claim action on October 14, 1988.

In November 1989, the county hired an engineering consultant to provide a project reconstruction to determine several areas of technical responsibility. As is evidenced, five years had elapsed between the initial contract signing and the employ of a consulting firm experienced in engineering design, construction management, and overall project management. The roadway was actually finished by the second general construction contractor approximately one year prior to the employ of the consultant.

Purpose and Significance
The case study is one of a highway construction project that "went bad" several times before it "got better." This type of scenario is not unique to the transportation sector and has been duplicated in the power industry sector, many industrial sector areas, and in research and development efforts, including the space program. This presentation will provide some definition of the width and breadth of this "new" technical field for project managers as well as offer a "road map" when implementing a technical team response. The authors believe that this is a significant new area for project management teams; the authors believe the following case study will present their reasons.

Case Study

Sequence of Events/Chronology of Actual Construction Process
To set the stage for this case study, a chronology of actual major events has been assembled. The name of the actual contractor is not relevant nor is the name of the involved county. Instead, for the purposes of this study, we will call the contractor "Urban Highway Construction, Inc. (UHCI)," and the county, "Southern USA." The major events as they occurred are included in Table 1.

In order to determine the party that most contributed to the failure of this project, a reconstruction of events was prepared. The first stage in this process was to obtain all letters, drawings, log books, notes, project specifications, a transcript of the job explanation meeting, progress photographs, contractor's daily logs, and any other piece of information that would shed light on the events that transpired throughout the life of the project. This information was read, summarized, and placed in chronological order. This effort was required so that an understanding could be acquired of not only the written word about the events that occurred but also to provide insight as to why certain actions were taken. Once this had been accomplished, the contractor was reviewed. Urban Highway Construction, Inc. did not update its schedule during the project.

Unfortunately, Southern USA did not keep track of activities either to reconstruct or update the schedule on a monthly basis as the contractor's services were utilized. It was estimated that the method of payment was based on completed activities; otherwise, it would have been difficult to achieve a realistic/believable progress curve. Manpower and equipment taken from the contractor's daily logs were overlaid onto the progress curve. The county site representative's daily logs were used to cross-check the accuracy of the contractor's information. (The importance of such diaries cannot be emphasized enough.) In this particular case, the site representative listed daily equipment and manpower working along the job site as well as non-working and broken down equipment. He also recorded equipment and manpower coming and going on a day-to-day basis. The importance of this information will be discussed later.

Once the reconstruction of events and rebuilding of the schedule was complete, the analysis of who, what, when, where, and why began.

Urban Highway Construction, Inc. based its claim on an event that occurred between contract award and notice to proceed. Others had removed two hundred thousand cubic yards of material from an area of the project. The contractor stated that he had planned to use this material elsewhere along the right-of-way and that the loss of this ability not only cost additional monies but severely disrupted his schedule and delayed progress. The contractor further stated that since Southern USA denied him access to this area, the workaround that resulted compounded this problem.

Southern USA's stated position was that it had tried to negotiate a fair settlement, but the UHCI refused to negotiate in good faith. The county finally awarded a contract to replace the fill to another contractor. This contractor reconstructed the right-of-way to the original lines and grades, as shown in the bid drawings.

This section did not please Urban Highway Construction, Inc. It claimed that although the material used exceeded the quality of the original soil, it was not compacted properly. To compound this argument, compaction tests were not taken during replacement nor were they taken at the completion of fill replacement.

It should be noted at this point that, concurrent with reconstruction and analyzing this project, depositions were being taken from all parties associated with the project that were available. The importance of preparing probing

Table 1

Event Date	Event Description
06/20/84	Bid opening by Southern USA.
10/02/84	Contract award to Urban Highway Construction, Inc. (UHCI)
11/09/84	Contract executed by Southern USA and UHCI.
01/22/85	During preconstruction meeting, UHCI reports fill taken from the right-of-way between Station 45+00 and Station 55+00. UHCI also advises the unit price of fill has increased since the job was bid.
02/05/85	Southern USA asks via certified mail for the detailed construction schedule as required by the contract before NTP.
02/18/97	Southern USA issues the NTP, effective 2/18/85, with job completion scheduled 8/11/86 (540-day contract period).
03/18/85	Work started. UHCI sent letter to Southern USA that it cannot work between Station 40+00 and 66+00 until the fill problem is resolved.
03/20/85	UHCI notified Southern USA that clearing and grubbing has been completed between Station 25+00 and Station 39+80.
03/25/85	The lawyer for UHCI notified Southern USA that an extension of time was required due to the differing site conditions from Station 40+00 through Station 67+55.
03/29/85	Southern USA issued a change order for $100 K for review by UHCI to cover cost for removing backfill and replacing same with in-specification fill.
05/02/85	UHCI notified Southern USA that the change order as proposed was unacceptable. Requested meeting to negotiate.
05/16/85	Meeting between parties; UHCI to prepare a supplemental agreement for Southern USA review regarding relief of problems resulting from the stolen fill and unacceptable backfill.
5/17–5/30/85	Work progress by UHCI almost stopped in most areas.
5/31/85	UHCI claims progress payment received late; asks for $1,423.52 in interest.
5/31–6/06/85	Work stopped.
06/06–06/17/85	Southern USA sends certified letter to UHCI stating that the approved construction schedule is not being implemented. County stated that if work is not resumed on a full-time basis within ten days, Southern USA will declare the contract in default.
07/03–07/30/85	Work sporadic
07/30/85	Southern USA sent UHCI letter requesting a show cause or immediate default.
08/02/85	UHCI acknowledged letter and enclosed plans on differing site conditions as reason for slow progress of work.
08/02–09/04/85	Work effort improved but not full force.
09/06/85	UHCI sent letter to Southern USA with notice of impact to construction schedule from work by a utility agency. Work was due to start on 9/5 but was delayed to either 9/9 or 9/10.
9/18/85	UHCI sent letter to Southern USA in response to their letter of 7/3/85. Offered to work on "force account basis" if the county could not issue a supplemented proposal based upon UHCI's counter proposal.
09/23–10/04/85	Work progressing.
10/03/85	Follow-up letter from UHCI to Southern USA requesting response to 9/18/85 letter proposal.
10/04/85	Letter from Southern USA to UHCI addresses cost proposals for replacement of fill removed and removal of debris. Debris removal to be accomplished on force account basis. Proposal cost for replacement of stolen fill not acceptable. Southern USA prepared to recommend time extension for removal of debris and replacement of fill only.
10/07–10/16/85	Work progressing.
10/17/85	UHCI sent letter addressing items of 10/4/85 letter. UHCI stated it would remove debris but refused to furnish replacement fill at contract cost basis. UHCI threatened suit for relief. UHCI stated that Southern USA's time extension plan was unacceptable; again threatened court intervention.
10/21–11/18/85	Work progressing.
11/19/85	Hurricane.
11/20–12/11/85	Work progressing.

Table 1 (con't)

Event Date	Event Description
12/12/85	UHCI notified Southern USA that it will suspend activities from 12/21–1/2/86 for Christmas holiday.
12/13/85	Southern USA refused the holiday as an extension of time authorization.
12/16/85–02/10/86	Work progressing.
02/11/86	Southern USA sent letter advising that it will replace the stolen fill at its own direct expense. This would include emplacement, compacted to the elevations shown on the construction plans.
02/12–03/18/86	Work progressing.
03/19/86	UHCI sent letter advising that the differing site conditions had not been resolved between Stations 85 and 95.
3/24/86	Southern USA notified UHCI that 610 cubic yards of lime-rock fill (recently placed by the county) had been taken by UHCI without authorization.
04/01/86	Southern USA notified UHCI that the county would contract an outside source to remove the debris between Stations 53 and 67 between 4/7/86 and 4/25/86.
04/17/86	Southern USA followed up letter of 3/19/86 and again stated the county will not be held liable for contractor not fully investigating site conditions before bid submittal; no additional compensation for time extension.
07/01/86	Southern USA sent certified letter to UHCI, invoking Section 8-8 of the contract, preliminary notice of delinquency. Further it was stated that a final notice would be issued in ten days from date of receipt if UHCI failed to take action to correct lack of progress and improper allocation of equipment and personnel.
07/22/86	UHCI sent letter acknowledging that the project cannot be completed on time and asked for an extension to December 31, 1986.
07/24/86	Southern USA issued notice of delinquency.
07/29/86	UCHI responded via certified letter that Southern USA's actions forced the project to be completed out of sequence.
08/01/86	Southern USA notified UHCI that the contract would not be extended beyond 08/21/86 and that after that date, UHCI would become liable for liquidation damages until final job completion by others.
08/22/86	A new attorney for UHCI hand-delivered a letter to Southern USA restating UHCI's position.
02/05/87	The Federal Highway Administration (FHWA) in a letter to Southern USA provided information for the basis of termination by the FHWA for default on the contract with UHCI.
07/01/87	UHCI sent Southern USA a certified letter citing the lack of cooperation by the county, the county's failure to pay for certain portions of the work, and *other* breaches of the contract as cause for them to stop work on the project and walked off the job.
07/09/87	Southern USA sent a certified letter to UHCI invoking Section 8-9, "Default and Termination of Contract," and sent a preliminary notice. The preliminary notice provided for UHCI to return to the job within ten days.
07/21/87	Southern USA sent a certified letter to UHCI declaring the contract in default.
10/22/87	Southern USA formally hired another contractor to complete the unfinished work for an approximate amount of $2.2 million with an NTP date of 11/9/87.

questions for these proceedings cannot be overemphasized. What might be construed as simple statements turn into insightful comments not only as to events but also, in some cases, as to the truth of what actually occurred.

It became evident that the missing fill was the cornerstone of the contractor's argument. To determine the true impact of this material, a MASS diagram was prepared. One might make the observation that this was an obvious exercise, but it only became "obvious" after hundreds of hours of research and reading of depositions. The MASS diagram revealed a starting spot; the area from which the fill had been removed was an area that required fill. Further, of the 200,000 cubic yards of material removed, only 30,000 had been located in the right-of-way. Once this "cornerstone" was removed, other areas of the contractor's actions came to a more meaningful interpretation.

The manpower and equipment data that were overlaid on the project curve were analyzed. The major dips in manpower/equipment also produced a flattening on the process curve. These time frames were investigated, and it was found that they were concurrent with other work accomplished by the contractor for other clients. The original argument by the contractor that this was due to lack of fill material dissipated with the knowledge that inputted fill requirements had not changed as originally perceived.

Urban Highway Construction, Inc., did not, however, back down. The company still believed that jury sympathy would be on its side, since it was a David and Goliath scenario: the "big bad county" against the "poor little contractor." The importance of this concept was not lost as first preparations were being completed. Poster board-sized graphics were prepared to give the jury a visual understanding of the project and the areas in question. This was done to help the jury, which most likely would not understand construction techniques and practices, to see in simple terms the root cause of what transpired during construction.

Urban Highway Construction, Inc., was represented not only be its own attorney but also by the bonding company. The trial took ten days to complete, including three days of jury deliberation. Urban Highway Construction, Inc., was awarded $164,000, which equaled its last invoice plus the Southern USA retention. Southern USA was awarded court costs, which amounted to nearly $100,000. The clear winner in this instance was the county, if one were to ignore the over one-year delay and costs associated with bringing in a second contractor to finish the work and all costs associated with this action. In actual fact, there was no winner.

The major lesson to be learned in cases such as these is to take "care of business" at the time it occurs. The county should have resolved the missing fill issue prior to notice to proceed. Everyone knew about the altered site conditions at the preconstruction conference. The contractor was the one to put the issue on the table. The county had all the options at hand to resolve the situation *prior* to notice to proceed. For unknown reasons, the issue was ignored, and the contractor was told to start work. The contractor, for whatever reason, tried to exploit this situation. He became, in the written opinion, greedy, and this became evident during the trial. No one really "wins" once a project enters into litigation. Legal fees, lost revenue, and the lost use of money all take their toll.

An Architect's View

PM Network (February 1990)

Introduction

In any given construction project, there are a set of tasks to be performed to ensure its success. As amazing as it may seem to those who are not truly familiar with our industry (i.e., most owners, many self-styled managers, and some regulatory officials) that those tasks and their appropriate patterns of undertaking are generally well known to architects, engineers, and builders. Who gets to do those tasks, under contract to whom, in what sequence, for how much money, and under what terms of reference, however, is the source of much frantic energy these days, especially in the private sector. Owners are often motivated to minimize their short-term costs (as opposed to obtaining the greatest long-term benefit) and are advised to maximize their control by breaking down the process into its smallest units and working at the greatest speed. Unfortunately, reputed advantages are often illusory because the natural outfall consists of larger numbers of working units, many more points of contact (read: gaps), loss of time for due consideration, and unhealthy pressure—without proper contractual definition. It then becomes exceedingly difficult to ensure responsible action and coordination. When that is further compounded by low bidder selection, the die is cast. "Cheap professional advice" is inherently contradictory. The Station Square delivery system had all the ingredients for trouble. Unfortunately, this time the recipe boiled over.

Management by Design

It is the AIBC's belief that while there were a host of factors—from technical incompetence to playing ostrich—variously contributing to the collapse, those factors are all byproducts of a more profound problem, i.e., fragmentation of the "traditional" delivery process, especially as it relates to the design and construction of the project for the owner. That process is becoming increasingly ill-defined by market forces (not public interest) and "bought" in shifting guises by uninformed or poorly advised owners within an insufficiently monitored and controlled operating context. Frequently, so-called "project managers" are no small part of the problem and give "project management" a bad name.

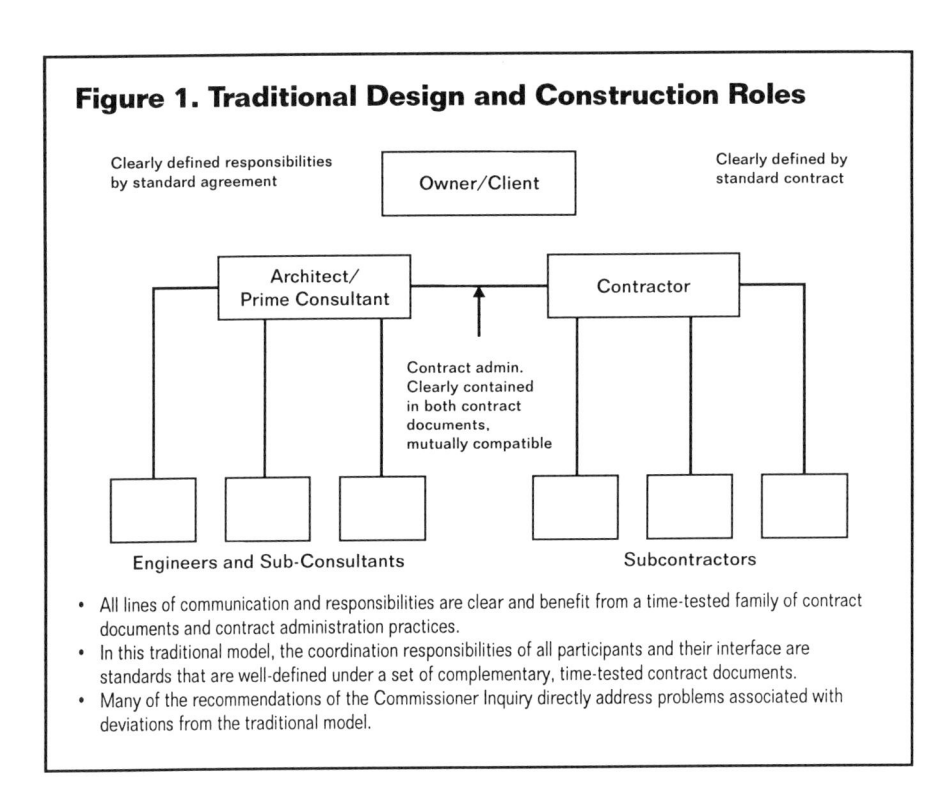

> **Figure 1. Traditional Design and Construction Roles**
>
> Clearly defined responsibilities by standard agreement — Owner/Client — Clearly defined by standard contract
>
> Architect/Prime Consultant — Contractor
>
> Contract admin. Clearly contained in both contract documents, mutually compatible
>
> Engineers and Sub-Consultants — Subcontractors
>
> - All lines of communication and responsibilities are clear and benefit from a time-tested family of contract documents and contract administration practices.
> - In this traditional model, the coordination responsibilities of all participants and their interface are standards that are well-defined under a set of complementary, time-tested contract documents.
> - Many of the recommendations of the Commissioner Inquiry directly address problems associated with deviations from the traditional model.

Let us make no mistake: the process-model by which specific people cause a project to happen is something which must not be allowed to happen by accident. What is needed is management by design so that there is a well communicated and understood clarity of roles and relationships that has been designed by persons who know what is necessary and how to achieve that in the best interest of all affected parties.

It is indeed possible and practical to have someone provide overall coordination, at least as far as the efforts of the "design" consultants are concerned, as to their review and certification of construction and the owner's related role. Most architects are darn good at it. That's a fundamental part of our background, approach, and skill. In those areas, other layers of management are both redundant and counterproductive. In fact, it is folly to allow the owner or an unqualified manager to define and allocate such project responsibilities (which happens now all too often).

Motivation and Trust

Very often the owner has little or no long-range commitment to the project, its users, or the public interest, seeking short-term gains and frequently for a quick flip (resale), at which point it becomes someone else's problem. The licensed

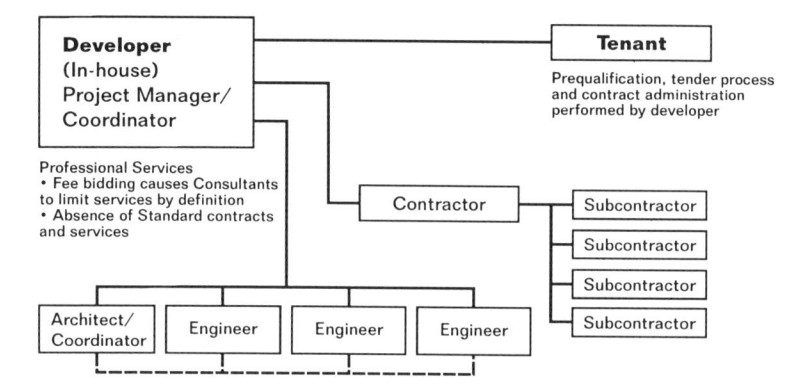

> **Figure 2. Sample Alternative Design and Construction Roles**
>
> ```
> Developer ─────────────────── Tenant
> (In-house)
> Project Manager/             Prequalification, tender process
> Coordinator                  and contract administration
>                              performed by developer
>
> Professional Services
> • Fee bidding causes Consultants
>   to limit services by definition    Contractor ── Subcontractor
> • Absence of Standard contracts                 ── Subcontractor
>   and services                                  ── Subcontractor
>                                                 ── Subcontractor
> Architect/    Engineer  Engineer  Engineer
> Coordinator
> ```
>
> - Prime consultant's role is compromised by lack of standard contracts, reduced control, unclear, and divided coordination roles.
> - Confusion of roles occurs particularly with respect to implications and coordination of changes to construction during fast tracking.
> - Absence of contract administration (e.g., coordination/impact of changes) by architect weakens control over quality and process, hence the need arises for letters of professional assurance.
> - Real Issue: Developer has assumed certain responsibilities from prime consultant yet it is unclear precisely what and how they will be managed. Inevitably, individual persons who must actually function in a manner consistent with the project's terms of reference are unable to do so in the absence of articulate mechanisms.
>
>   Frequently, persons who initiate "alternate" models are unaware that such problems exist or resist such a fact. The ensuing chaos undermines quality assurance; is contrary to objectives of project efficiency; and exacts an unnecessary toll in human relationships.

consultant, however, is in for the long run and has public responsibility, along with its attendant accountability and potential liability— even to his estate after death. The consultant (unlike the owner, builder, and manager) is regulated and could (should) stand on those grounds supported by his professional association and enforced government legislation, in opposition to unwise owner-parameters.

The authorities and any consumer (second or third parties) are entitled to expect and receive ethical and technically sound actions. Policing of that has to come from the professions; no other body is qualified.

Responsibility and Regulation

The missing components in the overall system are responsible owners, licensed constructors, and authorities' enforcement of regulations, all in the public interest.

Responsibility cannot be delegated. Notwithstanding the industry paranoia often fostered by insurance companies and legal counsel (all who urge parties to back away from responsibility), someone has to take charge of things and provide (or ensure) sufficient checks and balances. Whatever may be the scope of government inspection, the involvement of such authority does not alter the architect or engineer's responsibility, already derived from license and well defined under statute.

The typical (commercial) owner is in it to make money but is a construction-process innocent. That's a large problem in an entrepreneurial society wherein we cannot feasibly regulate an owner's competence, knowledge, or attitude. What we could do is regulate an owner's actions. That way, an innocent (or avaricious) owner or an unsuspecting public would not be victimized by recommendations to install fragmented delivery models that have the appearance of saving time and money but which effectively reduce coherence and quality while increasing risk unnecessarily.

Owners should be required to file (with the local authority) undertakings as to the project's delivery model, including roles and relationships of all consultants; nature of construction contract(s); and primary activity sequences. At the very least, the authority should be empowered to require that professional statutes and building regulations be adhered to and (in the event of a nontraditional model) that its appropriateness be demonstrated—all as a condition of permitting the project to proceed.

First Principles

Let us not forget that in advance of the real need for a proper checking regimen, there are a whole series of creative, constructive, integrative, and progressive tasks, i.e., the generation of ideas and the construction itself, which are far more difficult, time-consuming, and valuable than any after-the-fact monitoring. That is where the best management energies and strategies are needed; that is where professionals and owners need to make informed judgments first; and that is where we need to ensure that proper standards of engagement (including remuneration) and practice are both invoked and enforced.

It is absolutely essential that there be sound application of professional service, proper application of risk, and appropriate government involvement. All the participants need to understand roles and relationships, responsibility, and liability. The "Save-On-Foods" roof collapse or similarly unfortunate events must not be allowed to recur. There is a real need to ensure clarity and quality in the public interest.

Construction Delay Communication Computer System

Project Management Institute 26th Annual Seminar/Symposium (October 1995)

Introduction

Communicating pertinent information during decision processes at construction sites is a key element of successful projects, and the Construction Delay Communication Computer System was designed to assist with communications by providing a systematic analysis of delays during construction. Managing delays on construction projects requires analyzing available information and the formulation of summaries that aid decision-making processes. Construction personnel and managers require easy access to current and historical data and information in order to make more informed decisions. To meet this requirement a computer program was developed called the Construction Delay Analysis System (CDAS).

The CDAS computer program automates the process of construction delay management and assists in optimizing the lines of communication among key parties on a construction project. It helps identify and quantify delays encountered on both domestic and international projects. The CDAS program is an interactive system for reviewing and recording the production of individual activities and for monitoring and reporting on the overall status of a project. It provides a consistent, detailed, and systematic analysis of progress, causes of delays, and corrective actions at any time during the life cycle of a project. The system imports project schedules from project management software such as Openplan and Primavera, documents schedule delays, and tracks historical information for the purpose of delay claims.

The CDAS computer program was developed as part of a research project that was funded by two grants from the National Science Foundation Division of Structures and Building Systems. In addition to government funding, another essential element of the research was industry participation by contractors, owner organizations, engineers, and the division offices of the United States Army Corps of Engineers. The acquisition of actual project information was key in formulating the knowledge bases used in the computer system.

One of the major advantages of the Construction Delay Analysis System (CDAS) program is the consistency it introduces into decision-making processes. Another advantage is that it reduces the amount of time required to gather data for the dispute resolution process upon completion of projects. The process of apportioning equitable allocation of responsibility for delays is streamlined by the documentation provided by the CDAS computer program.

The CDAS program documents decision-making processes and forms a traceable link between project data and decisions. Using the CDAS program allows managers to review decisions made under similar circumstances, which helps them make more informed future decisions. The dynamic attributes of the program enhance information processing and decision-making on construction projects

It is important to understand that this program is a *decision support system*, which means that it is not designed to make decisions for the user but rather it provides pertinent information in an efficient and easily accessed format that allows users to make more informed decisions. This paper discusses the development of the CDAS computer program, the generation of industrial data for the knowledge acquisition system, the purpose of the CDAS program, development of the research project, data collection, the phases of development, technical parameters, program sub-models, databases, sample data, program features, and the research results.

Purpose of the Construction Delay Analysis System Program

The Construction Delay Analysis System (CDAS) computer program creates an interactive environment for knowledge acquisition that improves project management and project controls analysis processes. The program was designed to enhance decision-making abilities by providing project personnel with an integrated and intelligent system for obtaining a consistent, detailed, and systematic analysis of a project at any point in time. The research was undertaken to address the issue of making decisions when too much information is provided and there is not enough time to properly process all of the data required in order to make the decision.

The CDAS program is not a standalone project management system as it was designed to be used in conjunction with existing project management systems such as Openplan and Primavera. It models a functional simulation of the construction environment; tests for multiple influences; searches for trends, exceptions, comparisons, and patterns that indicate problems; and then highlights deviations from the baselines. This type of system eliminates handling the same data numerous times and provides historical documentation of decision processes.

The program simulates the process of delay determinations by comparing technical parameters; accessing knowledge matrices; determining which activities are all right or need immediate or later attention; suggests possible causes for delays; and suggests alternative courses of corrective action.

Development of the Research Project

There were several different organizations involved in the development of this research project. The initial concept was developed for use on a multiple prime construction project for an Iowa-based construction firm. The initial concept was refined when a research initiation grant was received from the National Science Foundation (NSF) to develop a pilot program. Based on the success of the pilot program the NSF provided an additional three years of funding to research and develop a commercial program. In addition to the NSF support, the Business Roundtable provided support services and contacts and the United States Army Corps of Engineers participated by providing data from its division offices.

Data Collection

The data used for this project was provided by firms from different construction-related business sectors including: commercial building, government, heavy industrial, infrastructure, institutional building, light industrial, power, and process. Data was received from owner organizations, contractors, and construction managers in forty different states and the United States Army Corps of Engineers.

Questionnaires were sent to a variety of different firms, and 198 responded with information about specific projects related to delays, technical causes of delays, and measures used to reduce delays. The industrial data collected was used to develop the computer program and databases.

Construction delays were analyzed from two distinct perspectives: delays encountered at the project level and delays encountered at the activity level. The conceptual and actual design of the program was based upon this distinction. Delay reductions measures were categorized to deal with delays at both levels.

The program contains several different knowledge bases that categorize the data by different business sectors. It also contains a database of Construction Specification Institute (CSI) abbreviations and codes, files with "seeded" delays and measures to reduce delays, databases for customized information, historical database files from current projects, and historical database files from previous projects.

Phases of Development

There were ten major phases required for this research project, as follows:

1988–1989	The pilot program was developed and tested on a multiple-prime construction project (1).
1990–1991	Data was collected on delays from domestic projects using a knowledge engineering system (2).
1990–1991	Several database files were developed for CSI codes and abbreviations, technical causes of delays, and corrective measures.
1991–1992	The computer program was written and coded (3, 4).
1992–1994	The computer program was rewritten to update its capabilities (5).
1993–1994	Data was collected on international delays.
1993–1994	The historical sub-model was developed for use during claims analysis.
1994–1995	The program was tested and validated (6).
1995–1996	The computer program will be released.

Technical Parameters

The Construction Delay Analysis System (CDAS) program analyzes delays at the activity level from two viewpoints: actual and proactive. In order to analyze delays the CDAS program imports the appropriate schedule from project management software programs such as Openplan or Primavera. The program accesses progress measures including the budgeted cost of work performed, budgeted cost of work scheduled, actual cost of work performed, schedule performance index (SPI), and cost performance index and evaluates these measures and indices with the total float of each activity to provide assessments about the activities.

In order to only analyze pertinent activities, the program queries through the records of all activities and selects only those that meet the following criteria:

- Total Float (TF) < 0 or SPI < 100
- OD <> RD (original duration not equal to remaining duration)
- TF < RD (TF is less than remaining duration)

The CDAS program monitors the SPI (the actual quantities to date divided by the scheduled quantities to date), performance factors (earned work minus work to date divided by actual work minus hours to date), cost performance index (actual costs to date divided by scheduled costs to date), and total float (the amount of time that an activity can be delayed without delaying the entire project).

Table 1. Construction Delay Analysis Sub-Models

Sub-Model #1 Program Introductions and Instructions	Sub-Model #2 Input Parameters—Project and Contract Information	Sub-Model #3 Access Control Data
Sub-Model #4 Activity Delay Calculations	Sub-Model #5 Processing of Delay Information	Sub-Model #5 WBS Level Summaries
Sub-Model #7 Report Generation	Sub-Model #8 Program Summary	

Program Sub-Models

The Construction Delay Analysis System (CDAS) program contains eight different sub-models that are processed during execution of the delay analysis. Table 1 contains a list of these eight sub-models that are processed when the program is accessed.

Sub-Model 1

The first sub-model provides information on how to use the program and how to access the help function and a master menu of options that allows users to select additional sub-models.

Sub-Model 2

The second sub-model prompts users to input project specific information such as the following:
- Project type: commercial building, heavy industrial, infrastructure, institutional building, light industrial, process, or power
- Regional location factors: Mid-Atlantic, Mountain Pacific, Midwest, Northeast, Southeast, Southwest, or West
- Type of firm: design/build, project management, construct only, E/P/C, owner, or government; type of contract: cost plus fee, lump sum, unit price, fixed fee, or guaranteed maximum
- Contract value (millions): 0–.5, 1–4.9, 5–49, 50–100, >100.

Sub-Model 3

After each of the parameters mentioned in Sub-Model 2 have been entered, the third sub-model processes the information and selects the appropriate database containing delay data for the particular parameters stipulated. The information contained in the databases was gathered from industry experts by the different types of parameters that are listed in Sub-Model 2.

Sub-Model 4
The fourth sub-model imports information from project management software programs. If the data imported currently lists activities by Construction Specification Institute (CSI) code, the technical parameters are directly imported. If another coding system is being used the program matches activities to the closest CSI keyword and assigns an appropriate CSI code so that the delay information can be stored according to the CSI standard code format.

Sub-Model 5
The fifth sub-model processes the technical parameters, as imported from the project management software program, and generates a listing of activities that are on schedule (all right), need attention, or need immediate action. For those activities that need attention and immediate action the program accesses the existing delay databases and generates a list of possible causes of delays and a list of possible measures to reduce delays (corrective actions).

Sub-Model 6
The sixth sub-model generates a summary of the information processed in Sub-model 5 according to the different work breakdown structure levels being used for the project.

Sub-Models 7 and 8
The seventh sub-model generates reports of the data, and the eighth sub-model summarizes program information.

Program Databases

Seeded Databases
The Construction Delay Analysis System (CDAS) program contains "seeded" databases that were created from the information provided by industry experts who work for construction-related firms. The data was collected according to the parameters provided in Sub-model 2 so program users have a choice as to whether they would like to use knowledge provided by experts or start with empty databases and create their own customized delay databases.

Historical Databases
In addition to the databases provided with the program, or the customized databases created by users for their own projects, the program also provides historical databases that contain a record of all of the information that has

been processed by the program. Historical information can be accessed by an activity number (and a record of all actions taken during the course of the project relative to that activity is generated), or a particular date could be input by the user (and information on all activities—and the actions being performed on that date—would be generated). This information aids in the dispute resolution process as users would have immediate access to information relative to any activity at any point in time.

Construction Delay Analysis System Computer Program

The Construction Delay Analysis System (CDAS) program was designed to take advantage of the attributes of a relational language while still being capable of conforming to a hierarchical structure. There are five levels of depth in the CDAS program. The master program is situated at the highest level, and it branches into a second sub-level with five options, each of which contains many different options. The implementation of a hierarchical design structure facilitates chronological program execution that is necessary for simplification of use and the utilization of overlays for memory management purposes. The program contains thirty database files and thirty-eight index files with fields assigned to the various database files as deemed necessary.

Program Use

The knowledge databases identify the delays associated with the inputs of the user, and the program ranks the delays based on an overall integrated weighting system. Only those delays that meet a certain established threshold are analyzed in the delay reduction database. The system generates a project level delay report that includes a project information summary, a list of possible causes of delays encountered or that could be encountered in the specified project, and related delay reduction measures.

The system allows users to input information about a specific project to be analyzed with five choices provided relating to project, company, geographical location, contract type, and managerial information. Each screen prompts the user to answer specific questions, and the answers are analyzed by the system.

A proactive analysis of activity level delays is performed through an activity delay knowledge database. Acknowledging that it is not realistic to include every possible construction activity in the databases, it was determined that the databases would only contain general classifications as set forth by the Construction Specification Institute (CSI). CSI system classifies all construction-related operations into sixteen divisions.

Table 2. Firm and Project Type Delays

Firm Type	Proj. Type	Delay #1	Wt. #1	Delay #2	Wt. #2	Delay #3	Wt. #3
Con. Only	Light Industrial	Design Modif.	12	Not Enough Labor	10	QC/ Inspection	10
Engr./ Proc./ Const.	Heavy Industrial	Labor Productivity	9	Late Engr.	9	Decision Delay	8
Proj. Man.	Com. Bldg.	Change Orders	8	Material Delivery	5	Site Conditions	5

Time/Cost Tradeoffs

After importing the project schedule, the program prompts users to indicate whether the CSI coding system has been used. If the CSI coding system is available, the program matches the first two digits of the identification number (ID) of each of the pertinent activities with the knowledge in the activity delay database to recommend actions. If the ID numbers in the project do not use the CSI coding system, then users have the choice of matching each activity or having the system match the first ten characters of the title of each activity with the title of activities contained in the delay database. Activity descriptions and appropriate CSI codes provided in the CSI manual key word index were entered into a computer database that selects the appropriate CSI code for each activity.

The Activity Level Delay Report generates an objective analysis on the tradeoff between cost and duration for activity specific delays. Utilizing the cost performance index (CPI), the system calculates another index labeled TCPI, denoting the CPI until completion. For activities that are behind schedule, the program calculates various dollar values for defined TCPI levels. It calculates the dollar increase per day for that specific activity under various TCPI benchmarks, along with the dollar value that would put that activity back on schedule, and its corresponding TCPI value.

Sample Data

Table 2 shows the type of data that is processed in the Construction Delay Analysis System (CDAS) program, and it has sample data from a database on the firm and project type delays. Table 2 also contains the respective weighting factors for each of the sample delay causes listed. Other types of delay categories include contract type value delays, location type delays, and contract value delays. Table 3 shows sample delay reduction measures.

Table 3. Delay Reduction Measures

Delay Cause	Delay Measure 1	Delay Measure 2	Delay Measure 3
Change Orders	QA Program	Work Critical Tasks	Increase Crew Size
Inaccurate Estimate	Cost Control Program	Improve Internal Reporting	Overtime
Labor Productivity	Increase Supervision	Increase Training	Increase Crew Size
Site Conditions	Overtime	Design Modifications	Organizational Modifications
Weather Delay	Overtime	Increase Crew Size	Work Critical Tasks

Once the information is processed a table is generated that lists the activity, or activities, in question and the system-generated recommendations. The program also allows users to input actual measures taken to rectify activity delays. This is critical for the documentation of decisions made at various stages of a project and for the examination of past project decisions.

Project Information
The project and the related information option allows users to customize the program for a particular project by entering project information such as project, company, geographical location, contract type, management type, and so on.

Construction Delay Analysis System Program Features

Main Menu
The program was designed to be user friendly in that it is menu driven with a help option that can assist users when they are not sure what to select from the menu. The main menu has five options: project and related information, schedule information, historical viewpoint, reports and queries, and system utilities menus. When a user selects one of the options, additional menus appear and allow the user to access a variety of options.

Schedule Information
The schedule option imports schedules from project management software.

Reports and Queries
The reports and queries option generates reports. There are five options: project information listings, project information query, and three delay-related reports. The first option generates a list summarizing information about all projects listed in the Project Names Table database. The second option generates pertinent project information through querying. The third and fourth options generate a Project Level Delay Report and an Activity Level Delay Report based on knowledge supplied by users in the User Knowledge Delay Table.

System Utilities
The system utilities option is used to update all system tables and knowledge bases if required or to customize the databases. The system code tables include project type, firm type, contract type, domestic location, international location, and Construction Specification Institute code tables. In addition to the knowledge bases provided with the program, a user knowledge table is also provided where users can document their data without altering the knowledge bases provided with the system.

Historical Viewpoint
The historical viewpoint option accesses information relating to a historical analysis of the project. This option provides users with the capability of evaluating or extracting past project performance measures. The program saves all of the measures imported from the schedule to a historical database along with a run date link. The program monitors the performance of individual activities along a certain time span or specific activities throughout the history of the project, or it reports on the performance of all activities in question at a certain specified date.

Analysis of Delay Causes and Reduction Factors
Since it was possible for respondents to indicate more than one reduction measure for each delay a total of 3,703 cases were documented. Both the delay cause—the independent variable—and the delay reduction factor—the dependent variable—were identified as categorical, and a cross-tabulation test was performed. The results of the test were used to develop databases used in the computer program.

The relationship between each of the sixteen Construction Specification Institute divisions and delay causes was analyzed using the surveys to create 676 documented cases. This analysis was used to create a database containing the three highest rated delay causes, weights, and databases of actual delays associated with activity classifications.

Research Results

The results obtained during the knowledge acquisition stage were utilized to develop the knowledge bases for the computer program. The data collected was documented, coded, classified, and statistically analyzed. The data was evaluated from five different perspectives. The first analysis examined various project information parameters with delay causes, and the second analysis paired delay causes with delay reduction factors. The third analysis covered hypothesis testing, the fourth included a subjective evaluation of the comments provided by the respondents, and the fifth examined activity level delays.

When different hypotheses were tested the only ones found to be significantly different were the following. Between lump sum and fixed fee projects there were different types of delays, and between projects in excess of $500 million and all other project values there were different types of delays. There were no significant differences in delays on different types of projects, among different types of firms, or at different project locations.

Conclusions

This research project demonstrated that additional techniques could be used to assist with the decision-making processes required in a project environment. Decision-makers need accurate, timely information that is often difficult to manually extract from previously existing computer programs and reports. In addition, the process of reconstructing delays at the end of construction is a tedious process that can be augmented with information available in the Construction Delay Analysis System (CDAS) program.

The intention of the research project was to explore new and innovative ways to assist in information processing in a construction environment. The CDAS program demonstrates that the knowledge required during construction can be captured in knowledge databases for use by others during construction, at the conclusion of construction, or on the construction of similar projects. The CDAS system also demonstrates that communication processes at construction sites can be improved through the proper use of computers. The right type of computer decision support systems can assist managers and construction personnel in decision-making processes and can also be used to capture these processes for further reference.

This paper discussed the research conducted to develop the CDAS computer program, including the purpose of the program, its technical parameters, data collection and analysis processes, development of the program, program sub-models, program features, and how the program can be used to assist construction personnel in analyzing project delays.

Each delay in a construction project generates experience and expertise in recognizing and rectifying mistakes. Acquiring this knowledge is costly to companies in the form of time, labor, and safety, as well as actual costs. This expertise can be accumulated, collated, and disseminated by the CDAS computer program to provide future managers with the benefits of experience without the cost of relearning the same lessons on each new project. It also provides new construction personnel with a useful technique for learning what has been done on previous projects and assists them in their decision-making processes.

The Construction Delay Analysis System (CDAS) is a new method whereby the data generated during projects related to delays can be categorized, quantified, and recorded so that the knowledge being generated can be captured for use during the remainder of the project or on similar types of future projects. The CDAS program provides an interactive technique that augments traditional methods for monitoring construction delays by highlighting causes of deviations and providing recommendations for rectification and prevention purposes.

The CDAS computer program is an excellent tool for the overall project communication system because it provides a documented process for recording the information that is communicated on projects related to delays. The system provides a method to document decisions and the information used to arrive at decisions in order to provide a traceable link for decision processes.

References

1. Rahbar, F. and J.K. Yates. 1990. "Executive Summary Status Report." *Transactions of the American Association of Cost Engineers Conference*. Boston, Massachusetts (June): D.3.1–D.3.9.

2. Rahbar, F., and J.K. Yates. 1991. "A Knowledge Engineering System for Inquiry-Feedback Project Management." *Proceedings of the American Society of Civil Engineers Construction Congress II*. Boston, Massachusetts (April): 704–709.

3. Rahbar, Fred, G. Spencer, and J.K. Yates. 1991. "Project Management Knowledge Engineering System." *Journal of the American Association of Cost Engineers* 33: 7 (July): 15–23.

4. Yates, J.K. 1992. "A Computerized Inquiry-Feedback Knowledge Engineering System." *Transactions of the American Association of Cost Engineers Annual Conference*. Orlando, Florida (June): R.1.1–R.1.7.

5. Yates, J.K. 1993. "Construction Decision Support System for Delay Analysis—CDAS." *Journal of the Construction Engineering and Management, American Society of Civil Engineers* 119: 2 (June): 1–9.

6. Aoude, H. 1995. *Computerized Construction Delay Management System*. Ph.D. Dissertation, Polytechnic University (June).

Appendix A: AIA Document A201-1997

Reproduced with permission of the American Institute of Architects under license number #97048. This license expires December 31, 1998. FURTHER REPRODUCTION IS PROHIBITED. Because AIA Documents are revised from time to time, users should ascertain from the AIA the current edition of this document. Copies of the current edition of this document may be purchased from The American Institute of Architects or its local distributors. The text of this document is not "model language" and is intended for use in other documents without permission of the AIA.

AIA DOCUMENT A201-1997

GENERAL INFORMATION

PURPOSE. AIA Document A201-1997, a general conditions form, is intended to be used as one of the contract documents forming the construction contract. In addition, it is frequently adopted by reference into a variety of other agreements, including the Owner-Architect agreements and the Contractor-Subcontractor agreements, to establish a common basis for the primary and secondary relationships on the typical construction project.

RELATED DOCUMENTS. A201-1997 is incorporated by reference into two AIA Owner-Contractor agreements (A101-1997 and A111-1997), the A401-1997 Contractor-Subcontractor agreement and several AIA Owner-Architect agreements (for example, B141-1997 and B151-1997). It is also incorporated by reference into two design-build agreements (A491-Part 2 and B901-Part 2) and two Owner-Construction Manager/constructor agreements (A121/CMc-Part 2 and A131/CMc-Part 2). A201-1997 may be adopted by indirect reference when the prime Agreement between the Owner and Architect adopts A201-1997 and is in turn adopted into Architect-Consultant agreements such as AIA Documents C141-1997 and C142-1997. Such incorporation by reference is a valid legal drafting method, and documents so incorporated are generally interpreted as part of the respective.

The Contract Documents, including A201-1997, record the Contract for Construction between the Owner and the Contractor. The other Contract Documents are:

©1997 AIA ® AIA Document A201–1997 Used with permission

Owner-Contractor Agreement Form (e.g., A101-1997 or A111-1997)
Supplementary Conditions
Drawings
Specifications
Modifications

Although the AIA does not produce standard documents for Supplementary Conditions, Drawings or Specifications, a variety of model and guide documents are available, including AIA's MASTERSPEC and AIA Document A511, Guide for Supplementary Conditions.

The A201-1997 document is considered the keystone document coordinating the many parties involved in the construction process. As mentioned above the diagrammed below, it is a vital document used to allocate the proper legal responsibilities of the parties.

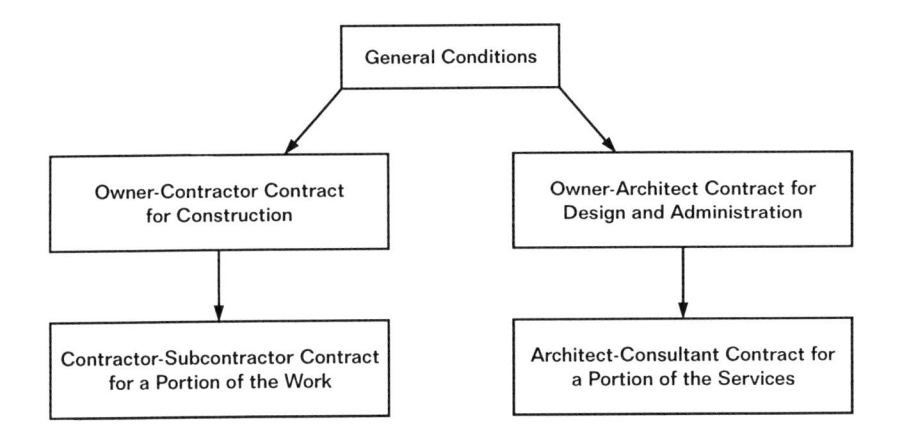

```
                    ┌─────────────────────┐
                    │  General Conditions │
                    └──────────┬──────────┘
                   ┌───────────┴───────────┐
                   ▼                       ▼
      ┌─────────────────────┐   ┌─────────────────────────┐
      │ Owner-Contractor    │   │ Owner-Architect Contract│
      │ Contract for        │   │ for Design and          │
      │ Construction        │   │ Administration          │
      └──────────┬──────────┘   └────────────┬────────────┘
                 ▼                           ▼
      ┌─────────────────────┐   ┌─────────────────────────┐
      │ Contractor-Subcon-  │   │ Architect-Consultant    │
      │ tractor Contract    │   │ Contract for a Portion  │
      │ for a Portion of    │   │ of the Services         │
      │ the Work            │   │                         │
      └─────────────────────┘   └─────────────────────────┘
```

REPRODUCTIONS. A201-1997 is a copyrighted work and may not be reproduced or excerpted from in substantial part without the express written permission of the AIA. This document is intended to be used as a consumable—that is, the original document purchased by the user is intended to be consumed in the course of being used. There is no implied permission to reproduce this document, nor does membership in the American Institute of Architects confer and further rights to reproduce A201-1997 in whole or in part.

This document may not be reproduced for Project Manuals. Rather, if a user wishes to include it as an example in a Project Manual, the normal practice is to purchase a quantity of the original forms and bind one in each of the Project Manuals. Modifications may be accomplished through the use of separate Supplementary Conditions, such as those derived from AIA Document A511.

©1997 AIA ® AIA Document A201–1997 Used with permission

Unlike many other AIA documents, A201-1997 does not carry with it a limited license to reproduce. The AIA will not permit the reproduction of this document or the use of substantial portions of language from it, except upon written application by a specific user to and after receipt of written permission from the AIA.

The AIA logo is printed in red on the original version of this document. This logo distinguishes an original AIA document from copies or counterfeits. To ensure accuracy and uniformity of language, purchasers should only use an original AIA document or one that has been reproduced from an original under a special limited license from the AIA. Documents generated by the software AIA Contract Documents: Electronic Format for Windows™ do not contain a red logo. Documents reproduced in this program may be accompanied by AIA Document D401, Certification of Document's Authority. In addition, all documents in the program contain the license number under which the document was reproduced and the date of expiration of the license.

CHANGES FROM THE PREVIOUS EDITION

AIA Document A201-1997 revises the 1987 edition of A201 to reflect changes in construction industry practices and the law. Comments and assistance in this revision were received from numerous individuals and organizations, including those representing owners, architects, engineers, specifiers, general contractors, independent insurance agents, sureties, attorneys and arbitrators.

A number of substantial changes have been made to the A201-1997 document. The changes are described below.
    Article 1: Protection of rights in Drawings, Specifications and other documents is now specifically extended to those of the Architect's consultants, and includes documents in electronic form.
    Article 2: The Owner is required to designate a representative empowered to act for the Owner on the Project. The Contractor is entitled to rely on the accuracy and completeness of information furnished by the Owner.
    Article 3: Procedures are given for Contractors review of field conditions and for review of instructions in the Contract Documents regarding construction means and methods. The rights and responsibilities of the parties with respect to incidental design by the Contractor are set out in detail.
    Articles 4: Mediation is included as a precursor to arbitration. The Owner and Contractor waive consequential damages (i.e., indirect damages) arising out of the Contract.
    Article 7: Amounts not in dispute under a Construction Change Directive must be included in Applications for Payment. Interim determinations as to amounts still in dispute will be made by the Architect.

©1997 AIA ® AIA Document A201–1997 Used with permission

Article 9: In the absence of a payment bond in the full amount of the contract sum, payments received by the Contractor for the Work of subcontractors are held by the Contractor for the subcontractors. Release of retainage on completed Work is required at substantial completion.

Article 10: Hazardous materials provisions have been expanded to cover materials other than asbestos and PCB, and indemnification of the Contractor under these provisions has been extended to cover remediation costs.

Article 11: Project Management Protective Liability insurance, covering risks of the Owner, Contractor and Architect, is now an option for the parties to the Contract.

Article 12: If during the correction period, the Owner discovers Work that is not in accordance with the Contract Documents, the Owner must notify the Contractor. Failure to do so results in a waiver of the Owner's rights under the correction of Work and warranty provisions.

Article 13: The Owner is permitted to assign the Contract to the lender without consent of the Contractor.

Article 14: The Owner is permitted to terminate the Contract for convenience, with appropriate payment to the Contractor.

USING THE A201-1997 FORM

MODIFICATIONS. Users are encouraged to consult an attorney before completing an AIA document. Particularly with respect to contractor's licensing laws, duties imposed by building codes, interest charges, arbitration and indemnification, this document may require modification with the assistance of legal counsel to fully comply with state or local laws regulating these matters.

Generally, necessary modifications to the General Conditions may be accomplished by supplementary conditions included in the Project Manual and referenced in the Owner-Contractor Agreement. See AIA Document A511, Guide for Supplementary Conditions, for model provisions and suggested format for the Supplementary Conditions.

Warning: Unlicensed photocopying violates U.S. copyright laws and will subject the violator to legal prosecution.

©1997 AIA ® AIA Document A201–1997 Used with permission

1997 EDITION

AIA DOCUMENT A201–1997

GENERAL CONDITIONS OF THE CONTRACT FOR CONSTRUCTION

TABLE OF ARTICLES

1. GENERAL PROVISIONS
2. OWNER
3. CONTRACTOR
4. ADMINISTRATION OF THE CONTRACT
5. SUBCONTRACTORS
6. CONSTRUCTION BY OWNER OR BY SEPARATE CONTRACTORS
7. CHANGES IN THE WORK
8. TIME
9. PAYMENTS AND COMPLETION
10. PROTECTION OF PERSONS AND PROPERTY
11. INSURANCE AND BONDS
12. UNCOVERING AND CORRECTION OF WORK
13. MISCELLANEOUS PROVISIONS
14. TERMINATION OR SUSPENSION OF THE CONTRACT

©1997 AIA ® AIA Document A201–1997 Used with permission

INDEX

Acceptance of Nonconforming Work
9.6.6, 9.9.3, 12.3
Acceptance of Work
9.6.6, 9.8.2, 9.9.3, 9.10.1, 9.10.3, 12.3
Access to Work
3.16, 6.2.1, 12.1
Accident Prevention
4.2.3, 10
Acts and Omissions
3.2, 3.3.2, 3.12.8, 3.18, 4.2.3, 4.3.8, 4.4.1, 8.3.1, 9.5.1, 10.2.5, 13.4.2,13.7, 14.1
Addenda
1.1.1, 3.11
Additional Costs, Claims for
4.3.4, 4.3.5, 4.3.6, 6.1.1, 10.3
Additional Inspections and Testing
9.8.3, 12.2,1, 13.5
Additional Time, Claims for
4.3.4, 4.3.7, 8.3.2
ADMINISTRATION OF THE CONTRACT
3.3.3, 4, 9.4, 9.5
Advertisement or Invitation to Bid
1.1.1
Aesthetic Effect
4.2.13, 4.5.1
Allowances
3.8
All-risk Insurance
11.4.1.1
Applications for Payment
4.2.5, 7.3.8, 9.2, 9.3, 9.4, 9.5.1, 9.6.3, 9.7.1, 9.8.5, 9.10, 11.1.3, 14.2.4, 14.4.3
Approvals
2.4, 3.1.3, 3.5, 3.10.2, 3.12, 4.2.7, 9.3.2,13.4.2, 13.5
Arbitration
4.3.3, 4.4, 4.5.1, 4.5.2, 4.6, 8.3.1, 9.7.1, 11.4.9, 11.4.10
Architect
4.1

Architect, Definition of
4.1.1
Architect, Extent of Authority
2.4, 3.12.7, 4.2, 4.3.6, 4.4, 5.2, 6.3, 7.1.2, 7.3.6, 7.4, 9.2, 9.3.1, 9.4, 9.5, 9.8.3, 9.10.1, 9.10.3, 12.1, 12.2.1, 13.5.1, 13.5.2,14.2.2, 14.2.4
Architect, Limitations of Authority and Responsibility
2.1.1, 3.3.3, 3.12.4, 3.12.8, 3.12.10, 4.1.2, 4.2.1, 4.2.2, 4.2.3, 4.2.6, 4.2.7, 4.2.10, 4.2.12, 4.2.13, 4.4, 5.2.1 7.4, 9.4.2, 9.6.4, 9.6.6
Architect's Additional Services and Expenses
2.4, 11.4.1.1, 12.2.1, 13.5.2,13.5.3, 14.2.4
Architect's Administration of the Contract
3.1.3, 4.2, 4.3.4, 4.4, 9.4, 9.5
Architect's Approvals
2.4, 3.1.3, 3.5.1, 3.10.2, 4.2.7
Architect's Authority to Reject Work
3.5.1, 4.2.6, 12.1.2, 12.2.1
Architect's Copyright
1.6
Architect's Decisions
4.2.6, 4.2.7, 4.2.11, 4.2.12, 4.2.13. 4.3.4, 4.4.1, 4.4.5, 4.4.6, 4.5, 6.3, 7.3.6, 7.3.8, 8.1.3, 8.3.1, 9.2, 9.4, 9.5.1, 9.8.4, 9.9.1, 13.5.2, 14.2.2, 14.2.4
Architect's Inspections
4.2.2, 4.2.9, 4.3.4, 9.4.2, 9.8.3, 9.9.2, 9.10.1, 13.5
Architect's Instructions
3.2.3, 3.3.1, 4.2.6, 4.2.7, 4.2.8, 7.4.1, 12.1, 13.5.2
Architect's Interpretations
4.2.11, 4.2.12, 4.3.6
Architect's Project Representative
4.2.10

©1997 AIA ® AIA Document A201–1997 Used with permission

Architect's Relationship with Contractor
  1.1.2, 1.6, 3.1.3, 3.2.1, 3.2.2, 3.2.3,
  3.3.1, 3.4.2, 3.5.1, 3.7.3, 3.10, 3.11,
  3.12, 3.16, 3.18, 4.1.2, 4.1.3, 4.2, 4.3.4,
  4.4.1, 4.4.7, 5.2, 6.2.2, 7, 8.3.1, 9.2,
  9.3, 9.4, 9.5, 9.7, 9.8, 9.9, 10.2.6, 10.3,
  11.3, 11.4.7, 12, 13.4.2, 13.5
Architect's Relationship with Subcontractors
  1.1.2, 4.2.3, 4.2.4, 4.2.6, 9.6.3, 9.6.4, 11.4.7
Architect's Representations
  9.4.2, 9.5.1, 9.10.1
Architect's Site Visits
  4.2.2, 4.2.5, 4.2.9, 4.3.4, 9.4.2, 9.5.1, 9.9.2, 9.10.1, 13.5
Asbestos
  10.3.1
Attorneys' Fees
  3.18.1, 9.10.2, 10.3.3
Award of Separate Contracts
  6.1.1, 6.1.2
Award of Subcontracts and Other Contracts for Portions of the Work
  5.2
Basic Definitions
  1.1
Bidding Requirements
  1.1.1, 1.1.7, 5.2.1, 11.5.1
Boiler and Machinery Insurance
  11.4.2
Bonds, Lien
  9.10.2
Bonds, Performance, and Payment
  7.3.6.4, 9.6.7, 9.10.3, 11.4.9, 11.5
Building Permit
  3.7.1
Capitalization
  1.3
Certificate of Substantial Completion
  9.8.3, 9.8.4, 9.8.5

Certificates for Payment
  4.2.5, 4.2.9, 9.3.3, 9.4, 9.5, 9.6.1, 9.6.6, 9.7.1, 9.10.1, 9.10.3, 13.7, 14.1.1.3, 14.2.4
Certificate of Inspection, Testing or Approval
  13.5.4
Certificates of Insurance
  9.10.2, 11.1.3
Change Orders
  1.1.1, 2.4.1, 3.4.2, 3.8.2.3, 3.11.1, 3.12.8, 4.2.8, 4.3.4, 4.3.9, 5.2.3, 7.1, 7.2, 7.3, 8.3.1, 9.3.1.1, 9.10.3, 11.4.1.2, 11.4.4, 11.4.9, 12.1.2
Change Orders, Definition of
  7.2.1
CHANGES IN THE WORK
  3.11, 4.2.8, 7, 8.3.1, 9.3.1.1, 11.4.9
Claim, Definition of
  4.3.1
Claims and Disputes
  3.2.3, 4.3, 4.4, 4.5, 4.6, 6.1.1, 6.3, 7.3.8, 9.3.3, 9.10.4, 10.3.3
Claims and Timely Assertion of Claims
  4.6.5
Claims for Additional Cost
  3.2.3, 4.3.4, 4.3.5, 4.3.6, 6.1.1, 7.3.8, 10.3.2
Claims for Additional Time
  3.2.3, 4.3.4, 4.3.7, 6.1.1, 8.3.2, 10.3.2
Claims for Concealed or Unknown Conditions
  4.3.4
Claims for Damages
  3.2.3, 3.18, 4.3.10, 6.1.1, 8.3.3, 9.5.1, 9.6.7, 10.3.3, 11.1.1, 11.4.5, 11.4.7, 14.1.3, 14.2.4
Claims Subject to Arbitration
  4.4.1, 4.5.1, 4.6.1
Cleaning Up
  3.15, 6.3

©1997 AIA ® AIA Document A201–1997 Used with permission

Commencement of Statutory Limitation Period
13.7

Commencement of the Work, Conditions Relating to
2.2.1, 3.2.1, 3.4.1, 3.7.1, 3.10.1, 3.12.6, 4.3.5, 5.2.1, 5.2.3, 6.2.2, 8.1.2, 8.2.2, 8.3.1, 11.1, 11.4.1, 11.4.6, 11.5.1

Commencement of the Work, Definition of
8.1.2

Communications Facilitating Contract Administration
3.9.1, 4.2.4

Completion, Conditions Relating to
1.6.1, 3.4.1, 3.11, 3.15, 4.2.2, 4.2.9, 8.2, 9.4.2, 9.8, 9.9.1, 9.10, 12.2, 13.7, 14.1.2

COMPLETION, PAYMENTS AND
9

Completion, Substantial
4.2.9, 8.1.1, 8.1.3, 8.2.3, 9.4.2, 9.8, 9.9.1, 9.10.3, 9.10.4.2, 12.2, 13.7

Compliance with Laws
1.6.1, 3.2.2, 3.6, 3.7, 3.12.10, 3.13, 4.1.1, 4.4.8, 4.6.4, 4.6.6, 9.6.4, 10.2.2, 11.1, 11.4, 13.1, 13.4, 13.5.1, 13.5.2, 13.6, 14.1.1, 14.2.1.3

Concealed or Unknown Conditions
4.3.4, 8.3.1, 10.3

Conditions of the Contract
1.1.1, 1.1.7, 6.1.1, 6.1.4

Content, Written
1.6, 3.4.2, 3.12.8, 3.14.2, 4.1.2, 4.3.4, 4.6.4, 9.3.2, 9.8.5, 9.9.1, 9.10.2, 9.10.3, 11.4.1, 13.2, 13.4.2

CONSTRUCTION BY OWNER OR BY SEPARATE CONTRACTORS
1.1.4, 6

Construction Change Directive, Definition of
7.3.1

Construction Change Directives
1.1.1, 3.12.8, 4.2.8, 4.3.9, 7.1, 7.3, 9.3.1.1

Construction Schedules, Contractor's
1.4.1.2, 3.10, 3.12.1, 3.12.2, 4.3.7.2, 6.1.3

Contingent Assignment of Subcontracts
5.4, 14.2.2.2

Continuing Contract Performance
4.3.3

Contract, Definition of
1.1.2

CONTRACT, TERMINATION OR SUSPENSION OF THE
5.4.1.1, 11.4.9, 14

Contract Administration
3.1.3, 4.9.4, 9.5

Contract Award and Execution, Conditions Relating to
3.7.1, 3.10, 5.2, 6.1, 11.1.3, 11.4.6, 11.5.1

Contract Documents, The
1.1, 1.2

Contract Documents, Copies Furnished and Use of
1.6, 2.2.5, 5.3

Contract Documents, Definition of
1.1.1

Contract Sum
3.8, 4.3.4, 4.3.5, 4.4.5, 5.2.3, 7.2, 7.3, 7.4, 9.1, 9.4.2, 9.5.1.4, 9.6.7, 9.7, 10.3.2, 11.4.1, 14.2.4, 14.3.2

Contract Sum, Definition of
9.1

Contract Time
4.3.4, 4.3.7, 4.4.5, 5.2.3, 7.2.1.3, 7.3, 7.4, 8.1.1, 8.2, 8.3.1, 9.5.1, 9.7, 10.3.2, 12.1.1, 14.3.2

Contract Time, Definition of
8.1.1

CONTRACTOR
3

©1997 AIA ® AIA Document A201-1997 Used with permission

Contractor, Definition of
   3.1, 6.1.2
Contractor's Construction Schedules
   1.4.1.2, 3.10, 3.12.1, 3.12.2, 4.3.7.2, 6.1.3
Contractor's Employees
   3.3.2, 3.4.3, 3.8.1, 3.9, 3.18.2, 4.2.3, 4.2.6, 10.2, 10.3, 11.1.1, 11.4.7, 14.1, 14.2.1.1
Contractor's Liability Insurance
   11.1
Contractor's Relationship with Separate Contractors and Owner's Forces
   3.12.5, 3.14.2, 4.2.4, 6, 11.4.7, 12.1.2, 12.2.4
Contractor's Relationship with Subcontractors
   1.2.2, 3.3.2, 3.18.1, 3.18.2, 5, 9.6.2, 9.6.7, 9.10.2, 11.4.1.2, 11.4.7, 11.4.8
Contractor's Relationship with the Architect
   1.1.2, 1.6, 3.1.3, 3.2.1, 3.2.2, 3.2.3, 3.3.1, 3.4.2, 3.5.1, 3.7.3, 3.10, 3.11, 3.12, 3.16, 3.18, 4.1.2, 4.1.3, 4.2, 4.3.4, 4.4.1, 4.4.7, 5.2, 6.2.2, 7, 8.3.1, 9.2, 9.3, 9.4, 5, 9.7, 9.8, 9.9, 10.2.6, 10.3, 11.3, 11.4.7, 12, 13.4.2, 13.5
Contractor's Representations
   1.5.2, 3.5.1, 3.12.6, 6.2.2, 8.2.1, 9.3.3, 9.8.2
Contractor's Responsibility for Those Performing the Work
   3.3.2, 3.18, 4.2.3, 4.3.8, 5.3.1, 6.1.3, 6.2, 6.3, 9.5.1, 10
Contractor's Review of Contract Documents
   1.5.2, 3.2, 3.7.3
Contractor's Right to Stop the Work
   9.7
Contractor's Right to Terminate the Contract
   4.3.10, 14.1

Contractor's Submittals
   3.10, 3.11, 3.12, 4.2.7, 5.2.1, 5.2.3, 7.3.6, 9.2, 9.3, 9.8.2, 9.8.3, 9.9.1, 9.10.2, 9.10.3, 11.1.3, 11.5.2
Contractor's Superintendent
   3.9, 10.2.6
Contractor's Supervision and Construction Procedures
   1.2.2, 3.3, 3.4, 3.12.10, 4.2.2, 4.2.7, 4.3.3, 6.1.3, 6.2.4, 7.1.3, 7.3.4, 7.3.6, 8.2, 10, 12, 14
Contractual Liability Insurance
   11.1.1.8, 11.2, 11.3
Coordination and Correlation
   1.2, 1.5.2, 3.3.1, 3.10, 3.12.6, 6.1.3, 6.2.1
Copies Furnished of Drawings and Specifications
   1.6, 2.2.5, 3.11
Copyrights
   1.6, 3.17
Correction of Work
   2.3, 2.4, 3.7.4, 4.2.1, 9.4.2, 9.8.2, 9.8.3, 9.9.1, 12.1.2, 12.2, 13.7.1.3
Correlation and Intent of the Contract Documents
   1.2
Cost, Definition of
   7.3.6
Costs
   2.4, 3.2.3, 3.7.4, 3.8.2, 3.15.2, 4.3, 5.4.2, 6.1.1, 6.2.3, 7.3.3.3, 7.3.6, 7.3.7, 7.3.8, 9.10.2, 10.3.2, 10.5, 11.3, 11.4, 12.1, 12.2.1, 12.2.4, 13.5, 14
Cutting and Patching
   6.2.5, 3.14
Damage to Construction of Owner or Separate Contractors
   3.14.2, 6.2.4, 9.2.1.5, 10.2.1.2, 10.2.5, 10.6, 11.1, 11.4, 12.2.4
Damage to the Work
   3.14.2, 9.9.1, 10.2.1.2, 10.2.5, 10.6, 11.4, 12.2.4

©1997 AIA ® AIA Document A201–1997 Used with permission

Damages, Claims for
3.2.3, 3.18, 4.3.10, 6.1.1, 8.3.3, 9.5.1, 9.6.7, 10.3.3, 11.1.1, 11.4.5, 11.4.7, 14.1.3, 14.2.4

Damages For Delay
6.1.1, 8.3.3, 9.5.1.6, 9.7, 10.3.2

Date of Commencement of the Work, Definition of
8.1.2

Date of Substantial Completion, Definition of
8.1.3

Day, Definition of
8.1.4

Decision of the Architect
4.2.6, 4.2.7, 4.2.11, 4.2.12, 4.2.13, 4.3.4, 4.4.1, 4.4.5, 4.4.6, 4.5, 6.3, 7.3.6, 7.3.8, 8.1.3, 8.3.1, 9.2, 9.4, 9.5.1, 9.8.4, 9.9.1, 13.5.2, 14.2.2, 14.2.4

Decisions to Withhold Certification
9.4.1, 9.5, 9.7, 14.1.1.3

Defective or Nonconforming Work, Acceptance, Rejection and Correction of
2.3, 2.4, 3.5.1, 4.2.6, 6.2.5, 9.5.1, 9.5.2, 9.6.6, 9.8.2, 9.9.3, 9.10.4, 12.2.1, 13.7.1.3

Defective Work, Definition of
3.5.1

Definitions
1.1, 2.1.1, 3.1, 3.5.1, 3.12.1, 3.12.2, 3.12.3, 4.1.1, 4.3.1, 5.1, 6.1.2, 7.2.1, 7.3.1, 7.3.6, 8.1, 9.1, 9.8.1

Delays and Extensions of Time
3.2.3, 4.3.1, 4.3.4, 4.3.7, 4.4.5, 5.2.3, 7.2.1, 7.3.1, 7.4.1, 7.5.1, 8.3, 9.5.1, 9.7.1, 10.3.2, 10.6.1, 14.3.2

Disputes
4.1.4, 4.3, 4.4, 4.5, 4.6, 6.3, 7.3.8

Documents and Samples at the Site
3.11

Drawings, Definition of
1.1.5

Drawings and Specifications, Use and Ownership of
1.1.1, 1.3, 2.2.5, 3.11, 5.3

Effective Date of Insurance
8.2.2, 11.1.2

Emergencies
4.3.5, 10.6, 14.1.1.2

Employees, Contractor's
3.3.2, 3.4.3, 3.8.1, 3.9, 3.18.2, 4.2.3, 4.2.6, 10.2, 10.3, 11.1.1, 11.4.7, 14.1, 14.2.1.1

Equipment, Labor, Materials and
1.1.3, 1.1.6, 3.4, 3.5.1, 3.8.2, 3.8.3, 3.12, 3.13, 3.15.1 4.2.6, 4.2.7, 5.2.1, 6.2.1, 7.3.6, 9.3.2, 9.3.3, 9.5.1.3, 9.10.2, 10.2.1, 10.2.4, 14.2.1.2

Execution and Progress of the Work
1.1.3, 1.2.1, 1.2.2, 2.2.3, 2.2.5, 3.1, 3.3, 3.4, 3.5, 3.7, 3.10, 3.12, 3.14, 4.2.2, 4.2.3, 4.3.3, 6.2.2, 7.1.3, 7.3.4, 8.2, 9.5, 9.9.1, 10.2, 10.3, 12.2, 14.2, 14.3

Extensions of Time
3.2.3, 4.3.1, 4.3.4, 4.3.7, 4.4.5, 5.2.3, 7.2.1, 7.3, 7.4.1, 9.5.1, 9.7.1, 10.3.2, 10.6.1, 14.3.2

Failure of Payment
4.3.6, 9.5.1.3, 9.7, 9.10.2, 14.1.1.3, 14.2.1.2, 13.6

Faulty Work
(See Defective or Nonconforming Work)

Final Completion and Final Payment
4.2.1, 4.2.9, 4.3.2, 9.8.2, 9.10, 11.1.2, 11.3, 11.4.1, 11.4.5, 12.3.1, 13.7 14.2.4, 14.4.3

Financial Arrangements, Owner's
2.2.1, 13.2.2, 14.1.1.5

Fire and Extended Coverage Insurance
11.4

GENERAL PROVISIONS
1

Governing Law
13.1

©1997 AIA ® AIA Document A201–1997 Used with permission

Guarantees (See Warranty)
Hazardous Materials
    10.2.4, 10.3, 10.5
Identification of Contract Documents
    1.5.1
Identification of Subcontractors and Suppliers
    5.2.1
Indemnification
    3.17, 3.18, 9.10.2, 10.3.3, 10.5, 11.4.1.2, 11.4.7
Information and Services Required of the Owner
    2.1.2, 2.2, 3.2.1, 3.12.4, 3.12.10, 4.2.7, 4.3.3, 6.1.3, 6.1.4, 6.2.5, 9.3.2, 9.6.1, 9.6.4, 9.9.2, 9.10.3, 10.3.3, 11.2, 11.4, 13.5.1, 13.5.2, 14.1.1.4, 14.1.4
Injury or Damage to Person or Property
    4.3.8, 10.2, 10.6
Inspections
    3.1.3, 3.3.3, 3.7.1, 4.2.2, 4.2.6, 4.2.9, 9.4.2, 9.8.2, 9.8.3, 9.9.2, 9.10.1, 12.2.1, 13.5
Instructions to Bidders
    1.1.1
Instructions to the Contractor
    3.2.3, 3.3.1, 3.8.1, 4.2.8, 5.2.1, 7, 12, 8.2.2, 13.5.2
Insurance
    3.18.1, 6.1.1, 7.3.6, 8.2.1, 9.3.2, 9.8.4, 9.9.1, 9.10.2, 9.10.5, 11
Insurance, Boiler and Machinery
    11.4.2
Insurance, Contractor's Liability
    11.1
Insurance, Effective Date of
    8.2.2, 11.1.2
Insurance, Loss of Use
    11.4.3
Insurance, Owner's Liability
    11.2

Insurance, Project Management Protective Liability
    11.3
Insurance, Property
    10.2.5, 11.4
Insurance, Stored Materials
    9.3.2, 11.4.1.4
INSURANCE AND BONDS
    11
Insurance Companies, Consent to Partial Occupancy
    9.9.1, 11.4.1.5
Insurance Companies, Settlement with
    11.4.10
Intent of the Contract Documents
    1.2.1, 4.2.7, 4.2.12, 4.2.13, 7.4
Interest
    13.6
Interpretation
    1.2.3, 1.4, 4.1.1, 4.3.1, 5.1, 6.1.2, 8.1.4
Interpretations, Written
    4.2.11, 4.2.12, 4.3.6
Joinder and Consolidation of Claims Required
    4.6.4
Judgment on Final Award
    4.6.6
Labor and Materials, Equipment
    1.1.3, 1.1.6, 3.4, 3.5.1, 3.8.2, 3.8.3, 3.12, 3.13, 3.15.1, 4.2.6, 4.2.7, 5.2.1, 6.2.1, 7.3.6, 9.3.2, 9.3.3, 9.5.1.3, 9.10.2, 10.2.1, 10.2.4, 14.2.1.2
Labor Disputes
    8.3.1
Laws and Regulations
    1.6, 3.2.2, 3.6, 3.7, 3.12.10, 3.13, 4.1.1, 4.4.8, 4.6, 9.6.4, 9.9.1, 10.2.2, 11.1, 11.4, 13.1, 13.4, 13.5.1, 13.5.2, 13.6, 14
Liens
    2.1.2, 4.4.8, 8.2.2, 9.3.3, 9.10
Limitation on Consolidation or Joinder
    4.6.4

©1997 AIA ® AIA Document A201–1997 Used with permission

Limitations, Statutes of
  4.6.3, 12.2.6, 13.7
Limitations of Liability
  2.3, 3.2.1, 3.5.1, 3.7.3, 3.12.8, 3.12.10,
  3.17, 3.18, 4.2.6, 4.2.7, 4.2.12, 6.2.2,
  9.4.2, 9.6.4, 9.6.7, 9.10.4, 10.3.3,
  10.2.5, 11.1.2, 11.2.1, 11.4.7, 12.2.5,
  13.4.2
Limitations of Time
  2.1.2, 2.2, 2.4, 3.2.1, 3.7.3, 3.10, 3.11,
  3.12.5, 3.15.1, 4.2.7, 4.3, 4.4, 4.5, 4.6,
  5.2, 5.3, 5.4, 6.2.4, 7.3, 7.4, 8.2, 9.2,
  9.3.1, 9.3.3, 9.4.1, 9.5, 9.6, 9.7, 9.8,
  9.9, 9.10, 11.1.3, 11.4.1.5, 11.4.6,
  11.4.10, 12.2, 13.5, 13.7, 14
Loss of Use Insurance
  11.4.3
Material Suppliers
  1.6, 3.12.1, 4.2.4, 4.2.6, 5.2.1, 9.3,
  9.4.2, 9.6, 9.10.5
Materials, Hazardous
  10.2.4, 10.3, 10.5
Materials, Labor, Equipment and
  1.1.3, .1.1.6, 1.6.1, 3.4, 3.5.1, 3.8.2,
  3.8.23, 3.12, 3.13, 3.15.1, 4.2.6, 4.2.7,
  5.2.1, 6.2.1, 7.3.6, 9.3.2, 9.3.3, 9.5.1.3,
  9.10.2, 10.2.1, 10.2.4, 14.2.1.2
Means, Methods, Techniques, Sequences
  and Procedures of Construction
  3.3.1, 3.12.10, 4.2.2, 4.2.7, 9.4.2
Mechanic's Lien
  4.4.8
Mediation
  4.4.1, 4.4.5, 4.4.6, 4.4.8, 4.5, 4.6.1,
  4.6.2, 8.3.1, 10.5
Minor Changes in the Work
  1.1.1, 3.12.8, 4.2.8, 4.3.6, 7.1, 7.4
MISCELLANEOUS PROVISIONS
  13
Modifications, Definition of
  1.1.1
Modifications to the Contract
  1.1.1, 1.1.2, 3.7.3, 3.11, 4.1.2, 4.2.1,
  5.2.3, 7, 8.3.1, 9.7, 10.3.2, 11.4.1

Mutual Responsibility
  6.2
Nonconforming Work, Acceptance of
  9.6.6, 9.9.3, 12.3
Nonconforming Work, Rejection and
  Correction of
  2.3, 2.4, 3.5.1, 4.2.6, 6.2.5, 9.5.1, 9.8.2,
  9.9.3, 9.10.4, 12.2.1, 13.7.1.3
Notice
  2.2.1, 2.3, 2.4, 3.2.3, 3.3.1, 3.7.2, 3.7.4,
  3.12.9, 4.3, 4.4.8, 4.6.5, 5.2.1, 8.2.2,
  9.5.1, 9.10, 10.2.2, 11.1.3, 11.4.6, 12.2.2,
  12.2.4, 13.3, 13.5.1 13.5.2, 14.1, 14.2
Notice, Written
  2.3, 2.4, 3.3.1, 3.9, 3.12.9, 3.12.10, 4.3,
  4.4.8, 4.6.5, 5.2.1, 8.2.2, 9.7, 9.10,
  10.2.2, 10.3, 11.1.3, 11.4.6, 12.2.2,
  12.2.4, 13.3, 14
Notice of Testing and Inspections
  13.5.1, 13.5.2
Notice to Proceed
  8.2.2
Notices, Permits, Fees and
  2.2.2, 3.7, 3.13, 7.3.6.4, 10.2.2
Observations, Contractors
  1.5.2, 3.2, 3.7.3, 4.3.4
Occupancy
  2.2.2, 9.6.6, 9.8, 11.4.1.5
Orders, Written
  1.1.1, 2.3, 3.9, 4.3.6, 7, 8.2.2, 11.4.9,
  12.1, 12.2, 13.5.2, 14.3.1
OWNER
  2
Owner, Definition of
  2.1
Owner, Information and Services
  Required of the
  2.1.2, 2.2, 3.2.1, 3.12.4, 3.12.10, 4.2.7,
  4.3.3, 6.1.3, 6.1.4, 6.2.5, 9.3.2, 9.6.1,
  9.6.4, 9.9.2, 9.10.3, 10.3.3, 11.2, 11.4,
  13.5.1, 13.5.2, 14.1.1.4, 14.1.4

©1997 AIA ® AIA Document A201–1997 Used with permission

Owner's Authority
  1.6, 2.1.1, 2.3, 2.4, 3.4.2, 3.8.1,
  3.12.10, 3.14.2, 4.1.2, 4.1.3, 4.2.4,
  4.2.9, 4.3.6, 4.4.7, 5.2.1, 5.2.4, 5.4.1,
  6.1, 6.3, 7.2.1, 7.3.1, 8.2.2, 8.3.1, 9.3.1,
  9.3.2, 9.5.1, 9.9.1, 9.10.2, 10.3.2,
  11.1.3, 11.3.1, 11.4.3, 11.4.10, 12.2.2,
  12.3.1, 13.2.2, 14.3, 14.4
Owner's Financial Capability
  2.2.1, 13.2.2, 14.1.1.5
Owner's Liability Insurance
  11.2
Owner's Loss of Use Insurance
  11.4.3
Owner's Relationship with Subcontractors
  1.1.2, 5.2, 5.3, 5.4, 9.6.4, 9.10.2, 14.2.2
Owner's Right to Carry Out the Work
  2.4, 12.2.4, 14.2.2.2
Owner's Right to Clean Up
  6.3
Owner's Right to Perform Construction and to Award Separate Contracts
  6.1
Owner's Right to Stop the Work
  2.3
Owner's Right to Suspend the Work
  14.3
Owner's Right to Terminate the Contract
  14.2
Ownership and Use of Drawings, Specifications and Other Instruments of Service
  1.1.1, 1.6, 2.2.5, 3.2.1, 3.11.1,
  3.17.1, 4.2.12, 5.3
Partial Occupancy or Use
  9.6.6, 9.9, 11.4.1.5
Patching, Cutting and
  3.14, 6.2.5
Patents
  3.17

Payment, Applications for
  4.2.5, 7.3.8, 9.2, 9.3, 9.4, 9.5.1, 9.6.3,
  9.7.1, 9.8.5, 9.10.1, 9.10.3, 9.10.5,
  11.1.3, 14.2.4, 14.4.3
Payment, Certificates for
  4.2.5, 4.2.9, 9.3.3, 9.4, 9.5, 9.6.1, 9.6.6,
  9.7.1, 9.10.1, 9.10.3, 13.7, 4.1.1.3,
  14.2.4
Payment, Failure of
  4.3.6, 9.5.1.3, 9.7, 9.10.2, 14.1.1.3,
  14.2.1.2, 13.6
Payment, Final
  4.2.1, 4.2.9, 4.3.2, 9.8.2, 9.10, 11.1.2,
  11.1.3, 11.4.1, 11.4.5, 12.3.1, 13.7,
  14.2.4, 14.4.3
Payment Bond, Performance Bond and
  7.3.6.4, 9.6.7, 9.10.3, 11.4.9, 11.5
Payments, Progress
  4.3.3, 9.3, 9.6, 9.8.5, 9.10.3, 13.6,
  14.2.3

PAYMENTS AND COMPLETION
  9
Payments to Subcontractors
  5.4.2, 9.5.1.3, 9.6.2, 9.6.5.3, 9.6.4,
  9.6.7, 11.4.8, 14.2.1.2
PCB
  10.3.1
Performance Bond and Payment Bond
  7.3.6.4, 9.6.7, 9.10.3, 11.4.9, 11.5
Permits, Fees and Notices
  2.2.2, 3.7, 3.13, 7.3.6.4, 10.2.2

PERSONS AND PROPERTY, PROTECTION OF
  10
Polychlorinated Biphenyl
  10.3.1
Product Data, Definition of
  3.12.2
Product Data and Samples, Shop Drawings
  3.11, 3.12, 4.2.7
Progress and Completion
  4.2.2, 4.3.3, 8.2, 9.8, 9.9.1, 14.1.4

©1997 AIA ® AIA Document A201–1997 Used with permission

173

Progress Payments
    4.3.3, 9.3, 9.6, 9.8.5, 9.10.3, 13.6, 14.2.3
Project, Definition of the
    1.1.4
Project Management Protective Liability Insurance
    11.3
Project Manual, Definition of the
    1.1.7
Project Manuals
    2.2.5
Project Representatives
    4.2.10
Property Insurance
    10.2.5, 11.4
PROTECTION OF PERSONS AND PROPERTY
    10
Regulations and Laws
    1.6, 3.2.2, 3.6, 3.7, 3.12.10, 3.13, 4.1.1, 4.4.8, 4.6, 9.6.4, 9.9.1, 10.2.2, 11.1, 11.4, 13.1, 13.4, 13.5.1, 13.5.2, 13.6, 14
Rejection of Work
    3.5.1, 4.2.6, 12.2.1
Releases and Waivers of Liens
    9.10.2
Representations
    1.5.2, 3.5.1, 3.12.6, 6.2.2, 8.2.1, 9.3.3, 9.4.2, 9.5.1, 9.8.2, 9.10.1
Representatives
    2.1.1, 3.1.1, 3.9, 4.1.1, 4.2.1, 4.2.10, 5.1.1, 5.1.2, 13.2.1
Resolution of Claims and Disputes
    4.4, 4.5, 4.6
Responsibility for Those Performing the Work
    3.3.2, 3.18, 4.2.3, 4.3.8, 5.3.1, 6.1.3, 6.2, 6.3, 9.5.1, 10
Retainage
    9.3.1, 9.6.2, 9.8.5, 9.9.1, 9.10.2, 9.10.3

Review of Contract Documents and Field Conditions by Contractor
    1.5.2, 3.2, 3.7.3, 3.12.7, 6.1.3
Review of Contractor's Submittals by Owner and Architect
    3.10.1, 3.10.2, 3.11, 3.12, 4.2, 5.2, 6.1.3, 9.2, 9.8.2
Review of Shop Drawings, Product Data and Samples by Contractor
    3.12
Rights and Remedies
    1.1.2, 2.3, 2.4, 3.5.1, 3.15.2, 4.2.6, 4.3.4, 4.5, 4.6, 5.3, 5.4, 6.1, 6.3, 7.3.1, 8.3, 9.5.1, 9.7, 10.2.5, 10.3, 12.2.2, 12.2.4, 13.4, 14
Royalties, Patents and Copyrights
    3.17
Rules and Notices for Arbitration
    4.6.2
Safety of Persons and Property
    10.2, 10.6
Safety Precautions and Programs
    3.3.1, 4.2.2, 4.2.7, 5.3.1, 10.1, 10.2, 10.6
Samples, Definition of
    3.12.3
Samples, Shop Drawings, Product Data and
    3.11, 3.12, 4.2.7
Samples at the Site, Documents and
    3.11
Schedule of Values
    9.2, 9.3.1
Schedules, Construction
    1.4.1.2, 3.10, 3.12.1, 3.12.2, 4.3.7.2, 6.1.3
Separate Contracts and Contractors
    1.1.4, 3.12.5, 3.14.2, 4.2.4, 4.2.7, 4.6.4, 6, 8.3.1, 11.4.7, 12.1.2, 12.2.5
Shop Drawings, Definition of
    3.12.1
Shop Drawings, Product Data and Samples
    3.11, 3.12, 4.2.7

©1997 AIA ® AIA Document A201–1997 Used with permission

Site, Use of
  3.13, 6.1.1, 6.2.1
Site Inspections
  1.2.2, 3.2.1, 3.3.3, 3.7.1, 4.2, 4.3.4, 9.4.2, 9.10.1, 13.5
Site Visits, Architect's
  4.2.2, 4.2.9, 4.3.4, 9.4.2, 9.5.1, 9.9.2, 9.10.1, 13.5
Special Inspections and Testing
  4.2.6, 12.2.1, 13.5
Specifications, Definition of the
  1.1.6
Specifications, The
  1.1.1, 1.1.6, 1.1.7, 1.2.2, 1.6, 3.11, 3.12.10, 3.17
Statute of Limitations
  4.6.3, 12.2.6, 13.7
Stopping the Work
  2.3, 4.3.6, 9.7, 10.3, 14.1
Stored Materials
  6.2.1, 9.3.2, 10.2.1.2, 10.2.4, 11.4.1.4
Subcontractor, Definition of
  5.1.1
SUBCONTRACTORS
  5
Subcontractors, Work by
  1,2.2, 3.3.2, 3.12.1, 4.2.3, 5.2.3, 5.3, 5.4, 9.3.1.2, 9.6.7
Subcontractual Relations
  5.3, 5.4, 9.3.1.2, 9.6, 9.10, 10.2.1, 11.4.7, 11.4.8, 14.1, 14.2.1, 14.3.2
Submittals
  1.6, 3.10, 3.11, 3.12, 4.2.7, 5.2.1, 5.2.3, 7.3.6, 9.2, 9.3, 9.8, 9.9.1, 9.10.2, 9.10.3, 11.1.3
Subrogation, Waivers of
  6.1.1, 11.4.5, 11.4.7
Substantial Completion
  4.2.9, 8.1.1, 8.1.3, 8.2.3, 9.4.2, 9.8, 9.9.1, 9.10.3, 9.10.4.2, 12.2, 13.7
Substantial Completion, Definition of
  9.8.1

Substitution of subcontractors
  5.2.3, 5.2.4
Substitution of Architect
  4.1.3
Substitutions of Materials
  3.4.2, 3.5.1, 7.3.7
Sub-subcontractor, Definition of
  5.1.2
Subsurface Conditions
  4.3.4
Successors and Assigns
  13.2
Superintendent
  3.9, 10.2.6
Supervision and Construction Procedures
  1.2.2, 3.3, 3.4, 3.12.10, 4.2.2, 4.2.7, 4.3.3, 6.1.3, 6.2.4, 7.1.3, 7.3.6, 8.2, 8.3.1, 9.4.2, 10, 12, 14
Surety
  4.4.7, 5.4.1.2, 9.8.5, 9.10.2, 9.10.3, 14.2.2
Surety, Consent of
  9.10.2, 9.10.3
Surveys
  2.2.3
Suspension by the Owner for Convenience
  14.4
Suspension of the Work
  5.4.2, 14.3
Suspension or Termination of the Contract
  4.3.6, 5.4.1.1, 11.4.9, 14
Taxes
  3.6, 3.8.2.1, 7.3.6.4
Termination by the Contractor
  4.3.10, 14.1
Termination by the Owner for Cause
  4.3.10, 5.4.1.1, 14.2
Termination of the Architect
  4.1.3

©1997 AIA ® AIA Document A201–1997 Used with permission

Termination of the Contractor
   14.2.2

TERMINATION OR SUSPENSION OF THE CONTRACT
   14

Tests and Inspections
   3.1.3, 3.3.3, 4.2.2, 4.2.6, 4.2.9, 9.4.2,
   9.8.3, 9.9.2, 9.10.1, 10.3.2, 11.4.1.1,
   12.2.1, 13.5

TIME
   8

Time, Delays and Extensions of
   3.2.3, 4.3.1, 4.3.4, 4.3.7, 4.4.5, 5.2.3,
   7.2.1, 7.3.1, 7.4.1, 7.5.1, 8.3, 9.5.1,
   9.7.1, 10.3.2, 10.6.1, 14 3.2

Time Limits
   2.1.2, 2.2, 2.4, 3.2.1, 3.7.3, 3.10, 3.11,
   3.12.5, 3.15.1, 4.2, 4.3, 4.4, 4.5, 4.6,
   5.2, 5.3, 5.4, 6.2.4, 7.3, 7.4, 8.2, 9.2,
   9.3.1, 9.3.3, 9.4.1, 9.5, 9.6, 9.7, 9.8,
   9.9, 9.10, 11.1.3, 11.4.1.5, 11.4.6,
   11.4.10, 12.2, 13.5, 13.7, 14

Time Limits on Claims
   4.3.2, 4.3.4, 4.3.8, 4.4, 4.5, 4.6

Title to Work
   9.3.2, 9.3.3

UNCOVERING AND CORRECTION OF WORK
   12

Uncovering of Work
   12.1

Unforeseen Conditions
   4.3.4, 8.3.1, 10.3

Unit Prices
   4.3.9, 7.3.3.2

Use of Documents
   1.1.1, 1.6, 2.2.5, 3.12.6, 5.3

Use of Site
   3.13, 6.1.1, 6.2.1

Values, Schedule of
   9.2, 9.3.1

Waiver of Claims by the Architect
   13.4.2

Waiver of Claims by the Contractor
   4.3.10, 9.10.5, 11.4.7, 13.4.2

Waiver of Claims by the Owner
   4.3.10, 9.9.3, 9.10.3, 9.10.4, 11.4.3,
   11.4.5, 11.4.7, 12.2.2.1, 13.4.2, 14.2.4

Waiver of Consequential Damages
   4.3.10, 14.2.4

Waiver of Liens
   9.10.2, 9.10.4

Waivers of Subrogation
   6.1.1, 11.4.5, 11.4.7

Warranty
   3.5, 4.2.9, 4.3.5.3, 9.3.3, 9.8.4, 9.9.1,
   9.10.4, 12.2.2, 13.7.1.3

Weather Delays
   4.3.7.2

Work, Definition of
   1.1.3

Written Consent
   1.6, 3.4.2, 3.12.8, 3.14.2, 4.1.2, 4.3.4,
   4.6.4, 9.3.2, 9.8.5, 9.9.1, 9.10.2. 9.10.3,
   11.4.1, 13.2, 13.4.2

Written Interpretations
   4.2.11, 4.2.12, 4.3.6

Written Notice
   2.3, 2.4, 3.3.1, 3.9, 3.12.9, 3.12.10, 4.3,
   4.4.8, 4.6.5, 5.2.1, 8.2.2. 9.7, 9.10,
   10.2.2, 10.3, 11.1.3., 11.4.6, 12.2.2,
   12.2.4, 13.3, 14

Written Orders
   1.1.1, 2.3, 3.9., 4.3.6, 7, 8.2.2, 11.4.9,
   12.1, 12.2, 13.5.2, 14.3.1

©1997 AIA ® AIA Document A201–1997 Used with permission

ARTICLE 1 GENERAL PROVISIONS

1.1 BASIC DEFINITIONS

1.1.1 THE CONTRACT DOCUMENTS

The Contract Documents consist of the Agreement between Owner and Contractor (hereinafter the Agreement), Conditions of the Contract (General, Supplementary and other Conditions), Drawings, Specifications, Addenda issued prior to execution of the Contract, other documents listed in the Agreement and Modifications issued after execution of the Contract. A Modification is (1) a written amendment to the Contract signed by both parties (2) a Change Order, (3) a Construction Change Directive or (4) a written order for a minor change in the Work issued by the Architect. Unless specifically enumerated in the Agreement, the Contract Documents do not include other documents such as bidding requirements (advertisement or invitation to bid, Instructions to Bidders, sample forms, the Contractor's bid or portions of Addenda relating to bidding requirements).

1.1.2 THE CONTRACT

The Contract Documents form the Contract for Construction. The Contract represents the entire and integrated agreement between the parties hereto and supersedes prior negotiations, representations or agreements, either written or oral. The Contract may be amended or modified only by a Modification. The Contract Documents shall not be construed to create a contractual relationship of any kind (1) between the Architect and Contractor, (2) between the Owner and a Subcontractor or Sub-subcontractor, (3) between the Owner and Architect or (4) between any persons or entities other than the Owner and Contractor. The Architect shall, however, be entitled to performance and enforcement of obligations under the Contract intended to facilitate performance of the Architect's duties.

1.1.3 THE WORK

The term "Work" means the construction and services required by the Contract Documents, whether completed or partially completed, and includes all other labor, materials, equipment and services provided or to be provided by the Contractor to fulfill the Contractor's obligations. The Work may constitute the whole or a part of the Project.

1.1.4 THE PROJECT

The Project is the total construction of which the Work performed under the Contract Documents may be the whole or a part and which may include construction by the Owner or by separate contractors.

1.1.5 THE DRAWINGS

The Drawings are the graphic and pictorial portions of the Contract

©1997 AIA ® AIA Document A201–1997 Used with permission

Documents showing the design, location and dimensions of the Work, generally including plans, elevations, sections, details, schedules and diagrams.

1.1.6 THE SPECIFICATIONS

The Specifications are that portion of the Contract Documents consisting of the written requirements for materials, equipment, systems, standards and workmanship for the Work, and performance of related services.

1.1.7 THE PROJECT MANUAL

The Project Manual is a volume assembled for the Work which may include the bidding requirements, sample forms, Conditions of the Contract and Specifications.

1.2 CORRELATION AND INTENT OF THE CONTRACT DOCUMENTS

1.2.1 The intent of the Contract Documents is to include all items necessary for the proper execution and completion of the Work by the Contractor. The Contract Documents are complementary and what is required by one shall be as binding as if required by all; performance by the Contractor shall be required only to the extent consistent with the Contract Document and reasonably inferable from them as being necessary to produce the indicated result.

1.2.2 Organization of the Specifications into divisions, sections and articles, and arrangement of Drawings shall not control the Contractor in dividing the Work among subcontractors or in establishing the extent of Work to be performed by any trade.

1.2.3 Unless otherwise stated in the Contract Documents, words which have well-known technical or construction industry meanings are used in the Contract Documents in accordance with such recognized meanings.

1.3 CAPITALIZATION

1.3.1 Terms capitalized in these General Conditions include those which are (1) specifically defined. (2) the titles of numbered articles and identified references to Paragraphs, Subparagraphs and Clauses in the document or (3) the titles of other documents published by the American Institute of Architects.

1.4 INTERPRETATION

1.4.1 In the interest of brevity the Contract Documents frequently omit modifying words such as "all" and "any" and articles such as "the" and "an," but

©1997 AIA ® AIA Document A201–1997 Used with permission

the fact that a modifier or an article is absent from one statement and appears in another is not intended to affect the interpretation of either statement.

1.5 EXECUTION OF CONTRACT DOCUMENTS

1.5.1 The Contract Documents shall be signed by the Owner and Contractor. If either the Owner or Contractor or both do not sign all the Contract Documents, the Architect shall identify such unsigned Documents upon request.

1.5.2 Execution of the Contract by the Contractor is a representation that the Contractor has visited the site, become generally familiar with local conditions under which the Work is to be performed and correlated personal observations with requirements of the Contract Documents.

1.6 OWNERSHIP AND USE OF DRAWINGS, SPECIFICATIONS AND OTHER INSTRUMENTS OF SERVICE

1.6.1 The Drawings, Specifications and other documents, including those in electronic form, prepared by the Architect and the Architect's consultants are instruments of Service through which the Work to be executed by the Contractor is described. The Contractor may retain one record set. Neither the Contractor nor any Subcontractor, Sub-subcontractor or material or equipment supplier shall own or claim a copyright in the Drawings, Specifications and other documents prepared by the Architect or the Architect's consultants, and unless otherwise indicated the Architect and the Architect's consultants shall be deemed the authors of them and will retain all common law, statutory and other reserved rights, in addition to the copyrights. All copies of Instruments of Service, except the Contractor's record set, shall be returned or suitably accounted for to the Architect, on request, upon completion of the Work. The Drawings, Specifications and other documents prepared by the Architect and the Architect's consultants, and copies thereof furnished to the Contractor, are for use solely with respect to this Project. They are not to be used by the Contractor or any Subcontractor, Sub-subcontractor or material or equipment supplier on other projects or for additions to this Project outside the scope of the Work without the specific written consent of the Owner, Architect and the Architect's consultants. The Contractor, Subcontractors, Sub-subcontractors and material or equipment suppliers are authorized to use and reproduce applicable portions of the Drawings, Specifications and other documents prepared by the Architect and the Architect's consultants appropriate to and for use in the execution of their Work under the Contract Documents. All copies made under this authorization shall bear the statutory copyright notice, if any, shown on the Drawings, Specifications and other documents prepared by the Architect and the Architect's consultants. Submittal or distribution to meet official regulatory requirements or for other purposes in connection with this Project is

©1997 AIA ® AIA Document A201–1997 Used with permission

not to be construed as publication in derogation of the Architect's or Architect's consultants' copyrights or other reserved rights.

ARTICLE 2   OWNER

2.1   GENERAL

2.1.1   The Owner is the person or entity identified as such in the Agreement and is referred to throughout the Contract Documents as if singular in number. The Owner shall designate in writing a representative who shall have express authority to bind the Owner with respect to all matters requiring the Owner's approval or authorization. Except as otherwise provided in Subparagraph 4.2.1, the Architect does not have such authority. The term "Owner" means the Owner or the Owner's authorized representative.

2.1.2   The Owner shall furnish to the Contractor within fifteen days after receipt of a written request, information necessary and relevant for the Contractor to evaluate, give notice of or enforce mechanic's lien rights. Such information shall include a correct statement of the record legal title to the property on which the Project is located, usually referred to as the site, and the Owner's interest therein.

2.2   INFORMATION AND SERVICES REQUIRED OF THE OWNER

2.2.1   The Owner shall, at the written request of the Contractor, prior to commencement of the Work and thereafter, furnish to the Contractor reasonable evidence that financial arrangements have been made to fulfill the Owner's obligations under the Contract. Furnishing of such evidence shall be a condition precedent to commencement or continuation of the Work. After such evidence has been furnished, the Owner shall not materially vary such financial arrangements without prior notice to the Contractor.

2.2.2   Except for permits and fees, including those required under Subparagraph 3.7.1, which are the responsibility of the Contractor under the Contract Documents, the Owner shall secure and pay for necessary approvals, easements, assessments and charges required for construction, use or occupancy of permanent structures or for permanent changes in existing facilities.

2.2.3   The Owner shall furnish surveys describing physical characteristics, legal limitations and utility locations for the site of the Project, and a legal description of the site. The Contractor shall be entitled to rely on the accuracy of

©1997 AIA ® AIA Document A201–1997 Used with permission

information furnished by the Owner but shall exercise proper precautions relating to the safe performance of the Work.

2.2.4 Information or services required of the Owner by the Contract Documents shall be furnished by the Owner with reasonable promptness. Any other information or services relevant to the Contractor's performance of the Work under the Owner's control shall be furnished by the Owner after receipt from the Contractor of a written request for such information or services.

2.2.5 Unless otherwise provided in the Contract Documents, the Contractor will be furnished, free of charge, such copies of Drawings and Project Manuals as are reasonably necessary for execution of the Work.

2.3 OWNERS RIGHT TO STOP THE WORK

2.3.1 If the Contractor fails to correct Work which is not in accordance with the requirements of the Contract Documents as required by Paragraph 12.2 or persistently fails to carry out Work in accordance with the Contract Documents, the Owner may issue a written order to the Contractor to stop the Work, or any portion thereof, until the cause Car for such order has been eliminated; however, the right of the Owner to stop the Work shall not give rise to a duty on the part of the Owner to exercise this right for the benefit of the Contractor or any other person or entity, except to the extent required by Subparagraph 6.1.3.

2.4 OWNER'S RIGHT TO CARRY OUT THE WORK

2.4.1 If the Contractor defaults or neglects to carry out the Work in accordance with the Contract Documents and fails within a seven-day period after receipt of written notice from the Owner to commence and continue correction of such default or neglect with diligence and promptness, the Owner may after such seven-day period give the Contractor a second written notice to correct such deficiencies within a three-day period. If the Contractor within such three-day period after receipt of such second notice fails to commence and continue to correct any deficiencies, the Owner may, without prejudice to other remedies the Owner may have, correct such deficiencies. In such case an appropriate Change Order shall be issued deducting from payments then or thereafter due the Contractor the reasonable cost of correcting such deficiencies, including Owner's expenses and compensation for the Architect's additional services made necessary by such default, neglect or failure. Such action by the Owner and amounts charged to the Contractor are both subject to prior approval of the Architect. If payments then or thereafter due the Contractor are not sufficient to cover such amounts, the Contractor shall pay the difference to the Owner.

©1997 AIA ® AIA Document A201–1997 Used with permission

ARTICLE 3 CONTRACTOR

3.1 GENERAL

3.1.1 The Contractor is the person or entity identified as such in the Agreement and is referred to throughout the Contract Documents as if singular in number. The term "Contractor" means the Contractor or the Contractor's authorized representative.

3.1.2 The Contractor shall perform the Work in accordance with the Contract Documents.

3.1.3 The Contractor shall not be relieved of obligations to perform the Work in accordance with the Contract Documents either by activities or duties of the Architect in the Architect's administration of the Contract, or by tests, inspections or approvals required or performed by persons other than the Contractor.

3.2 REVIEW OF CONTRACT DOCUMENTS AND FIELD CONDITIONS BY CONTRACTOR

3.2.1 Since the Contract Documents are complementary, before starting each portion of the Work, the Contractor shall carefully study and compare the various Drawings and other Contract Documents relative to that portion of the Work, as well as the information furnished by the Owner pursuant to Subparagraph 2.2.3, shall take field measurements of any existing conditions related to that portion of the Work and shall observe any conditions at the site affecting it. These obligations are for the purpose of facilitating construction by the Contractor and are not for the purpose of discovering errors, omissions, or inconsistencies in the Contract Documents; however, any errors, inconsistencies or omissions discovered by the Contractor shall be reported promptly to the Architect as a request for information in such form as the Architect may require.

3.2.2 Any design errors or omissions noted by the Contractor during this review shall be reported promptly to the Architect, but it is recognized that the Contractor's review is made in the Contractor's capacity as a contractor and not as a licensed design professional unless otherwise specifically provided in the Contract Documents. The Contractor is not required to ascertain that the Contract Documents are in accordance with applicable laws, statutes, ordinances, building codes, and rules and regulations, but any nonconformity discovered by or made known to the Contractor shall he reported promptly to the Architect.

3.2.3 If the Contractor believes that additional cost or time is involved because of clarifications or instructions issued by the Architect in response to the Contractor's notices or requests for information pursuant to Subparagraphs 3.2.1 and 3.2.2, the Contractor shall make Claims as provided in Subparagraphs 4.3.6

©1997 AIA ® AIA Document A201–1997 Used with permission

and 4.3.7. If the Contractor fails to perform the obligations of subparagraphs 3.2.1 and 3.2.2, the Contractor shall pay such costs and damages to the Owner as would have been avoided if the Contractor had performed such obligations. The Contractor shall not be liable to the Owner or Architect for damages resulting from errors, inconsistencies or omissions in the Contract Documents or for differences between field measurements or conditions and the Contract Documents unless the Contractor recognized such error, inconsistency, omission or difference and knowingly railed to report it to the Architect

3.3 SUPERVISION AND CONSTRUCTION PROCEDURES

3.3.1 The Contractor shall supervise and direct the Work, using the Contractor's best skill and attention. The Contractor shall be solely responsible for and have control over construction means, methods, techniques, sequences and procedures and for coordinating all portions of the Work under the Contract, unless the Contract Documents give other specific instructions concerning these matters. If the Contract Documents give specific instructions concerning construction means, methods, techniques, sequences or procedures, the Contractor shall evaluate the jobsite safety thereof and, except as stated below, shall be fully and solely responsible for the jobsite safety of such means, methods, techniques, sequences or procedures. If the Contractor determines that such means, methods, techniques, sequences or procedures may not be safe, the Contractor shall give timely written notice to the Owner and Architect and shall not proceed with that portion of the Work without further written instructions from the Architect. If the Contractor is then instructed to proceed with the required means, methods, techniques, sequences or procedures without acceptance of changes proposed by the Contractor, the Owner shall be solely responsible for any resulting loss or damage.

3.3.2 The Contractor shall be responsible to the Owner for acts and omissions of the Contractor's employees, Subcontractors and their agents and employees, and other persons or entities performing portions of the Work for or on behalf of the Contractor or any of its Subcontractors.

3.3.3 The Contractor shall be responsible for inspection of portions of Work already performed to determine that such portions are in proper condition to receive subsequent Work.

3.4 LABOR AND MATERIALS

3.4.1 Unless otherwise provided in the Contract Documents, the Contractor shall provide and pay for labor, materials, equipment, tools, construction equipment and machinery, water, heat, utilities, transportation, and other facilities and

©1997 AIA ® AIA Document A201–1997 Used with permission

services necessary for proper execution and completion of the Work, whether temporary or permanent and whether or not incorporated or to be incorporated in the Work.

3.4.2 The Contractor may make substitutions only with the consent of the Owner, after evaluation by the Architect and in accordance with a Change Order.

3.4.3 The Contractor shall enforce strict discipline and good order among the Contractor's employees and other persons carrying out the Contract. The Contractor shall not permit employment of unfit persons or persons not skilled in tasks assigned to them.

3.5   WARRANTY

3.5.1 The Contractor warrants to the Owner and Architect that materials and equipment furnished under the Contract will be of good quality and new unless otherwise required or permitted by the Contract Documents, that the Work will be free from defects not inherent in the quality required or permitted, and that the Work will conform to the requirements of the Contract Documents. Work not conforming to these requirements. including substitutions not properly approved and authorized, may be considered defective. The Contractor's warranty excludes remedy for damage or defect caused by abuse, modifications not executed by the Contractor, improper or insufficient maintenance, improper operation, or normal wear and tear and normal usage. If required by the Architect, the Contractor shall furnish satisfactory evidence as to the kind and quality of materials and equipment.

3.6   TAXES

3.6.1 The Contractor shall pay sales, consumer, use and similar taxes for the Work provided by the Contractor which are legally enacted when bids are received or negotiations concluded, whether or not yet effective or merely scheduled to go into effect.

3.7   PERMITS, FEES AND NOTICES

3.7.1 Unless otherwise provided in the Contract Documents, the Contractor shall secure and pay for the building permit and other permits and governmental fees, licenses and inspections necessary for proper execution and completion of the Work which are customarily secured after execution of the Contract and which are legally required when bids are received or negotiations concluded.

©1997 AIA ® AIA Document A201–1997 Used with permission

3.7.2 The Contractor shall comply with and give notices required by laws, ordinances, rules, regulations and lawful orders of public authorities applicable to performance of the Work.

3.7.3 It is not the Contractor's responsibility to ascertain that the Contract Documents are in accordance with applicable laws, statutes, ordinances, building codes, and rules and regulations. However, if the Contractor observes that portions of the Contract Documents are at variance therewith, the Contractor shall promptly notify the Architect and Owner in writing, and necessary changes shall be accomplished by appropriate Modification.

3.7.4 If the Contractor performs Work knowing it to be contrary to laws, statutes, ordinances, building codes, and rules and regulations without such notice to the Architect and Owner, the Contractor shall assume appropriate responsibility for such Work and shall bear the costs attributable to correction.

3.8 ALLOWANCES

3.8.1 The Contractor shall include in the Contract Sum all allowances stated in the Contract Documents. Items covered by allowances shall be supplied for such amounts and by such persons or entities as the Owner may direct, but the Contractor shall not be required to employ persons or entities to whom the Contractor has reasonable objection.

3.8.2 Unless otherwise provided in the Contract Documents:

.1 allowances shall cover the cost to the Contractor of materials and equipment delivered at the site and all required taxes, less applicable trade discounts;

.2 Contractor's costs for unloading and handling at the site, labor, installation costs, overhead, profit and other expenses contemplated for stated allowance amounts shall be included in the Contract Sum but not in the allowances;

.3 when costs are more than or less than allowances, the Contract Sum shall be adjusted accordingly by Change Order. The amount of the Change Order shall reflect (1) the difference between actual costs and the allowances under Clause 3.8.2.1 and (2) changes in Contractor's costs under Clause 3.8.2.2.

3.8.3 Materials and equipment under an allowance shall be selected by the Owner in sufficient time to avoid delay in the Work.

©1997 AIA ® AIA Document A201–1997 Used with permission

3.9 SUPERINTENDENT

3.9.1 The Contractor shall employ a competent superintendent and necessary assistants who shall be in attendance at the Project site during performance of the Work. The superintendent shall represent the Contractor, and communications given to the superintendent shall be as binding as if given to the Contractor. Important communications shall be confirmed in writing. Other communications shall be similarly confirmed on written request in each case.

3.10 CONTRACTOR'S CONSTRUCTION SCHEDULES

3.10.1 The Contractor, promptly after being awarded the Contract, shall prepare and submit for the Owner's and Architect's information a Contractor's construction schedule for the Work. The schedule shall not exceed time limits current under the Contract Documents, shall be revised at appropriate intervals as required by the conditions of the Work and Project, shall be related to the entire Project to the extent required by the Contract Documents, and shall provide for expeditious and practicable execution of the Work.

3.10.2 The Contractor shall prepare and keep current, for the Architect's approval, a schedule of submittals which is coordinated with the Contractor's construction schedule and allows the Architect reasonable time to review submittals.

3.10.3 The Contractor shall perform the Work in general accordance with the most recent schedules submitted to the Owner and Architect.

3.11 DOCUMENTS AND SAMPLES AT THE SITE

3.11.1 The Contractor shall maintain at the site for the Owner one record copy of the Drawings, Specifications, Addenda, Change Orders and other Modifications, in good order and marked currently to record field changes and selections made during construction, and one record copy of approved Shop Drawings, Product Data, Samples and similar required submittals. These shall be available to the Architect and shall be delivered to the Architect for submittal to the Owner upon completion of the Work.

3.12 SHOP DRAWINGS; PRODUCT DATA AND SAMPLES

3.12.1 Shop Drawings are drawings, diagrams, schedules and other data specially prepared for the Work by the Contractor or a Subcontractor, Sub-subcontractor, manufacturer, supplier or distributor to illustrate some portion of the Work.

©1997 AIA ® AIA Document A201–1997 Used with permission

3.12.2 Product Data are illustrations, standard schedules, performance charts, instructions, brochures, diagrams and other information furnished by the Contractor to illustrate materials or equipment for some portion of the Work.

3.12.3 Samples are physical examples which illustrate materials, equipment or workmanship and establish standards by which the Work will be judged.

3.12.4 Shop Drawings, Product Data, Samples and similar submittals are not Contract Documents. The purpose of their submittal is to demonstrate for those portions of the Work for which submittals are required by the Contract Documents the way by which the Contractor proposes to conform to the information given and the design concept expressed in the Contract Documents. Review by the Architect is subject to the limitations of Subparagraph 4.2.7. Informational submittals upon which the Architect is not expected to take responsive action may be so identified in the Contract Documents. Submittals which are not required by the Contract Documents may be returned by the Architect without action.

3.12.5 The Contractor shall review for compliance with the Contract Documents, approve and submit to the Architect Shop Drawings, Product Data, Samples and similar submittals required by the Contract Documents with reasonable promptness and in such sequence as to cause no delay in the Work or in the activities of the Owner or of separate contractors. Submittals which are not marked as reviewed for compliance with the Contract Documents and approved by the Contractor may be returned by the Architect without action.

3.12.6 By approving and submitting shop Drawings, Product Data, Samples and similar submittals, the Contractor represents that the Contractor has determined and verified materials, field measurements and field construction criteria related thereto, or will do so, and has checked and coordinated the information contained within such submittals with the requirements of the Work and of the Contract Documents.

3.12.7 The Contractor shall perform no portion of the Work for which the Contract Documents require submittal and review of Shop Drawings, Product Data, Samples or similar submittals until the respective submittal has been approved by the Architect.

3.12.8 The Work shall be in accordance with approved submittals except that the Contractor shall not be relieved of responsibility for deviations from requirements of the Contract Documents by the Architect's approval of Shop Drawings, Product Data, Samples or similar submittals unless the Contractor has specifically informed the Architect in writing of such deviation at the time of submittal and (1) the Architect has given written approval to the specific deviation as a minor change in the work, or (2) a Change Order or Construction Change Directive

©1997 AIA ® AIA Document A201–1997 Used with permission

has been issued authorizing the deviation. The Contractor shall not be relieved of responsibility for errors or omissions in Shop Drawings. Product Data, Samples or similar submittals by the Architect's approval thereof.

3.12.9 The Contractor shall direct specific attention, in writing or on resubmitted Shop Drawings, Product Data, Samples or similar submittals, to revisions other than those requested by the Architect on previous submittals. In the absence of such written notice the Architect's approval of a resubmission shall not apply to such revisions.

3.12.10 The Contractor shall not be required to provide professional services which constitute the practice of architecture or engineering unless such services are specifically required by the Contract Documents for a portion of the Work or unless the Contractor needs to provide such services in order to carry out the Contractor's responsibilities for construction means, methods, techniques, sequences and procedures. The Contractor shall not be required to provide professional services in violation of applicable law. If professional design services or certifications by a design professional related to systems, materials or equipment are specifically required of the Contractor by the Contract Documents, the Owner and the Architect will specify all performance and design criteria that such services must satisfy. The Contractor shall cause such services or certifications to be provided by a properly licensed design professional, whose signature and seal shall appear on all drawings, calculations, specifications, certifications, Shop Drawings and other submittals prepared by such professional. Shop Drawings and other submittals related to the Work designed or certified by such professional, if prepared by others, shall bear such professional's written approval when submitted to the Architect. The Owner and the Architect shall be entitled to rely upon the adequacy, accuracy and completeness of the services, certifications or approvals performed by such design professionals, provided the Owner and Architect have specified to the Contractor all performance and design criteria that such services must satisfy. Pursuant to this Subparagraph 3.12.10, the Architect will review, approve or take other appropriate action on submittals only for the limited purpose of checking for conformance with information given and the design concept expressed in the Contract Documents. The Contractor shall not be responsible for the adequacy of the performance or design criteria required by the Contract Documents.

3.13 USE OF SITE

3.13.1 The Contractor shall confine operations at the site to areas permitted by law, ordinances, permits and the Contract Documents and shall not unreasonably encumber the site with materials or equipment.

©1997 AIA ® AIA Document A201–1997 Used with permission

3.14 CUTTING AND PATCHING

3.14.1 The Contractor shall be responsible for cutting, fitting or patching required to complete the Work or to make its parts fit together properly.

3.14.2 The Contractor shall not damage or endanger a portion of the Work or fully or partially completed construction of the Owner or separate contractors by cutting, patching or otherwise altering such construction, or by excavation. The Contractor shall not cut or otherwise alter such construction by the Owner or a separate contractor except with written consent of the Owner and of such separate contractor; such consent shall not be unreasonably withheld. The Contractor shall not unreasonably withhold from the Owner or a separate contractor the Contractor's consent to cutting or otherwise altering the Work.

3.15 CLEANING UP

3.15.1 The Contractor shall keep the premises and surrounding area free from accumulation of waste materials or rubbish caused by operations under the Contract. At completion of the Work, the Contractor shall remove from and about the Project waste materials, rubbish, the Contractor's tools, construction equipment, machinery and surplus materials.

3.15.2 If the Contractor fails to clean up as provided in the Contract Documents, the Owner may do so and the cost thereof shall be charged to the Contractor.

2.16 ACCESS TO WORK

3.16.1 The Contractor shall provide the Owner and Architect access to the Work in preparation and progress wherever located.

3.17 ROYALTIES, PATENTS AND COPYRIGHTS

3.17.1 The Contractor shall pay all royalties and license fees. The Contractor shall defend suits or claims for infringement of copyrights and patent rights and shall hold the Owner and Architect harmless from loss on account thereof, but shall not be responsible for such defense or loss when a particular design, process or product of a particular manufacturer or manufacturers is required by the Contract Documents or where the copyright violations are contained in Drawings, Specifications or other documents prepared by the Owner or Architect. However, if the Contractor has reason to believe that the required design, process or product is an infringement of a copyright or a patent, the Contractor shall be responsible for such loss unless such information is promptly furnished to the Architect.

©1997 AIA ® AIA Document A201–1997 Used with permission

3.18 INDEMNIFICATION

3.18.1 To the fullest extent permitted by law and to the extent claims, damages, losses or expenses are not covered by Project Management Protective Liability insurance purchased by the Contractor in accordance with Paragraph 11.3, the Contractor shall indemnify and hold harmless the Owner, Architect, Architect's consultants, and agents and employees of any of them from and against claims, damages, losses and expenses, including but not limited to attorneys' fees, arising out of or resulting from performance of the Work, provided that such claim, damage, loss or expense is attributable to bodily injury, sickness, disease or death, or to injury to or destruction of tangible property (other than the Work itself), but only to the extent caused by the negligent acts or omissions of the Contractor, a Subcontractor, anyone directly or indirectly employed by them or anyone for whose acts they may be liable, regardless of whether or not such claim, damage, loss or expense is caused in part by a party indemnified hereunder. Such obligation shall not be construed to negate, abridge, or reduce other rights or obligations of indemnity which would otherwise exist as to a party or person described in this Paragraph 3.18.

3.18.2 In claims against any person or entity indemnified under this Paragraph 3.18 by an employee of the Contractor, a Subcontractor, anyone directly or indirectly employed by them or anyone for whose acts they may be liable, the indemnification obligation under Subparagraph 3.18.1 shall not be limited by a limitation on amount or type of damages, compensation or benefits payable by or for the Contractor or a Subcontractor under workers' compensation acts, disability benefit acts or other employee benefit acts.

ARTICLE 4   ADMINISTRATION OF THE CONTRACT

4.1   ARCHITECT

4.1.1 The Architect is the person lawfully licensed to practice architecture or an entity lawfully practicing architecture identified as such in the Agreement and is referred to throughout the Contract Documents as if singular in number. The term "Architect" means the Architect or the Architect's authorized representative.

4.1.2 Duties, responsibilities and limitations of authority of the Architect as set forth in the Contract Documents shall not be restricted, modified or extended without written consent of the Owner, Contractor and Architect. Consent shall not be unreasonably withheld.

4.1.3 If the employment of the Architect is terminated, the Owner shall employ a new Architect against whom the Contractor has no reasonable objec-

©1997 AIA ® AIA Document A201–1997 Used with permission

tion and whose status under the Contract Documents shall be that of the former Architect.

4.2 ARCHITECT'S ADMINISTRATION OF THE CONTRACT

4.2.1 The Architect will provide administration of the Contract as described in the Contract Documents, and will be an Owner's representative (1) during construction, (2) until final payment is due and (3) with the Owner's concurrence, from time to time during the one-year period for correction of Work described in Paragraph 12.2. The Architect will have authority to act on behalf of the Owner only to the extent provided in the Contract Documents, unless otherwise modified in writing in accordance with other provisions of the Contract.

4.2.2 The Architect, as a representative of the Owner, will visit the site at intervals appropriate to the stage of the Contractor's operations (1) to become generally familiar with and to keep the Owner informed about the progress and quality of the portion of the Work completed, (2) to endeavor to guard the Owner against defects and deficiencies in the Work, and (3) to determine in general if the Work is being performed in a manner indicating that the Work, when fully completed, will be in accordance with the Contract Documents. However, the Architect will not be required to make exhaustive or continuous on-site inspections to check the quality or quantity of the Work. The Architect will neither have control over or charge of, nor be responsible for, the construction means, methods, techniques, sequences or procedures, or for the safety precautions and programs in connection with the Work, since these are solely the Contractor's rights and responsibilities under the Contract Documents, accept as provided in Subparagraph 3.3.1.

4.2.3 The Architect will not be responsible for the Contractor's failure to perform the Work in accordance with the requirements of the Contract Documents. The Architect will not have control over or charge of and will not be responsible for acts or omissions of the Contractor, Subcontractors, or their agents or employees, or any other persons or entities performing portions of the Work.

4.2.4 Communications Facilitating Contract Administration. Except as otherwise provided in the Contract Documents or when direct communications have been specially authorized, the Owner and Contractor shall endeavor to communicate with each other through the Architect about matters arising out of or relating to the Contract. Communications by and with the Architect's consultants shall be through the Architect. Communications by and with Subcontractors and material suppliers shall be through the Contractor. Communications by and with separate contractors shall be through the Owner.

©1997 AIA ® AIA Document A201–1997 Used with permission

4.2.5   Based on the Architect's evaluations of the Contractor's Applications for Payment, the Architect will review and certify the amounts due the Contractor and will issue Certificates for Payment in such amounts.

4.2.6   The Architect will have authority to reject Work that does not conform to the Contract Documents. Whenever the Architect considers it necessary or advisable, the Architect will have authority to require inspection or testing of the work in accordance with Subparagraphs 13.5.2 and 13.5.3, whether or not such Work is fabricated, installed or completed. However, neither this authority of the Architect nor a decision made in good faith either to exercise or not to exercise such authority shall give rise to a duty or responsibility of the Architect to the Contractor, Subcontractors, material and equipment suppliers, their agents or employees, or other persons or entities performing portions of the Work.

4.2.7   The Architect will review and approve or take other appropriate action upon the Contractor's submittals such as Shop Drawings, Product Data and Samples, but only for the limited purpose of checking for conformance with information given and the design concept expressed in the Contract Documents. The Architect's action will be taken with such reasonable promptness as to cause no delay in the Work or in the activities of the Owner, Contractor or separate contractors, while allowing sufficient time in the Architect's professional judgment to permit adequate review. Review of such submittals is not conducted for the purpose of determining the accuracy and completeness of other details such as dimensions and quantities, or for substantiating instructions for installation or performance of equipment or systems, all of which remain the responsibility of the Contractor as required by the Contract Documents. The Architect's review of the Contractor's submittals shall not relieve the Contractor of the obligations under Paragraphs 3.3, 3.5 and 3.12. The Architect's review shall not constitute approval of safety precautions or, unless otherwise specifically stated by the Architect, of any construction means, methods, techniques, sequences or procedures. The Architect's approval of a specific item shall not indicate approval of an assembly of which the item is a component.

4.2.8   The Architect will prepare Change Orders and Construction Change Directives, and may authorize minor changes in the Work as provided in Paragraph 7.4.

4.2.9   The Architect will conduct inspections to determine the date or dates of Substantial Completion and the date of final completion, will receive and forward to the Owner, for the Owner's review and records, written warranties and related documents required by the Contract and assembled by the Contractor, and will issue a final Certificate for Payment upon compliance with the requirements of the Contract Documents.

©1997 AIA ® AIA Document A201–1997 Used with permission

4.2.10 If the Owner and Architect agree, the Architect will provide one or more project representatives to assist in carrying out the Architect's responsibilities at the site. The duties, responsibilities and limitations of authority of such project representatives shall be as set forth in an exhibit to be incorporated in the Contract Documents.

4.2.11 The Architect will interpret and decide matters concerning performance under, and requirements of, the Contract Documents on written request of either the Owner or Contractor. The Architect's response to such requests will be made in writing within any time limits agreed upon or otherwise with reasonable promptness. If no agreement is made concerning the time within which interpretations required of the Architect shall be furnished in compliance with this Paragraph 4.2, then delay shall not be recognized on account of failure by the Architect to furnish such interpretations until 15 days after written request is made for them.

4.2.12 Interpretations and decisions of the Architect will be consistent with the intent of and reasonably inferable from the Contract Documents and will be in writing or in the form of drawings. When making such interpretations and initial decisions, the Architect will endeavor to secure faithful performance by both Owner and Contractor, will not show partiality to either and will not be liable for results of interpretations or decisions so rendered in good faith.

4.2.13 The Architect's decisions on matters relating to aesthetic effect will be final if consistent with the intent expressed in the Contract Documents.

4.3   CLAIMS AND DISPUTES

4.3.1   Definition. A Claim is a demand or assertion by one of the parties seeking, as a matter of right, adjustment or interpretation of Contract terms, payment of money, extension of time or other relief with respect to the terms of the Contract. The term "Claim" also includes other disputes and matters in question between the Owner and Contractor arising out of or relating to the Contract. Claims must be initiated by written notice. The responsibility to substantiate Claims shall rest with the party making the Claim.

4.3.2   Time Limits on Claims. Claims by either party must be initiated within 21 days after occurrence of the event giving rise to such Claim or within 21 days after the claimant first recognizes the condition giving rise to the Claim, whichever is later. Claims must be initiated by written notice to the Architect and the other party.

©1997 AIA ® AIA Document A201–1997 Used with permission

4.3.3 **Continuing Contract Performance.** Pending final resolution of a Claim except as otherwise agreed in writing or as provided in Subparagraph 9.7.1 and Article 14 the Contractor shall proceed diligently with performance of the Contract and the Owner shall continue to make payments in accordance with the Contract Documents.

4.3.4 **Claims for Concealed or Unknown Conditions.** If conditions are encountered at the site which are (1) subsurface or otherwise concealed physical conditions which differ materially from those indicated in the Contract Documents or (2) unknown physical conditions of an unusual nature, which differ materially from those ordinarily found to exist and generally recognized as inherent in construction activities of the character provided for in the Contract Documents, then notice by the observing party shall be given to the other party promptly before conditions are disturbed and in no event later than 21 days after first observance of the conditions. The Architect will promptly investigate such conditions and, if they differ materially and cause an increase or decrease in the Contractor's cost of, or time required for, performance of any part of the Work, will recommend an equitable adjustment in the Contract Sum or Contract Time, or both. If the Architect determines that the conditions at the site are not materially different from those indicated in the Contract Documents and that no change in the terms of the Contract is justified, the Architect shall so notify the Owner and Contractor in writing, stating the reasons. Claims by either party in opposition to such determination must be made within 21 days after the Architect has given notice of the decision. If the conditions encountered are materially different, the Contract Sum and Contract Time shall be equitably adjusted, but if the Owner and Contractor cannot agree on an adjustment in the Contract Sum or Contract Time, the adjustment shall be referred to the Architect for initial determination, subject to further proceedings pursuant to Paragraph 4.4.

4.3.5 **Claims for Additional Cost.** If the Contractor wishes to make Claim for an increase in the Contract Sum, written notice as provided herein shall he given before proceeding to execute the Work. Prior notice is not required for Claims relating to an emergency endangering life or property arising under Paragraph 10.6.

4.3.6 If the Contractor believes additional cost is involved for reasons including but not limited to (1) a written interpretation from the Architect, (2) an order by the Owner to stop the Work where the Contractor was not at fault, (3) a written order for a minor change in the Work issued by the Architect, (4) failure of payment by the Owner, (5) termination of the Contract by the Owner, (6) Owner's suspension or (7) other reasonable grounds. Claim shall be filed in accordance with this Paragraph 4.3.

©1997 AIA ® AIA Document A201–1997 Used with permission

4.3.7   CLAIMS FOR ADDITIONAL TIME

4.3.7   If the Contractor wishes to make Claim for an increase in the Contract Time, written notice as provided herein shall be given. The Contractor's Claim shall include an estimate of cost and of probable effect of delay on progress of the Work. In the case of a continuing delay only one Claim is necessary.

4.3.7.2   If adverse weather conditions are the basis for a Claim for additional time, such Claim shall be documented by data substantiating that weather conditions were abnormal for the period of time, could not have been reasonably anticipated and had an adverse effect on the scheduled construction.

4.3.8   Injury or Damage to Person or Property. If either party to the Contract suffers injury or damage to person or property because of an act of omission of the other party, or of others for whose acts such party is legally responsible, written notice of such injury or damage, whether or not insured, shall be given to the other party within a reasonable time not exceeding 21 days after discovery. The notice shall provide sufficient detail to enable the other party to investigate the matter.

4.3.9   If unit prices are stated in the Contract Documents or subsequently agreed upon, and if quantities originally contemplated are materially changed in a proposed Change Order or Construction Change Directive so that application of such unit prices to quantities of Work proposed will cause substantial inequity to the Owner or Contractor, the applicable unit prices shall be equitably adjusted.

4.3.10   Claims for Consequential Damages. The Contractor and Owner waive Claims against each other for consequential damages arising out of or relating to this Contract. This mutual waiver includes:

> .1 damages incurred by the Owner for rental expenses, for losses of use, income, profit, financing, business and reputation, and for loss of management or employee productivity or of the services of such persons; and
>
> .2 damages incurred by the Contractor for principal office expenses including the compensation of personnel stationed there, for losses of financing, business and reputation, and for loss of profit except anticipated profit arising directly from the Work.

This mutual waiver is applicable, without limitation, to all consequential damages due to either party's termination in accordance with Article 14. Nothing contained in this Subparagraph 4.3.10 shall be deemed to preclude

©1997 AIA ® AIA Document A201–1997 Used with permission

an award of liquidated direct damages, when applicable, in accordance with the requirements of the Contract Documents.

4.4 RESOLUTION OF CLAIMS AND DISPUTES

4.4.1 **Decision of Architect**. Claims, including those alleging an error or omission by the Architect but excluding those arising under Paragraphs 10.3 through 10.5, shall be referred initially to the Architect for decision. An initial decision by the Architect shall be required as a condition precedent to mediation, arbitration or litigation of all Claims between the Contractor and Owner arising prior to the date final payment is due, unless 30 days have passed after the Claim has been referred to the Architect with no decision having been rendered by the Architect. The Architect will not decide disputes between the Contractor and persons or entities other than the Owner.

4.4.2 The Architect will review Claims and within ten days of the receipt of the Claim take one or more of the following actions: (1) request additional supporting data from the claimant or a response with supporting data from the other party, (2) reject the Claim in whole or in part, (3) approve the Claim, (4) suggest a compromise, or (5) advise the parties that the Architect is unable to resolve the Claim if the Architect lacks sufficient information to evaluate the merits of the Claim or if the Architect concludes that, in the Architect's sole discretion, it would be inappropriate for the Architect to resolve the Claim.

4.4.3 In evaluating Claims, the Architect may, but shall not be obligated to, consult with or seek information from either party or from persons with special knowledge or expertise who may assist the Architect in rendering a decision. The Architect may request the Owner to authorize retention of such persons at the Owner's expense.

4.4.4 If the Architect requests a party to provide a response to a Claim or to furnish additional supporting data, such party shall respond, within ten days after receipt of such request, and shall either provide a response on the requested supporting data, advise the Architect when the response or supporting data will be furnished or advise the Architect that no supporting data will be furnished. Upon receipt of the response or supporting data, if any, the Architect will either reject or approve the Claim in whole or in part.

4.4.5 The Architect will approve or reject Claims by written decision, which shall state the reasons therefor and which shall notify the parties or any change in the Contract Sum or Contract Time or both. The approval or rejection of a Claim by the Architect shall be final and binding on the parties but subject to mediation and arbitration.

©1997 AIA ® AIA Document A201–1997 Used with permission

4.4.6 When a written decision of the Architect states that (1) the decision is final but subject to mediation and arbitration and (2) a demand for arbitration of a Claim covered by such decision must be made within 30 days after the date on which the party making the demand receives the final written decision, then failure to demand arbitration within said 30 days' period shall result in the Architect's decision becoming final and binding upon the Owner and Contractor. If the Architect renders a decision after arbitration proceedings have been initiated, such decision may be entered as evidence, but shall not supersede arbitration proceedings unless the decision is acceptable to all parties concerned.

4.4.7 Upon receipt of a Claim against the Contractor or at any time thereafter, the Architect or the Owner may, but is not obligated to, notify the surety, if any, of the nature and amount of the Claim. If the Claim relates to a possibility of a Contractor's default, the Architect or the Owner may, but is not obligated to, notify the surety and request the surety's assistance in resolving the controversy.

4.4.8 If a Claim relates to or is the subject of a mechanic's lien, the party asserting such Claim may proceed in accordance with applicable law to comply with the lien notice or filing deadlines prior to resolution of the Claim by the Architect, by mediation or by arbitration.

4.5 MEDIATION

4.5.1 Any Claim arising out of or related to the Contract, except Claims relating to aesthetic effect and except those waived as provided for in Subparagraphs 4.3.10, 9.10.4 and 9.10.5 shall, after initial decision by the Architect or 30 days after submission of the Claim to the Architect, be subject to mediation as a condition precedent to arbitration or the institution of legal or equitable proceedings by either party.

4.5.2 The parties shall endeavor to resolve their Claims by mediation which, unless the parties mutually agree otherwise, shall be in accordance with the Construction Industry Mediation Rules of the American Arbitration Association currently in effect. Request for mediation shall be filed in writing with the other party to the Contract and with the American Arbitration Association. The request may be made concurrently with the filing of a demand for arbitration but, in such event, mediation shall proceed in advance of arbitration or legal or equitable proceedings, which shall be stayed pending mediation for a period of 60 days from the date of filing, unless stayed for a longer period by agreement of the parties or court order.

©1997 AIA ® AIA Document A201–1997 Used with permission

4.5.3 The parties shall share the mediator's fee and any filing fees equally. The mediation shall be held in the place where the Project is located, unless another location is mutually agreed upon. Agreements reached in mediation shall be enforceable as settlement agreements in any court having jurisdiction thereof.

4.6 ARBITRATION

4.6.1 Any Claim arising out of or related to the Contract, except Claims relating to aesthetic effect and except those waived as provided for in Subparagraphs 4.3.10, 9.10.4 and 9.10.5, shall, after decision by the Architect or 30 days after submission of the Claim to the Architect, be subject to arbitration. Prior to arbitration, the parties shall endeavor to resolve disputes by mediation in accordance with the provisions of Paragraph 4.5.

4.6.2 Claims not resolved by mediation shall be decided by arbitration which, unless the parties mutually agree otherwise, shall be in accordance with the Construction Industry Arbitration Rules of the American Arbitration Association currently in effect. The demand for arbitration shall be filed in writing with the other party to the Contract and with the American Arbitration Association, and a copy shall be filed with the Architect.

4.6.3 A demand for arbitration shall be made within the time limits specified in Subparagraphs 4.4.6 and 4.6.1 as applicable, and in other cases within a reasonable time after the Claim has arisen, and in no event shall it be made after the date when institution of legal or equitable proceedings based on such Claim would be barred by the applicable statute of limitations as determined pursuant to Paragraph 13.7.

4.6.4 Limitation on Consolidation or Joinder. No arbitration arising out of or relating to the Contract shall include, by consolidation or joinder or in any other manner, the Architect, the Architect's employees or consultants, except by written consent containing specific reference to the Agreement and signed by' the Architect, Owner, Contractor and any other person or entity sought to be joined. No arbitration shall include, by consolidation or joinder or in any other manner, parties other than the Owner, Contractor, a separate contractor as described in Article 6 and other persons substantially involved in a common question of fact or law whose presence is required if complete relief is to be accorded in arbitration. No person or entity other than the Owner, Contractor or a separate contractor as described in Article 6 shall be included as an original third party or additional third party to an arbitration whose interest or responsibility is insubstantial. Consent to arbitration involving an additional person or entity shall not constitute consent to arbi-

©1997 AIA ® AIA Document A201–1997 Used with permission

tration of a Claim not described therein or with a person or entity not named or described therein. The foregoing agreement to arbitrate and other agreements to arbitrate with an additional person or entity duly consented to by parties to the Agreement shall be specifically enforceable under applicable law in any court having jurisdiction thereof.

4.6.5 **Claims and Timely Assertion of Claims**. The party filing a notice or demand for arbitration must assert in the demand all Claims then known to that party on which arbitration is permitted to be demanded.

4.6.6 **Judgment on Final Award**. The award rendered by the arbitrator or arbitrators shall be final, and judgment may be entered upon it in accordance with applicable law in any court having jurisdiction thereof.

ARTICLE 5 SUBCONTRACTORS

5.1 DEFINITIONS

5.1.1 A Subcontractor is a person or entity who has a direct contract with the Contractor to perform a portion of the Work at the site. The term "Subcontractor" is referred to throughout the Contract Documents as if singular in number and means a Subcontractor or an authorized representative of the Subcontractor. The term "Subcontractor" does not include a separate contractor or subcontractors of a separate contractor.

5.1.2 A Sub-subcontractor is a person or entity who has a direct or indirect contract with a Subcontractor to perform a portion of the Work at the site. The term "Sub-subcontractor" is referred to throughout the Contract Documents as if singular in number and means a Sub-subcontractor or an authorized representative of the Sub-subcontractor.

5.2 AWARD OF SUBCONTRACTS AND OTHER CONTRACTS FOR PORTIONS OF THE WORK

5.2.1 Unless otherwise stated in the Contract Documents or the bidding requirements, the Contractor, as soon as practicable after award of the Contract, shall furnish in writing to the Owner through the Architect the names of persons or entities (including those who are to furnish materials or equipment fabricated to a special design) proposed for each principal portion of the Work. The Architect will promptly reply to the Contractor in writing stating whether or not the Owner or the Architect, after due investigation, has reasonable objection to any such proposed person or entity. Failure of the Owner or Architect to reply promptly shall constitute notice of no reasonable objection.

©1997 AIA ® AIA Document A201–1997 Used with permission

5.2.2 The Contractor shall not contract with a proposed person or entity to whom the Owner or Architect has made reasonable and timely objection. The Contractor shall not be required to contract with anyone to whom the Contractor has made reasonable objection.

5.2.3 If the Owner or Architect has reasonable objection to a person or entity proposed by the Contractor, the Contractor shall propose another to whom the Owner or Architect has no reasonable objection. If the proposed but rejected Subcontractor was reasonably capable of performing the Work, the Contract Sum and Contract Time shall be increased or decreased by the difference, if any, occasioned by such change, and an appropriate Change Order shall be issued before commencement of the substitute Subcontractor's Work. However, no increase in the Contract Sum or Contract Time shall be allowed for such change unless the Contractor has acted promptly and responsively in submitting names as required.

5.2.4 The Contractor shall not change a Subcontractor, person or entity previously selected if the Owner or Architect makes reasonable objection to such substitute.

5.3 SUBCONTRACTUAL RELATIONS

5.3.1 By appropriate agreement, written where legally required for validity, the Contractor shall require each Subcontractor, to the extent of the Work to be performed by the Subcontractor, to be bound to the Contractor by terms of the Contract Documents, and to assume toward the Contractor all the obligations and responsibilities, including the responsibility for safety of the Subcontractor's Work, which the Contractor, by these Documents, assumes toward the Owner and Architect. Each subcontract agreement shall preserve and protect the rights of the Owner and Architect under the Contract Documents with respect to the Work to be performed by the Subcontractor so that subcontracting thereof will not prejudice such rights, and shall allow to the Subcontractor, unless specifically provided otherwise in the subcontract agreement, the benefit of all rights, remedies and redress against the Contractor that the Contractor, by the Contract Documents, has against the Owner. Where appropriate, the Contractor shall require each Subcontractor to enter into similar agreements with Sub-subcontractors. The Contractor shall make available to each proposed Subcontractor, prior to the execution of the subcontract agreement, copies of the Contract Documents to which the Subcontractor will be bound, and, upon written request of the Subcontractor, identify to the Subcontractor terms and conditions of the proposed subcontract agreement which may be at variance with the Contract

©1997 AIA ® AIA Document A201–1997 Used with permission

Documents. Subcontractors will similarly make copies of applicable portions of such documents available to their respective proposed Sub-subcontractors.

5.4 CONTINGENT ASSIGNMENT OF SUBCONTRACTS

5.4.1 Each subcontract agreement for a portion of the Work is assigned by the Contractor to the Owner provided that:

.1 assignment is effective only after termination of the Contract by the Owner for cause pursuant to Paragraph 14.2 and only for those subcontract agreements which the Owner accepts by notifying the Subcontractor and Contractor in writing; and

.2 assignment is subject to the prior rights of the surety, if any, obligated under bond relating to the Contract.

5.4.2 Upon such assignment, if the Work has been suspended for more than 30 days, the Subcontractor's compensation shall be equitably adjusted for increases in cost resulting from the suspension.

ARTICLE 6 CONSTRUCTION BY OWNER OR BY SEPARATE CONTRACTORS

6.1 OWNER'S RIGHT TO PERFORM CONSTRUCTION AND TO AWARD SEPARATE CONTRACTS

6.1.1 The Owner reserves the right to perform construction or operations related to the Project with the Owner's own forces, and to award separate contracts in connection with other portions of the Project or other construction or operations on the site under Conditions of the Contract identical or substantially similar to these including those portions related to insurance and waiver of subrogation. If the Contractor claims that delay or additional cost is involved because of such action by the Owner, the Contractor shall make such Claim as provided in Paragraph 4.3.

6.1.2 When separate contracts are awarded for different portions of the Project or other construction or operations on the site, the term "Contractor" in the Contract Documents in each case shall mean the Contractor who executes each separate Owner-Contractor Agreement.

6.1.3 The Owner shall provide for coordination of the activities of the Owner's own forces and of each separate contractor with the Work of the Contractor, who shall cooperate with them. The Contractor shall participate with other separate contractors and the Owner in reviewing their construction schedules when directed to do so. The Contractor shall make any revisions to the construction schedule deemed necessary after a joint review and

©1997 AIA ® AIA Document A201–1997 Used with permission

mutual agreement. The construction schedules shall then constitute the schedules to be used by the Contractor, separate contractors and the Owner until subsequently revised.

6.1.4 Unless otherwise provided in the Contract Documents, when the Owner performs construction or operations related to the Project with the Owner's own forces, the Owner shall be deemed to be subject to the same obligations and to have the same rights which apply to the Contractor under the Conditions of the Contract, including, without excluding others, those stated in Article 3, this Article 6 and Articles 10, 11 and 12.

6.2   MUTUAL RESPONSIBILITY

6.2.1   The Contractor shall afford the Owner and separate contractors reasonable opportunity for introduction and storage of their materials and equipment and performance of their activities, and shall connect and coordinate the Contractor's construction and operations with theirs as required by the Contract Documents.

6.2.2   If part of the Contractor's Work depends for proper execution or results upon construction or operations by the Owner or a separate contractor, the Contractor shall, prior to proceeding with that portion of the Work, promptly report to the Architect apparent discrepancies or defects in such other construction that would render it unsuitable for such proper execution and results. Failure of the Contractor so to report shall constitute an acknowledgment that the Owner's or separate contractor's completed or partially completed construction is fit and proper to receive the Contractor's Work, except as to defects not then reasonably discoverable.

6.2.3   The Owner shall be reimbursed by the Contractor for costs incurred by the Owner which are payable to a separate contractor because of delays, improperly timed activities or defective construction of the Contractor. The Owner shall be responsible to the Contractor for costs incurred by the Contractor because of delays, improperly timed activities, damage to the Work or defective construction of a separate contractor.

6.2.4   The Contractor shall promptly remedy damage wrongfully caused by the Contractor to completed or partially completed construction or to property of the Owner or separate contractors as provided in Subparagraph 10.2.5.

6.2.5   The Owner and each separate contractor shall have the same responsibilities for cutting and patching as are described for the Contractor in Subparagraph 3.14.

©1997 AIA ® AIA Document A201–1997 Used with permission

6.3 OWNERS RIGHT TO CLEAN UP

6.3.1 If a dispute arises among the Contractor, separate contractors and the Owner as to the responsibility under their respective contracts for maintaining the premises and surrounding area free from waste materials and rubbish, the Owner may clean up and the Architect will allocate the cost among those responsible.

ARTICLE 7   CHANGES IN THE WORK

7.1 GENERAL

7.1.1 Changes in the Work may be accomplished after execution of the Contract and without invalidating the Contract, by Change Order, Construction Change Directive or order for a minor change in the Work, subject to the limitations stated in this Article 7 and elsewhere in the Contract Documents.

7.1.2 A Change Order shall be based upon agreement among the Owner, Contractor and Architect; a Construction Change Directive requires agreement by the Owner and Architect and may or may not be agreed to by the Contractor; an order for a minor change in the Work may be issued by the Architect alone.

7.1.3 Changes in the Work shall be performed under applicable provisions of the Contract Documents, and the Contractor shall proceed promptly, unless otherwise provided in the Change Order, Construction Change Directive or order for a minor change in the Work.

7.2 CHANGE ORDERS

7.2.1 A Change Order is a written instrument prepared by the Architect and signed by the Owner, Contractor and Architect, stating their agreement upon all of the following:
   .1 change in the Work;
   .2 the amount of the adjustment, if any, in the Contract Sum; and
   .3 the extent of the adjustment, if any, in the Contract Time.

7.2.2 Methods used in determining adjustments to the Contract Sum include those listed in Subparagraph 7.3.3.

7.3 CONSTRUCTION CHANGE DIRECTIVES

7.3.1 A Construction Change Directive is a written order prepared by the Architect and signed by the Owner and Architect, directing a change in the Work prior to agreement on adjustment, if any, in the Contract Sum or

©1997 AIA ® AIA Document A201–1997 Used with permission

Contract Time, or both. The Owner may by Construction Change Directive, without invalidating the Contract, order changes in the Work within the general scope of the Contract consisting of additions, deletions or other revisions, the Contract Sum and Contract Time being adjusted accordingly.

7.3.2 A Construction Change Directive shall be used in the absence of total agreement on the terms of a Change Order.

7.3.3 If the Construction Change Directive provides for an adjustment to the Contract Sum, the adjustment shall be based on one of the following methods:

    .1 mutual acceptance of a lump sum properly itemized and supported by sufficient substantiating data to permit evaluation;

    .2 unit prices stated in the Contract Documents or subsequently agreed upon;

    .3 cost to be determined in a manner agreed upon by the parties and a mutually acceptable fixed or percentage fee; or

    .4 as provided in Subparagraph 7.3.6.

7.3.4 Upon receipt of a Construction Change Directive, the Contractor shall promptly proceed with the change in the Work involved and advise the Architect of the Contractor's agreement or disagreement with the method, if any, provided in the Construction Change Directive for determining the proposed adjustment in the Contract Sum or Contract Time

7.3.5 A Construction Change Directive signed by the Contractor indicates the agreement of the Contractor therewith, including adjustment in Contract Sum and Contract Time or the method for determining them. Such agreement shall be effective immediately and shall be recorded as a Change Order.

7.3.6 If the Contractor does not respond promptly or disagrees with the method for adjustment in the Contract Sum, the method and the adjustment shall be determined by the Architect on the basis of reasonable expenditures and savings of those performing the Work attributable to the change, including, in case of an increase in the Contract Sum, a reasonable allowance for overhead and profit. In such case, and also under Clause 7.3.3.3, the Contractor shall keep and present, in such form as the Architect may prescribe, an itemized accounting together with appropriate supporting data. Unless otherwise provided in the Contract Documents, costs for the purposes of this Subparagraph 7.3.6 shall be limited to the following:

    .1 costs of labor, including social security, old age and unemployment insurance, fringe benefits required by agreement or custom, and workers' compensation insurance;

©1997 AIA ® AIA Document A201–1997 Used with permission

.2 costs of materials, supplies and equipment, including cost of transportation, whether incorporated or consumed;

.3 rental costs of machinery and equipment, exclusive of hand tools, whether rented from the Contractor or others;

.4 costs of premiums for all bonds and insurance, permit fees, and sales, use or similar taxes related to the Work; and

.5 additional costs of supervision and field office personnel directly attributable to the change.

7.3.7 The amount of credit to be allowed by the Contractor to the Owner for a deletion or change which results in a net decrease in the Contract Sum shall be actual net cost as confirmed by the Architect. When both additions and credits covering related Work or substitutions are involved in a change, the allowance for overhead and profit shall be figured on the basis of net increase, if any, with respect to that change.

7.3.8 Pending final determination of the total cost of a Construction Change Directive to the Owner, amounts not in dispute for such changes in the Work shall be included in Applications for Payment accompanied by a Change Order indicating the parties' agreement with part or all of such costs. For any portion of such cost that remains in dispute, the Architect will make an interim determination for purposes of monthly certification for payment for those costs. That determination of cost shall adjust the Contract Sum on the same basis as a Change Order, subject to the right of either party to disagree and assert a claim in accordance with Article 4.

7.3.9 When the Owner and Contractor agree with the determination made by the Architect concerning the adjustments in the Contract Sum and Contract Time, or otherwise reach agreement upon the adjustments, such agreement shall be effective immediately and shall be recorded by preparation and execution of an appropriate Change Order.

7.4 MINOR CHANGES IN THE WORK

7.4.1 The Architect will have authority to order minor changes in the Work not involving adjustment in the Contract Sum or extension of the Contract Time and not inconsistent with the intent of the Contract Documents. Such changes shall be effected by written order and shall be binding on the Owner and Contractor. The Contractor shall carry out such written orders promptly.

ARTICLE 8 TIME

8.1 DEFINITIONS

©1997 AIA ® AIA Document A201–1997 Used with permission

8.1.1 Unless otherwise provided, Contract Time is the period of time, including authorized adjustments, allotted in the Contract Documents for Substantial Completion of the Work.

8.1.2 The date of commencement of the Work is the date established in the Agreement.

8.1.3 The date of Substantial Completion is the date certified by the Architect in accordance with Paragraph 9.8.

8.1.4 The term "day" as used in the Contract Documents shall mean calendar day unless otherwise specifically defined.

8.2 PROGRESS AND COMPLETION

8.2.1 Time limits stated in the Contract Documents are of the essence of the Contract. By executing the Agreement the Contractor confirms that the Contract Time is a reasonable period for performing the Work.

8.2.2 The Contractor shall not knowingly, except by agreement or instruction of the Owner in writing, prematurely commence operations on the site or elsewhere prior to the effective date of insurance required by Article 11 to be furnished by the Contractor and Owner. The date of commencement of the Work shall not be changed by the effective date of such insurance. Unless the date of commencement is established by the Contract Documents or a notice to proceed given by the Owner, the Contractor shall notify the Owner in writing not less than five days or other agreed period before commencing the Work to permit the timely filing of mortgages, mechanic's liens and other security interests.

8.2.3 The Contractor shall proceed expeditiously with adequate forces and shall achieve Substantial Completion within the Contract Time.

8.3 DELAYS AND EXTENSIONS OF TIME

8.3.1 If the Contractor is delayed at any time in the commencement or progress of the Work by an act or neglect of the Owner or Architect, or of an employee of either, or of a separate contractor employed by the Owner, or by changes ordered in the Work, or by labor disputes, fire, unusual delay in deliveries, unavoidable casualties or other causes beyond the Contractor's control, or by delay authorized by the Owner pending mediation and arbitration, or by other causes which the Architect determines may justify delay, then the Contract Time shall be extended by Change Order for such reasonable time as the Architect may determine.

©1997 AIA ® AIA Document A201–1997 Used with permission

8.3.2 Claims relating to time shall he made in accordance with applicable provisions of Paragraph 4.3.

8.3.3 This Paragraph 8.3 does not preclude recovery of damages for delay by either party under other provisions of the Contract Documents.

ARTICLE 9   PAYMENTS AND COMPLETION
9.1   CONTRACT SUM

9.1.1 The Contract Sum is stated in the Agreement and, including authorized adjustments, is the total amount payable by the Owner to the Contractor for performance of the Work under the Contract Documents.

9.2   SCHEDULE OF VALUES

9.2.1 Before the first Application for Payment, the Contractor shall submit to the Architect a schedule of values allocated to various portions of the Work, prepared in such form and supported by such data to substantiate its accuracy as the Architect may require. This schedule, unless objected to by the Architect, shall be used as a basis for reviewing the Contractor's Applications for Payment.

9.3   APPLICATIONS FOR PAYMENT

9.3.1 At least ten days before the date established for each progress payment, the Contractor shall submit to the Architect an itemized Application for Payment for operations completed in accordance with the schedule of values. Such application shall be notarized, if required, and supported by such data substantiating the Contractor's right to payment as the Owner or Architect may require, such as copies or requisitions from Subcontractors and material suppliers, and reflecting retainage if provided for in the Contract Documents.

9.3.1.1 As provided in Subparagraph 7.3.8, such applications may include requests for payment on account of changes in the Work which have been properly authorized by Construction Change Directives, or by interim determinations of the Architect, but not yet included in Change Orders.

9.3.1.2 Such applications may not include requests for payment for portions of the Work for which the Contractor does not intend to pay to a Subcontractor or material supplier, unless such Work has been performed by others whom the Contractor intends to pay.

©1997 AIA ® AIA Document A201–1997 Used with permission

9.3.2 Unless otherwise provided in the Contract Documents, payments shall be made on account of materials and equipment delivered and suitably stored at the site for subsequent incorporation in the Work. If approved in advance by the Owner, payment may similarly be made for materials and equipment suitably stored off the site at a location agreed upon in writing. Payment for materials and equipment stored on or off the site shall be conditioned upon compliance by the Contractor with procedures satisfactory to the Owner to establish the Owner's title to such materials and equipment or otherwise protect the Owner's interest, and shall include the costs of applicable insurance, storage and transportation to the site for such materials and equipment stored off the site.

9.3.3 The Contractor warrants that title to all Work covered by an Application for Payment will pass to the Owner no later than the time of payment. The Contractor further warrants that upon submittal of an Application for Payment all Work for which Certificates for Payment have been previously issued and payments received from the Owner shall, to the best of the Contractor's knowledge, information and belief, be free and clear of liens, claims, security interests or encumbrances in favor of the Contractor, Subcontractors, material suppliers, or other persons or entities making a claim by reason of having provided labor, materials and equipment relating to the Work.

9.4 CERTIFICATES FOR PAYMENT

9.4.1 The Architect will, within seven days after receipt of the Contractor's Application for Payment, either issue to the Owner a Certificate for Payment, with a copy to the Contractor, for such amount as the Architect determines is properly due, or notify the Contractor and Owner in writing of the Architect's reasons for withholding certification in whole or in part as provided in Subparagraph 9.5.1.

9.4.2 The issuance of a Certificate for Payment will constitute a representation by the Architect to the Owner, based on the Architect's evaluation of the Work and the data comprising the Application for Payment, that the Work has progressed to the point indicated and that, to the best of the Architect's knowledge, information and belief, the quality of the Work is in accordance with the Contract Documents. The foregoing representations are subject to an evaluation of the Work for conformance with the Contract Documents upon Substantial Completion, to results of subsequent tests and inspections, to correction of minor deviations from the Contract Documents prior to completion and to specific qualifications expressed by the Architect. The issuance of a Certificate for Payment will further constitute a representa-

©1997 AIA ® AIA Document A201–1997 Used with permission

tion that the Contractor is entitled to payment in the amount certified. However, the issuance of a Certificate for Payment will not be a representation that the Architect has (1) made exhaustive or continuous on-site inspections to check the quality or quantity of the Work, (2) reviewed construction means, methods, techniques, sequences or procedures, (3) reviewed copies of requisitions received from Subcontractors and material suppliers and other data requested by the Owner to substantiate the Contractor's right to payment, or (4) made examination to ascertain how or for what purpose the Contractor has used money previously paid on account of the Contract Sum.

9.5 DECISIONS TO WITHHOLD CERTIFICATION

9.5.1 The Architect may withhold a Certificate for Payment in whole or in part, to the extent reasonably necessary to protect the Owner, if in the Architect's opinion the representations to the Owner required by Subparagraph 9.4.2 cannot be made. If the Architect is unable to certify payment in the amount of the Application, the Architect will notify the Contractor and Owner as provided in Subparagraph 9.4.1. If the Contractor and Architect cannot agree on a revised amount, the Architect will promptly issue a Certificate for Payment for the amount for which the Architect is able to make such representations to the Owner. The Architect may also withhold a Certificate for Payment, or, because of subsequently discovered evidence, may nullify the whole or a part of a Certificate for Payment previously issued, to such extent as may be necessary in the Architect's opinion to protect the Owner from loss for which the Contractor is responsible, including loss resulting from acts and omissions described in Subparagraph 3.3.2, because of:

    .1 defective Work not remedied;

    .2 third party claims filed or reasonable evidence indicating probable filing of such claims unless security acceptable to the Owner is provided by the Contractor;

    .3 failure of the Contractor to make payments properly to Subcontractors or for labor, materials or equipment;

    .4 reasonable evidence that the Work cannot be completed for the unpaid balance of the Contract Sum;

    .5 damage to the Owner or another contractor;

    .6 reasonable evidence that the Work will not be completed within the Contract Time, and that the unpaid balance would not be adequate to cover actual or liquidated damages for the anticipated delay; or

    .7 persistent failure to carry out the Work in accordance with the Contract Documents.

©1997 AIA ® AIA Document A201–1997 Used with permission

9.5.2 When the above reasons for withholding certification are removed, certification will be made for amounts previously withheld.

9.6 PROGRESS PAYMENTS

9.6.1 After the Architect has issued a Certificate for Payment, the Owner shall make payment in the manner and within the time provided in the Contract Documents, and shall so notify the Architect.

9.6.2 The Contractor shall promptly pay each Subcontractor, upon receipt of payment from the Owner, out of the amount paid to the Contractor on account of such Subcontractor's portion of the Work, the amount to which said Subcontractor is entitled, reflecting percentages actually retained from payments to the Contractor on account of such Subcontractor's portion of the Work. The Contractor shall, by appropriate agreement with each Subcontractor, require each Subcontractor to make payments to Sub-subcontractors in a similar manner.

9.6.3 The Architect will, on request, furnish to a Subcontractor, if practicable information regarding percentages of completion or amounts applied for by the Contractor and action taken thereon by the Architect and Owner on account of portions of the Work done by such Subcontractor.

9.6.4 Neither the Owner nor Architect shall have an obligation to pay or to see to the payment of money to a Subcontractor except as may otherwise be required by law.

9.6.5 Payment to material suppliers shall be treated in a manner similar to that provided in Subparagraphs 9.6.2, 9.6.3 and 9.6.4.

9.6.6 A Certificate for Payment, a progress payment, or partial or entire use or occupancy of the Project by the Owner shall not constitute acceptance of work not in accordance with the Contract Documents.

9.6.7 Unless the Contractor provides the Owner with a payment bond in the full penal sum of the Contract Sum, payments received by the Contractor for Work properly performed by Subcontractors and suppliers shall be held by the Contractor for those Subcontractors or suppliers who performed Work or furnished materials, or both, under contract with the Contractor for which payment was made by the Owner. Nothing contained herein shall require money to be placed in a separate account and not commingled with money of the Contractor, shall create any fiduciary liability or tort liability on the part of the Contractor for breach of trust or shall entitle any person or entity to an award of punitive damages against the Contractor for breach of the requirements of this provision.

©1997 AIA ® AIA Document A201-1997 Used with permission

9.7 FAILURE OF PAYMENT

9.7.1 If the Architect does not issue a Certificate for Payment, through no fault of the Contractor, within seven days after receipt of the Contractor's Application for Payment, or if the Owner does not pay the Contractor within seven days after the date established in the Contract Documents the amount certified by the Architect or awarded by arbitration, then the Contractor may, upon seven additional days' written notice to the Owner and Architect, stop the Work until payment of the amount owing has been received. The Contract Time shall be extended appropriately and the Contract Sum shall be increased by the amount of the Contractor's reasonable costs of shut-down, delay and start-up, plus interest as provided for in the Contract Documents.

9.8 SUBSTANTIAL COMPLETION

9.8.1 Substantial Completion is the stage in the progress of the Work when the Work or designated portion thereof is sufficiently complete in accordance with the Contract Documents so that the Owner can occupy or utilize the Work for its intended use.

9.8.2 When the Contractor considers that the Work, or a portion thereof which the Owner agrees to accept separately, is substantially complete, the Contractor shall prepare and submit to the Architect a comprehensive list of items to be completed or corrected prior to final payment. Failure to include an item on such list does not alter the responsibility of the Contractor to complete all Work in accordance with the Contract Documents.

9.8.3 Upon receipt of the Contractor's list, the Architect will make an inspection to determine whether the Work or designated portion thereof is substantially complete. If the Architect's inspection discloses any item, whether or not included on the Contractor's list, which is not sufficiently complete in accordance with the Contract Documents so that the Owner can occupy or utilize the Work or designated portion thereof for its intended use, the Contractor shall, before issuance of the Certificate of Substantial Completion, complete or correct such item upon notification by the Architect. In such case, the Contractor shall then submit a request for another inspection by the Architect to determine Substantial Completion.

9.8.4 When the Work or designated portion thereof is substantially complete, the Architect will prepare a Certificate of Substantial Completion which shall establish the date of Substantial Completion, shall establish responsibilities of the Owner and Contractor for security, maintenance, heat, utilities, damage to the Work and insurance, and shall fix the time within which the Contractor shall finish all items on the list accompanying the

©1997 AIA ® AIA Document A201–1997 Used with permission

Certificate. Warranties required by the Contract Documents shall commence on the date of Substantial Completion of the Work or designated portion thereof unless otherwise provided in the Certificate of Substantial Completion.

9.8.5 The Certificate of Substantial Completion shall be submitted to the Owner and Contractor for their written acceptance of responsibilities assigned to them in such Certificate. Upon such acceptance and consent of surety, if any, the Owner shall make payment of retainage applying to such Work or designated portion thereof. Such payment shall be adjusted for Work that is incomplete or not in accordance with the requirements of the Contract Documents.

9.9 PARTIAL OCCUPANCY OR USE

9.9.1 The Owner may occupy or use any completed or partially completed portion of the Work at any stage when such portion is designated by separate agreement with the Contractor, provided such occupancy or use is consented to by the insurer as required under Clause 11.4.1.5 and authorized by public authorities having jurisdiction over the Work. Such partial occupancy or use may commence whether or not the portion is substantially complete, provided the Owner and Contractor have accepted in writing the responsibilities assigned to each of them for payments, retainage, if any, security, maintenance, heat, utilities, damage to the Work and insurance, and have agreed in writing concerning the period for correction of the Work and commencement of warranties required by the Contract Documents. When the Contractor considers a portion substantially complete, the Contractor shall prepare and submit a list to the Architect as provided under Subparagraph 9.8.2. Consent of the Contractor to partial occupancy or use shall not be unreasonably withheld. The stage of the progress of the Work shall be determined by written agreement between the Owner and Contractor or, if no agreement is reached, by decision of the Architect.

9.9.2 Immediately prior to such partial occupancy or use, the Owner, Contractor and Architect shall jointly inspect the area to be occupied or portion of the Work to be used in order to determine and record the condition of the Work.

9.9.3 Unless otherwise agreed upon, partial occupancy or use of a portion or portions of the Work shall not constitute acceptance of Work not complying with the requirements of the Contract Documents.

©1997 AIA ® AIA Document A201–1997 Used with permission

9.10 FINAL COMPLETION AND FINAL PAYMENT

9.10.1 Upon receipt of written notice that the Work is ready for final inspection and acceptance and upon receipt of a final Application for Payment, the Architect will promptly make such inspection and, when the Architect finds the Work acceptable under the Contract Documents and the Contract fully performed, the Architect will promptly issue a final Certificate for Payment stating that to the best of the Architect's knowledge, information and belief, and on the basis of the Architect's on-site visits and inspections, the Work has been completed in accordance with terms and conditions of the Contract Documents and that the entire balance found to be due the Contractor and noted in the final Certificate is due and payable. The Architect's final Certificate for Payment will constitute a further representation that conditions listed in Subparagraph 9.10.2 as precedent to the Contractor's being entitled to final payment have been fulfilled.

9.10.2 Neither final payment nor any remaining retained percentage shall become due until the Contractor submits to the Architect (1) an affidavit that payrolls, bills for materials and equipment, and other indebtedness connected with the Work for which the Owner or the Owner's property might be responsible or encumbered (less amounts withheld by Owner) have been paid or otherwise satisfied, (2) a certificate evidencing that insurance required by the Contract Documents to remain in force after final payment is currently in effect and will not be canceled or allowed to expire until at least 30 days' prior written notice has been given to the Owner, (3) a written statement that the Contractor knows of no substantial reason that the insurance will not be renewable to cover the period required by the Contract Documents, (4) consent of surety, if any, to final payment and (5), if required by the Owner, other data establishing payment or satisfaction of obligations, such as receipts, releases and waivers of liens, claims, security interests or encumbrances arising out of the Contract, to the extent and in such form as may be designated by the Owner. If a Subcontractor refuses to furnish a release or waiver required by the Owner, the Contractor may furnish a bond satisfactory to the Owner to indemnify the Owner against such lien. If such lien remains unsatisfied after payments are made, the Contractor shall refund to the Owner all money that the Owner may be compelled to pay in discharging such lien, including all costs and reasonable attorneys' fees.

9.10.3 If, after Substantial Completion of the Work, final completion thereof is materially delayed through no fault of the Contractor or by issuance of Change Orders affecting final completion, and the Architect so confirms, the Owner shall, upon application by the Contractor and certification by the Architect, and without terminating the Contract, make payment of

©1997 AIA ® AIA Document A201–1997 Used with permission

the balance due for that portion of the Work fully completed and accepted. If the remaining balance for Work not fully completed or corrected is less than retainage stipulated in the Contract Documents, and if bonds have been furnished, the written consent of surety to payment of the balance due for that portion of the Work fully completed and accepted shall be submitted by the Contractor to the Architect prior to certification of such payment. Such payment shall be made under terms and conditions governing final payment, except that it shall not constitute a waiver of claims.

9.10.4 The making of final payment shall constitute a waiver of Claims by the Owner except those arising from:

    .1 liens, Claims, security interests or encumbrances arising out of the Contract and unsettled;

    .2 failure of the Work to comply with the requirements of the Contract Documents; or

    .3 terms of special warranties required by the Contract Documents.

9.10.5 Acceptance of final payment by the Contractor, a Subcontractor or material supplier shall constitute a waiver of claims by that payee except those previously made in writing and identified by that payee as unsettled at the time of final Application for Payment.

ARTICLE 10   PROTECTION OF PERSONS AND PROPERTY

10.1   SAFETY PRECAUTIONS AND PROGRAMS

10.1.1 The Contractor shall be responsible for initiating, maintaining and supervising all safety precautions and programs in connection with the performance of the Contract.

10.2   SAFETY OF PERSONS AND PROPERTY

10.2.1 The Contractor shall take reasonable precautions for safety of, and shall provide reasonable protection to prevent damage, injury or loss to:

    .1 employees on the Work and other persons who may be affected thereby;

    .2 the Work and materials and equipment to be incorporated therein, whether in storage on or off the site, under care, custody or control of the Contractor or the Contractor's Subcontractors or Sub-subcontractors; and

    .3 other property at the site or adjacent thereto, such as trees, shrubs, lawns, walks, pavements, roadways, structures and utilities not designated for removal, relocation or replacement in the course of construction.

©1997 AIA ® AIA Document A201–1997 Used with permission

10.2.2 The Contractor shall give notices and comply with applicable laws, ordinances, rules, regulations and lawful orders of public authorities bearing on safety of persons or property or their protection from damage, injury or loss.

10.2.3 The Contractor shall erect and maintain, as required by existing conditions and performance of the Contract, reasonable safeguards for safety and protection, including posting danger signs and other warnings against hazards, promulgating safety regulations and notifying owners and users of adjacent sites and utilities.

10.2.4 When use or storage of explosives or other hazardous materials or equipment or unusual methods are necessary for execution of the Work, the Contractor shall exercise utmost care and carry on such activities under supervision of properly qualified personnel.

10.2.5 The Contractor shall promptly remedy damage and loss (other than damage or loss insured under property insurance required by the Contract Documents) to property referred to in Clauses 10.2.1.2 and 10.2.1.3 caused in whole or in part by the Contractor, a Subcontractor, a Sub-subcontractor, or anyone directly or indirectly employed by any of them, or by anyone for whose acts they may be liable and for which the Contractor is responsible under Clauses 10.2.1.2 and 10.2.1.3, except damage or loss attributable to acts or omissions of the Owner or Architect or anyone directly or indirectly employed by either of them, or by anyone for whose acts either of them may be liable, and not attributable to the fault or negligence of the Contractor. The foregoing obligations of the Contractor are in addition to the Contractor's obligations under Paragraph 3.18.

10.2.6 The Contractor shall designate a responsible member of the Contractor's organization at the site whose duty shall be the prevention of accidents. This person shall be the Contractor's superintendent unless otherwise designated by the Contractor in writing to the Owner and Architect.

10.2.7 The Contractor shall not load or permit any part of the construction or site to be loaded so as to endanger its safety.

10.3 HAZARDOUS MATERIALS

10.3.1 If reasonable precautions will be inadequate to prevent foreseeable bodily injury or death to persons resulting from a material or substance, including but not limited to asbestos or polychlorinated biphenyl (PCB), encountered on the site by the Contractor, the Contractor shall, upon recognizing the condition, immediately stop Work in the affected area and report the condition to the Owner and Architect in writing.

©1997 AIA ® AIA Document A201–1997 Used with permission

10.3.2 The Owner shall obtain the services of a licensed laboratory to verify the presence or absence of the material or substance reported by the Contractor and, in the event such material or substance is found to be present, to verify that it has been rendered harmless. Unless otherwise required by the Contract Documents, the Owner shall furnish in writing to the Contractor and Architect the names and qualifications of persons or entities who are to perform tests verifying the presence or absence of such material or substance or who are to perform the task of removal or safe containment of such material or substance. The Contractor and the Architect will promptly reply to the Owner in writing stating whether or not either has reasonable objection to the persons or entities proposed by the Owner. If either the Contractor or Architect has an objection to a person or entity proposed by the Owner, the Owner shall propose another to whom the Contractor and the Architect have no reasonable objection. When the material or substance has been rendered harmless, Work in the affected area shall resume upon written agreement of the Owner and Contractor. The Contract Time shall be extended appropriately and the Contract Sum shall be increased in the amount of the Contractor's reasonable additional costs of shut-down, delay and start-up, which adjustments shall be accomplished as provided in Article 7.

10.3.3 To the fullest extent permitted by law, the Owner shall indemnify and hold harmless the Contractor, Subcontractors, Architect, Architect's consultants and agents and employees of any of them from and against claims, damages, losses and expenses, including but not limited to attorneys' fees, arising out of or resulting from performance of the Work in the affected area if in fact the material or substance presents the risk of bodily injury or death as described in Subparagraph 10.3.1 and has not been rendered harmless, provided that such claim, damage, loss or expense is attributable to bodily injury, sickness, disease or death, or to injury to or destruction of tangible property (other than the Work itself) and provided that such damage, loss or expense is not due to the sole negligence of a party seeking indemnity.

10.4 The Owner shall not be responsible under Paragraph 10.3 for materials and substances brought to the site by the Contractor unless such materials or substances were required by the Contract Documents.

10.5 If, without negligence on the part of the Contractor, the Contractor is held liable for the cost of remediation of a hazardous material or substance solely by reason of performing Work as required by the Contract Documents, the Owner shall indemnify the Contractor for all cost and expense thereby incurred.

©1997 AIA ® AIA Document A201–1997 Used with permission

10.6 EMERGENCIES

10.6.1 In an emergency affecting safety of persons or property, the Contractor shall act, at the Contractor's discretion, to prevent threatened damage, injury or loss. Additional compensation or extension of time claimed by the Contractor on account of an emergency shall be determined as provided in Paragraph 4.3 and Article 7.

ARTICLE 11 INSURANCE AND BONDS

11.1 CONTRACTOR'S LIABILITY INSURANCE

11.1.1 The Contractor shall purchase from and maintain in a company or companies lawfully authorized to do business in the jurisdiction in which the Project is located such insurance as will protect the Contractor from claims set forth below which may arise out of or result from the Contractor's operations under the Contract and for which the Contractor may be legally liable, whether such operations be by the Contractor or by a Subcontractor or by anyone directly or indirectly employed by any of them, or by anyone for whose acts any of them may be liable:

.1 claims under workers' compensation, disability benefit and other similar employee benefit acts which are applicable to the Work to be performed;

.2 claims for damages because of bodily injury, occupational sickness or disease, or death of the Contractor's employees;

.3 claims for damages because of bodily injury, sickness or disease, or death of any person other than the Contractor's employees;

.4 claims for damages insured by usual personal injury liability coverage;

.5 claims for damages, other than to the Work itself, because of injury to or destruction of tangible property, including loss of use resulting therefrom;

.6 claims for damages because of bodily injury, death of a person or property damage arising out of ownership, maintenance or use of a motor vehicle;

.7 claims for bodily injury or property damage arising out of completed operations; and

.8 claims involving contractual liability insurance applicable to the Contractor's obligations under Paragraph 3.18.

11.1.2 The insurance required by Subparagraph 11.1.1 shall be written for not less than limits of liability specified in the Contract Documents or required by law, whichever coverage is greater. Coverages, whether written on

©1997 AIA ® AIA Document A201–1997 Used with permission

an occurrence or claims-made basis, shall be maintained without interruption from date of commencement of the Work until date of final payment and termination of any coverage required to be maintained after final payment.

11.1.3 Certificates of insurance acceptable to the Owner shall be filed with the Owner prior to commencement of the Work. These certificates and the insurance policies required by this Paragraph 11.1 shall contain a provision that coverages afforded under the policies will not be canceled or allowed to expire until at least 30 days' prior written notice has been given to the Owner. If any of the foregoing insurance coverages are required to remain in force after final payment and are reasonably available, an additional certificate evidencing continuation of such coverage shall be submitted with the final Application for Payment as required by Subparagraph 9.10.2. Information concerning reduction of coverage on account of revised limits or claims paid under the General Aggregate, or both, shall be furnished by the Contractor with reasonable promptness in accordance with the Contractor's information and belief.

11.2 OWNER'S LIABILITY INSURANCE

11.2.1 The Owner shall be responsible for purchasing and maintaining the Owner's usual liability insurance.

11.3 PROJECT MANAGEMENT PROTECTIVE LIABILITY INSURANCE

11.3.1 Optionally, the Owner may require the Contractor to purchase and maintain Project Management Protective Liability insurance from the Contractor's usual sources as primary coverage for the Owner's, Contractor's and Architect's vicarious liability for construction operations under the Contract. Unless otherwise required by the Contract Documents, the Owner shall reimburse the Contractor by increasing the Contract Sum to pay the cost of purchasing and maintaining such optional insurance coverage, and the Contractor shall not be responsible for purchasing any other liability insurance on behalf of the Owner. The minimum limits of liability purchased with such coverage shall be equal to the aggregate of the limits required for Contractor's Liability Insurance under Clauses 11.1.1.2 through 11.1.1.5.

11.3.2 To the extent damages are covered by Project Management Protective Liability insurance, the Owner, Contractor and Architect waive all rights against each other for damages, except such rights as they may have to the proceeds of such insurance. The policy shall provide for such waivers of subrogation by endorsement or otherwise.

©1997 AIA ® AIA Document A201–1997 Used with permission

11.3.3 The Owner shall not require the Contractor to include the Owner, Architect or other persons or entities as additional insureds on the Contractor's Liability Insurance coverage under Paragraph 11.1.

11.4 PROPERTY INSURANCE

11.4.1 Unless otherwise provided, the Owner shall purchase and maintain, in a company or companies lawfully authorized to do business in the jurisdiction in which the Project is located, property insurance written on a builder's risk "all-risk" or equivalent policy form in the amount of the initial Contract Sum, plus value of subsequent Contract modifications and cost of materials supplied or installed by others, comprising total value for the entire Project at the site on a replacement cost basis without optional deductibles. Such property insurance shall be maintained, unless otherwise provided in the Contract Documents or otherwise agreed in writing by all persons and entities who are beneficiaries of such insurance, until final payment has been made as provided in Paragraph 9.10 or until no person or entity other than the Owner has an insurable interest in the property required by this Paragraph 11.4 to be covered, whichever is later. This insurance shall include interests of the Owner, the Contractor, Subcontractors and Sub-subcontractors in the Project.

11.4.1.1 Property insurance shall be on an "all-risk" or equivalent policy form and shall include, without limitation, insurance against the perils of fire (with extended coverage) and physical loss or damage including, without duplication of coverage, theft, vandalism, malicious mischief, collapse, earthquake, flood, windstorm, falsework, testing and startup, temporary buildings and debris removal including demolition occasioned by enforcement of any applicable legal requirements, and shall cover reasonable compensation for Architect's and Contractor's services and expenses required as a result of such insured loss.

11.4.1.2 If the Owner does not intend to purchase such property insurance required by the Contract and with all of the coverages in the amount described above, the Owner shall so inform the Contractor in writing prior to commencement of the Work. The Contractor may then effect insurance which will protect the interests of the Contractor, Subcontractors and Sub-Subcontractors in the Work, and by appropriate Change Order the cost thereof shall be charged to the Owner. If the Contractor is damaged by the failure or neglect of the Owner to purchase or maintain insurance as described above, without so notifying the Contractor in writing, then the Owner shall bear all reasonable costs properly attributable thereto.

©1997 AIA ® AIA Document A201–1997 Used with permission

11.4.1.3 If the property insurance required deductibles, the Owner shall pay costs not covered because of such deductibles.

11.4.1.4 This property insurance shall cover portions of the Work stored off the site, and also portions of the work in transit.

11.4.1.5 Partial occupancy or use in accordance with Paragraph 9.9 shall not commence until insurance company or companies providing property insurance have consented to such partial occupancy or use by endorsement or otherwise. The Owner and the Contractor shall take reasonable steps to obtain consent of the insurance company or companies and shall, without mutual written consent, take no action with respect to partial occupancy or use that would cause cancellation, lapse or reduction of insurance.

11.4.2   Boiler and Machinery Insurance. The Owner shall purchase and maintain boiler and machinery insurance required by the Contract Documents or by law, which shall specifically cover such insured objects during installation and until final acceptance by the Owner; this insurance shall include interests of the Owner, Contractor, Subcontractors and Sub-subcontractors in the Work, and the Owner and Contractor shall be named insureds.

11.4.3   Loss of Use Insurance. The Owner, at the Owner's option, may purchase and maintain such insurance as will insure the Owner against loss of use of the Owner's property due to fire or other hazards, however caused. The Owner waives all rights of action against the Contractor for loss of use of the Owner's property, including consequential losses due to fire or other hazards however caused.

11.4.4   If the Contractor requests in writing that insurance for risks other than those described herein or other special causes of loss be included in the property insurance policy, the Owner shall, if possible, include such insurance, and the cost thereof shall be charged to the Contractor by appropriate Change Order.

11.4.5   If during the Project construction period the Owner insures properties, real or personal or both, at or adjacent to the site by property insurance under policies separate from those insuring the Project, or if after final payment property insurance is to be provided on the completed Project through a policy or policies other than those insuring the Project during the construction period, the Owner shall waive all rights in accordance with the terms of Subparagraph 11.4.7 for damages caused by fire or other causes of loss covered by this separate property insurance. All separate policies shall provide this waiver of subrogation by endorsement or otherwise.

©1997 AIA ® AIA Document A201–1997 Used with permission

11.4.6 Before an exposure to loss may occur, the Owner shall file with the Contractor a copy of each policy that includes insurance coverages required by this Paragraph 11.4. Each policy shall contain all generally applicable conditions, definitions, exclusions and endorsements related to this Project. Each policy shall contain a provision that the policy will not be canceled or allowed to expire, and that its limits will not be reduced, until at least 30 days' prior written notice has been given to the Contractor.

11.4.7 Waivers of Subrogation. The Owner and Contractor waive all rights against (1) each other and any of their subcontractors, sub-subcontractors, agents and employees, each of the other, and (2) the Architect, Architect's consultants, separate contractors described in Article 6, if any, and any of their subcontractors, sub-subcontractors, agents and employees, for damages caused by fire or other causes of loss to the extent covered by property insurance obtained pursuant to this Paragraph 11.4 or other property insurance applicable to the Work, except such rights as they have to proceeds of such insurance held by the Owner as fiduciary. The Owner or Contractor, as appropriate, shall require of the Architect, Architect's consultants, separate contractors described in Article 6, if any, and the subcontractors, sub-subcontractors, agents and employees or any of them, by appropriate agreements, written where legally required for validity, similar waivers each in favor of other parties enumerated herein. The policies shall provide such waivers of subrogation by endorsement or otherwise. A waiver of subrogation shall be effective as to a person or entity even though that person or entity would otherwise have a duty of indemnification, contractual or otherwise, did not pay the insurance premium directly or indirectly, and whether or not the person or entity had an insurable interest in the property damaged.

11.4.8 A loss insured under Owner's property insurance shall be adjusted by the Owner as fiduciary and made payable to the Owner as fiduciary for the insureds, as their interests may appear, subject to requirements of any applicable mortgagee clause and of Subparagraph 11.4.10. The Contractor shall pay Subcontractors their just shares of insurance proceeds received by the Contractor, and by appropriate agreements, written where legally required for validity, shall require Subcontractors to make payments to their Sub-subcontractors in similar manner,

11.4.9 If required in writing by a party in interest, the Owner as fiduciary shall, upon occurrence of an insured loss, give bond for proper performance of the Owner's duties. The cost of required bonds shall be charged against proceeds received as fiduciary. The Owner shall deposit in a separate account proceeds so received, which the Owner shall distribute in accordance with such agreement as the parties in interest may reach, or in accordance with an

©1997 AIA ® AIA Document A201–1997 Used with permission

arbitration award in which case the procedure shall be as provided in Paragraph 4.6. If after such loss no other special agreement is made and unless the Owner terminates the Contract for convenience, replacement of damaged property shall be performed by the Contractor after notification of a Change in the Work in accordance with Article 7.

11.4.10 The Owner as fiduciary shall have power to adjust and settle a loss with insurers unless one of the parties in interest shall object in writing within five days after occurrence of loss to the Owner's exercise of this power; if such objection is made, the dispute shall be resolved as provided in Paragraphs 4.5 and 4.6. The Owner as fiduciary shall, in the case of arbitration, make settlement with insurers in accordance with directions of the arbitrators. If distribution of insurance proceeds by arbitration is required, the arbitrators will direct such distribution.

11.5 PERFORMANCE BOND AND PAYMENT BOND

11.5.1 The Owner shall have the right to require the Contractor to furnish bonds covering faithful performance of the Contract and payment of obligations arising thereunder as stipulated in bidding requirements or specifically required in the Contract Documents on the date of execution of the Contract.

11.5.2 Upon the request of any person or entity appearing to be a potential beneficiary of bonds covering payment of obligations arising under the Contract, the Contractor shall promptly furnish a copy of the bonds or shall permit a copy to be made.

ARTICLE 12   UNCOVERING AND CORRECTION OF WORK

12.1   UNCOVERING OF WORK

12.1.1 If a portion of the Work is covered contrary to the Architect's request or to requirements specifically expressed in the Contract Documents, it must, if required in writing by the Architect, be uncovered for the Architect's examination and be replaced at the Contractor's expense without change in the Contract Time.

12.1.2 If a portion of the Work has been covered which the Architect has not specifically requested to examine prior to its being covered, the Architect may request to see such Work and it shall be uncovered by the Contractor. If such Work is in accordance with the Contract Documents, costs of uncovering and replacement shall, by appropriate Change Order, be at the Owner's expense. If such Work is not in accordance with the Contract Documents,

©1997 AIA ® AIA Document A201–1997 Used with permission

correction shall be at the Contractor's expense unless the condition was caused by the Owner or a separate contractor in which event the Owner shall be responsible for payment of such costs.

12.2 CORRECTION OF WORK

12.2.1 BEFORE OR AFTER SUBSTANTIAL COMPLETION

12.2.1.1 The Contractor shall promptly correct Work rejected by the Architect or failing to conform to the requirements of the Contract Documents, whether discovered before or after Substantial Completion and whether or not fabricated, installed or completed. Costs of correcting such rejected Work, including additional testing and inspections and compensation for the Architect's services and expenses made necessary thereby, shall be at the Contractor's expense.

12.2.2 AFTER SUBSTANTIAL COMPLETION

12.2.2.1 In addition to the Contractor's obligations under Paragraph 3.5, if, within one year after the date of Substantial Completion of the Work or designated portion thereof or after the date for commencement of warranties established under Subparagraph 9.9.1 or by terms of an applicable special warranty required by the Contract Documents, any of the Work is found to be not in accordance with the requirements of the Contract Documents, the Contractor shall correct it promptly after receipt of written notice from the Owner to do so unless the Owner has previously given the Contractor a written acceptance of such condition. The Owner shall give such notice promptly after discovery of the condition. During the one-year period for correction of Work, if the Owner fails to notify the Contractor and give the Contractor an opportunity to make the correction, the Owner waives the rights to require correction by the Contractor and to make a claim for breach of warranty. If the Contractor fails to correct nonconforming Work within a reasonable time during that period after receipt of notice from the Owner or Architect, the Owner may correct it in accordance with Paragraph 2.4.

12.2.2.2 The one-year period for correction of Work shall be extended with respect to portions of Work first performed after Substantial Completion by the period of time between Substantial Completion and the actual performance of the Work.

12.2.2.3 The one-year period for correction of Work shall not be extended by corrective Work performed by the Contractor pursuant to this Paragraph 12.2.

©1997 AIA ® AIA Document A201–1997 Used with permission

12.2.3 The Contractor shall remove from the site portions of the Work which are not in accordance with the requirements of the Contract Documents and are neither corrected by the Contractor nor accepted by the Owner.

12.2.4 The Contractor shall bear the cost of correcting destroyed or damaged construction, whether completed or partially completed, of the Owner or separate contractors caused by the Contractor's correction or removal of Work which is not in accordance with the requirements of the Contract Documents.

12.2.5 Nothing contained in this Paragraph 12.2 shall be construed to establish a period of limitation with respect to other obligations which the Contractor might have under the Contract Documents. Establishment of the one-year period for correction of Work as described in Subparagraph 12.2.2 relates only to the specific obligation of the Contractor to correct the Work, and has no relationship to the time within which the obligation to comply with the Contract Documents may be sought to be enforced, nor to the time within which proceedings may be commenced to establish the Contractor's liability with respect to the Contractor's obligations other than specifically to correct the Work.

12.3 ACCEPTANCE OF NONCONFORMING WORK

12.3.1 If the Owner prefers to accept Work which is not in accordance with the requirements of the Contract Documents, the Owner may do so instead of requiring its removal and correction, in which case the Contract Sum will be reduced as appropriate and equitable. Such adjustment shall be effected whether or not final payment has been made.

ARTICLE 13   MISCELLANEOUS PROVISIONS

13.1 GOVERNING LAW

13.1.1 The Contract shall be governed by the law of the place where the Project is located.

13.2 SUCCESSORS AND ASSIGNS

13.2.1 The Owner and Contractor respectively bind themselves, their partners, successors, assigns and legal representatives to the other party hereto and to partners, successors, assigns and legal representatives of such other party in respect to covenants, agreements and obligations contained in the Contract Documents. Except as provided in Subparagraph 13.2.2, neither

©1997 AIA ® AIA Document A201–1997 Used with permission

party to the Contract shall assign the Contract as a whole without written consent of the other. If either party attempts to make such an assignment without such consent, that party shall nevertheless remain legally responsible for all obligations under the Contract.

13.2.2 The Owner may, without consent of the Contractor, assign the Contract to an institutional lender providing construction financing for the Project. In such event, the lender shall assume the Owner's rights and obligations under the Contract Documents. The Contractor shall execute all consents reasonably required to facilitate such assignment.

13.3 WRITTEN NOTICE

13.3.1 Written notice shall be deemed to have been duly served if delivered in person to the individual or a member of the firm or entity or to an officer of the corporation for which it was intended, or if delivered at or sent by registered or certified mail to the last business address known to the party giving notice.

13.4 RIGHTS AND REMEDIES

13.4.1 Duties and obligations imposed by the Contract Documents and rights and remedies available thereunder shall be in addition to and not a limitation of duties, obligations, rights and remedies otherwise imposed or available by law.

13.4.2 No action or failure to act by the Owner, Architect or Contractor shall constitute a waiver of a right or duty afforded them under the Contract, nor shall such action or failure to act constitute approval of or acquiescence in a breach thereunder except as may be specifically agreed in writing.

13.5 TESTS AND INSPECTIONS

13.5.1 Tests, inspections and approvals of portions of the Work required by the Contract Documents or by laws, ordinances, rules, regulations or orders of public authorities having jurisdiction shall be made at an appropriate time. Unless otherwise provided, the Contractor shall make arrangements for such tests, inspections and approvals with an independent testing laboratory or entity acceptable to the Owner, or with the appropriate public authority, and shall bear all related costs of tests, inspections and approvals. The Contractor shall give the Architect timely notice of when and where tests and inspections are to be made so that the Architect may be present for such procedures. The

©1997 AIA ® AIA Document A201–1997 Used with permission

Owner shall bear costs of tests, inspections or approvals which do not become requirements until after bids are received or negotiations concluded.

13.5.2 If the Architect, Owner or public authorities having jurisdiction determine that portions of the Work require additional testing, inspection or approval not included under Subparagraph 13.5.1, the Architect will, upon written authorization from the Owner, instruct the Contractor to make arrangements for such additional testing, inspection or approval by an entity acceptable to the Owner, and the Contractor shall give timely notice to the Architect of when and where tests and inspections are to be made so that the Architect may be present for such procedures. Such costs, except as provided in Subparagraph 13.5.3, shall be at the Owner's expense.

13.5.3 If such procedures for testing, inspection or approval under Subparagraphs 13.5.1 and 13.5.2 reveal failure of the portions of the Work to comply with requirements established by the Contract Documents, all costs made necessary by such failure including those of repeated procedures and compensation for the Architect's services and expenses shall be at the Contractor's expense.

13.5.4 Required certificates of testing, inspection or approval shall, unless otherwise required by the Contract Documents, be secured by the Contractor and promptly delivered to the Architect.

13.5.5 If the Architect is to observe tests, inspections or approvals required by the Contract Documents, the Architect will do so promptly and, where practicable, at the normal place of testing.

13.5.6. Tests or inspections conducted pursuant to the Contract Documents shall be made promptly to avoid unreasonable delay in the Work.

13.6 INTEREST

13.6.1 Payments due and unpaid under the Contract Documents shall bear interest from the date payment is due at such rate as the parties may agree upon in writing or, in the absence thereof, at the legal rate prevailing from time to time at the place where the Project is located.

13.7 COMMENCEMENT OF STATUTORY LIMITATION PERIOD

13.7.1 As between the Owner and Contractor:

.1 **Before Substantial Completion.** As to acts or failures to act occurring prior to the relevant date of Substantial Completion, any applicable statute of limitations shall commence to run and any

©1997 AIA ® AIA Document A201–1997 Used with permission

alleged cause of action shall be deemed to have accrued in any and all events not later than such date of Substantial Completion;

.2 **Between Substantial Completion and Final Certificate for Payment.** As to acts or failures to act occurring subsequent to the relevant date of Substantial Completion and prior to issuance of the final Certificate for Payment, any applicable statute of limitations shall commence to run and any alleged cause of action shall be deemed to have accrued in any and all events not later than the date of issuance of the final Certificate for Payment; and

.3 **After Final Certificate for Payment.** As to acts or failures to act occurring after the relevant date of issuance of the final Certificate for Payment, any applicable statute of limitations shall commence to run and any alleged cause of action shall be deemed to have accrued in any and all events not later than the date of any act or failure to act by the Contractor pursuant to any Warranty provided under Paragraph 3.5, the date of any correction of the Work or failure to correct the Work by the Contractor under Paragraph 12.2, or the date of actual commission of any other act or failure to perform any duty or obligation by the Contractor or Owner, whichever occurs last.

ARTICLE 14   TERMINATION OR SUSPENSION OF THE CONTRACT

14.1   TERMINATION BY THE CONTRACTOR

14-1.1 The Contractor may terminate the Contract if the Work is stopped for a period of 30 consecutive days through no act or fault of the Contractor or a Subcontractor, Sub-subcontractor or their agents or employees or any other persons or entities performing portions of the Work under direct or indirect contract with the Contractor, for any of the following reasons:

.1 issuance of an order of a court or other public authority having jurisdiction which requires all Work to be stopped;

.2 an act of government, such as a declaration of national emergency which requires all Work to be stopped;

.3 because the Architect has not issued a Certificate for Payment and has not notified the Contractor of the reason for withholding certification as provided in Subparagraph 9.4.1, or because the Owner has not made payment on a Certificate for Payment within the time stated in the Contract Documents; or

©1997 AIA ® AIA Document A201–1997 Used with permission

.4 the Owner has failed to furnish to the Contractor promptly, upon the Contractor's request, reasonable evidence as required by Subparagraph 2.2.1.

14.1.2 The Contractor may terminate the Contract if, through no act or fault of the Contractor or a Subcontractor, Sub-subcontractor or their agents or employees or any other persons or entities performing portions of the Work under direct or indirect contract with the Contractor, repeated suspensions, delays or interruptions of the entire Work by the Owner as described in Paragraph 14.3 constitute in the aggregate more than 100 percent of the total number of days scheduled for completion, or 120 days in any 365-day period, whichever is less.

14.1.3 If one of the reasons described in Subparagraph 14.1.1 or 14.1.2 exists, the Contractor may, upon seven days' written notice to the Owner and Architect, terminate the Contract and recover from the Owner payment for Work executed and for proven loss with respect to materials, equipment, tools, and construction equipment and machinery, including reasonable overhead, profit and damages.

14.1.4 If the Work is stopped for a period of 60 consecutive days through no act or fault of the Contractor or a Subcontractor or their agents or employees or any other persons performing portions of the Work under contract with the Contractor because the Owner has persistently failed to fulfill the Owner's obligations under the Contract Documents with respect to matters important to the progress of the Work, the Contractor may, upon seven additional days' written notice to the Owner and the Architect, terminate the Contract and recover from the Owner as provided in Subparagraph 14.1.3.

14.2 **TERMINATION BY THE OWNER FOR CAUSE**

14.2.1 The Owner may terminate the Contract if the Contractor:
.1 persistently or repeatedly refuses or fails to supply enough properly skilled workers or proper materials;
.2 fails to make payment to Subcontractors for materials or labor in accordance with the respective agreements between the Contractor and the Subcontractors;
.3 persistently disregards laws, ordinances, or rules, regulations or orders of a public authority having jurisdiction; or
.4 otherwise is guilty of substantial breach of a provision of the Contract Documents.

©1997 AIA ® AIA Document A201–1997 Used with permission

4.2.2 When any of the above reasons exist, the Owner, upon certification by the Architect that sufficient cause exists to justify such action, may without prejudice to any other rights or remedies of the Owner and after giving the Contractor and the Contractor's surety, if any, seven days' written notice, terminate employment of the Contractor and may, subject to any prior rights of the surety:

    .1 take possession of the site and of all materials, equipment, tools, and construction equipment and machinery thereon owned by the Contractor;

    .2 accept assignment of subcontracts pursuant to Paragraph 5.4; and

    .3 finish the Work by whatever reasonable method the Owner may deem expedient. Upon request of the Contractor, the Owner shall furnish to the Contractor a detailed accounting of the costs incurred by the Owner in finishing the Work.

14.2.3 When the Owner terminates the Contract for one of the reasons stated in Subparagraph 14.2.1, the Contractor shall not be entitled to receive further payment until the Work is finished.

14.2.4 If the unpaid balance of the Contract Sum exceeds costs of finishing the Work, including compensation for the Architect's services and expenses made necessary thereby, and other damages incurred by the Owner and not expressly waived, such excess shall be paid to the Contractor. If such costs and damages exceed the unpaid balance, the Contractor shall pay the difference to the Owner. The amount to be paid to the Contractor or Owner, as the case may be, shall be certified by the Architect, upon application, and this obligation for payment shall survive termination of the Contract.

14.3 SUSPENSION BY THE OWNER FOR CONVENIENCE

14.3.1 The Owner may, without cause, order the Contractor in writing to suspend, delay or interrupt the Work in whole or in part for such period of time as the Owner may determine.

14.3.2 The Contract Sum and Contract Time shall be adjusted for increases in the cost and time caused by suspension, delay or interruption as described in Subparagraph 14.3.1. Adjustment of the Contract Sum shall include profit. No adjustment shall be made to the extent:

    .1 that performance is, was or would have been so suspended, delayed or interrupted by another cause for which the Contractor is responsible; or

©1997 AIA ® AIA Document A201–1997 Used with permission

.2 that an equitable adjustment is made or denied under another provision of the Contract.

14.4 TERMINATION BY THE OWNER FOR CONVENIENCE

14.4.1 The Owner may, at any time, terminate the Contract for the Owner's convenience and without cause.

14.4.2 Upon receipt of written notice from the Owner of such termination for the Owner's convenience, the Contractor shall:
.1 cease operations as directed by the Owner in the notice;
.2 take actions necessary, or that the Owner may direct, for the protection and preservation of the Work; and
.3 except for Work directed to be performed prior to the effective date of termination stated in the notice, terminate all existing subcontracts and purchase orders and enter into no further subcontracts and purchase orders.

14.4.3 In case of such termination for the Owner's convenience, the Contractor shall be entitled to receive payment for Work executed, and costs incurred by reason of such termination, along with reasonable overhead and profit on the Work not executed.

©1997 AIA ® AIA Document A201–1997 Used with permission

Appendix B: Effective Project Management in Bureaucracies

*The **traditional project management process** should be adapted to the owner's organizational structure to maximize its effectiveness. Public-sector owner organizations tend to be functionally compartmentalized and bureaucratic. Applying current project management techniques in these organizations has met with mixed results. The authors discuss a theoretical approach for implementing effective project management, given the characteristics of the functionally compartmentalized owner organization and a subjective assessment of three consequential variables (project-specific, owner-specific, and market-specific). Effective project management is viewed from the least perspective of what combination of five "right" project management practices (contracting strategy, feedback mechanisms, cost management, schedule management, and dispute avoidance/resolution) makes the most sense.*

Ever since humans began building major projects for the public good, the search to manage these projects effectively has continued. The public sector requires that its projects be managed in a basic, no-nonsense fashion and at the lowest possible cost. However, public-sector project management organizations tend to be functionally compartmentalized, with conservative, slow-response time, and bureaucratic cultures. These are commonly believed to be undesirable qualities and detrimental to effective project management. Many project management consultants advise their clients to reorganize to take better advantage of current project management techniques. The authors, however, believe that these qualities exist for good reasons, which should be acknowledged. The authors also believe that the functionally compartmentalized owner's organizational structure will always exist in the public sector because it provides for accountability to constituents, a clear chain of command, and a system of checks and balances. The purpose of this paper is to explore the ways current project management techniques can be adapted to increase the effectiveness of project management efforts without reorganizing functionally compartmentalized organizations.

To understand our goal of effective project management, one must understand our view of effectiveness. Effectiveness is the degree to which a system accomplishes what it sets out to accomplish [6]. *Effective project management* involves at least three criteria: quality, quantity, and timeliness. Quality addresses doing the "right" things in the "right" way. Quantity addresses getting all of the "right" things done. And, timeliness addresses getting the "right" things done on time.

With a combined experience of over forty years in the administration and construction of public facilities, the authors realize that much of the following discussion is subjective and based on our experiences. However, we have attempted to develop the foundation of a good theory based on what we believe to be the "right" project management practices.

Project management within a bureaucracy is aimed at ensuring that the organization's resources are being used in ways consistent with its disparate goals and objectives. However, attempting to match an owner's organizational structure to an effective project management process regularly nets mixed results. Refinements in technology, coupled with the evolution of the construction, design, and legal professions, have spawned many variations of the traditional project management process and many new tools and methodologies. The authors believe that, of these, five project management practices have particular significance for the public sector, and we have chosen to refer to them as "right" management practices, or RMPs. The five are:

- construction contracting strategy,
- feedback mechanisms during design and construction,
- cost management,
- schedule management, and
- dispute avoidance and resolution mechanisms.

Our theory involves examining the five RMPs in light of three consequential variables (adapted from Gordon [2]).

1. *Project-Specific Variables* (including time constraints, uncertain and changing objectives, technical difficulty and complexity, and financial constraints);

2. *Owner-Specific Variables* (including construction sophistication, current capabilities and staffing limitations, risk aversion, restrictions on methods, geographical dispersion, size and number of projects being administered simultaneously, and other external factors such as bureaucratic restrictions and politics); and

3. *Market-Specific Variables* (including availability of appropriate contractors, availability of labor; material and equipment; current competitive state of the market; etc.).

We seek to address the question. Given a specific owner, project, and market conditions and a bureaucratic organizational structure, what is the most effective combination of RMP components? To find the answer, we will first discuss the characteristics of the functionally compartmentalized organization. Then, we will discuss the relevancy of the three consequential project variables. And finally, we will discuss the range of RMP components available to the project management organization.

The Owner's Project Management Organization

Most public-sector owner organizations are functionally compartmentalized and bureaucratic. The functionally compartmentalized organization (FCO) exists in many government entities, from medium-sized cities to huge state and federal bureaucracies, and in some large private entities as well.

The project management group within these organizations can vary in size from about 100 people to several thousand people.

To understand the functionally compartmentalized organizational structure, it is helpful to contrast it with two other basic organizational structures: the interdisciplinary (e.g., product-market-geographic area) structure and the matrix structure. At the opposite end of the continuum from the FCO is the purely interdisciplinary organization. It contains teams organized by some variable other than function (e.g., geographical location, type of work, or client). For instance, post offices and bakeries are organized by population areas. In the middle area of the continuum is the matrix organization. It typically contains interdisciplinary teams with members drawn from functional areas. Although there have been attempts in the public sector to organize in a manner other than functionally, the majority of large public sector organizations remain functionally compartmentalized.

The public-sector project management organization is segmented into functional areas for a variety of reasons. One obvious reason is that it maintains specialization. Specialization focuses the necessary knowledge, skills, professional training, work process, and career paths in an area and thereby seeks to improve competence and efficiency. In addition, compartmentalization is sometimes undertaken, especially in government organizations, in order to segregate the steps in the procurement process. It sets up a system of checks and balances (similar to the United States form of government). An important result of this structure is that it tends to minimize the chance of manipulating the process for financial gain. Third, the chain of command is explicit. Responsibility is readily understood and accountability is therefore easily traced. Common functional areas are described in Table 1.

In the FCO [functionally compartmentalized organization], the process of conceptualizing, funding, designing, constructing, and operating a project (or program) involves all parts of the organization at various times in a linear or relay-race fashion. Essentially, primary responsibility for the project is "handed off" during its lifetime from facilities planning to design to construction to operation and maintenance. Support is provided throughout the process from the financial management, legal, and contracting/procurement areas. A common variation on the pure FCO is to have the group that is responsible for coordinating the efforts of the rest of the organization throughout all or some portion of the project's lifetime.

In addition to the problems that are inherent in all projects (e.g., contract disagreements, technical errors, resource limits, changing owner requirements,

Table 1. Functional Areas in a Compartmentalized Organization

Functional Area	Functions Performed
Financial management	Budgeting, accounting, vendor/contractor payments
Facilities planning	Determine requirements, master planning
Design	Preparation of plans and specifications (or oversight thereof); technical expertise during construction
Construction	Construction contract administration, including inspection, interpretation of contract documents, progress assessment, approval of payments
Operation and Maintenance	Operation and maintenance of completed facilities warrantee enforcement
Legal	Legal review of contract awards, provisions, and interpretations, including changes and claims
Contracting/Procurement	Administrative/non-technical contract provisions contractor selection and award non-technical aspects of contract interpretations, including changes and claims

differing site conditions), the FCO tends to bring with it a set of challenges that flows from its very nature. In other words, the structure produces a specific set of behaviors. This set of behaviors results from an assumption of independence within functions. The focus of employees is on their own areas of expertise, with little understanding of how what they do impacts others. The functional areas within a FCO only realize their interdependence when there is a breakdown in the system. When something goes wrong, the assumption is that someone screwed up. Much effort is put into finding someone to blame. Little thought is given to the notion that perhaps the breakdown was the result of a systemic problem rather than a human problem [5].

The authors believe that the solution to improving project management in these organizations lies with getting the individuals within them to think in system-wide terms. Individuals and functional groups must see the consequences of their actions. The appropriate use of "right management practices" can foster system-wide, interdependent thinking within these types of organizations, and help them to adjust themselves from within according to the project at hand.

Information flow is crucial for effective project management. The interface problems associated with independent organizational parts often results in less-than-adequate information transfer. This should not be surprising when one considers the tremendous volume of knowledge that is associated with a major construction project. The problem is exacerbated, however, because the information is required for decision-making. Incorrect or suboptimal decisions may be made in the absence of the necessary information. Easy solutions become more difficult to discover. Also. when each part of the organization operates independently from the others and is only responsible for the project during a short time period, its members may tend to have a short-term outlook and to make decisions using only their own narrow areas of expertise, experience, and vested interests.

Problems also occur when the costs are incurred by one functional area and the benefits accrue to a different area. For instance, the operations and maintenance staff of a facility benefits by having on-site construction contractors perform routine maintenance functions during the course of construction (such as cleaning sludge lagoons while constructing new retention basins). This is often done by change order and results in the costs being charged against the construction budget rather than the operations budget. Some of these decisions are legitimate, and some are not.

To further aggravate the basic problem, performance incentive structures can cause a lack of accountability for "downstream" problems. Over time, turf battles occur and psychological barriers form between groups. Groups that are responsible for later phases of projects may feel that they bear a disproportionate share of the burden because that is when problems will manifest themselves if not mitigated earlier. Legal restrictions (such as laws requiring that all contracts be bid) and political or strategic considerations further intensify the problem.

Three Consequential Variables to be Managed

There are at least twenty separate variables that are considered to be consequential for effective project management; however, for ease of discussion each seems more or less to fit into one of Gordon's group of three "drivers": project, owner, and market [1].

Project-Specific Variables

Consequential project-specific variables include time constraints, uncertain and changing objectives, technical difficulty and complexity, and financial constraints.

A time constraint is typically manifested by less time being available than is reasonably required for the entire project process or a portion of the project. This may be due to an extended design phase, an uninterruptible operation, weather, bureaucratic deadlines, etc. Often, there is a need to address the trade-off between meeting the time constraint and other constraints, especially cost. Contract arrangements and cost and schedule management must be tailored to fit the circumstances.

Uncertain or changing objectives are particularly difficult to deal with because the phases of the design and construction process are so highly interdependent. Changing objectives impact time and cost explicitly as well as having less obvious effects (such as damage to morale). The further into the process one proceeds, the more effect changing objectives can have. The cost and time effects can be surprisingly far reaching (e.g., domino or ripple effect of one design change on multiple contractors' sequencing, suppliers' production times, labor and material availability, good weather periods, etc.), particularly in the construction phase.

Project complexity and technical difficulty beyond what is typically encountered tend to add stress to the owner's project management organization, thereby reducing its effectiveness. The increased use of experts, specialty consultants, and specialty contractors, coupled with a reduction in the pool of available talent to manage such projects, can cause problems. Owner-perceived risk increases. Project management ineffectiveness often results from inaccurately identifying and quantifying risk, and then misallocating it contractually.

Financial constraints can take the form of an extremely tight budget or an absolute maximum that may not be exceeded. This can be either for the project as a whole or for a portion of it. When managing a project with a financial constraint one must consider the full range of options for dealing with it. Time and scope control is critical to effectively managing this consequential variable.

Owner-Specific Variables

Consequential owner-specific variables include construction sophistication, current capabilities and staffing limitations, risk aversion, geographical dispersion, the size and number of projects being administered simultaneously, and other external factors such as bureaucratic restrictions and politics.

The capabilities of the owner's staff should be regularly and carefully assessed. This is especially true when recent project management difficulties have been experienced and on those occasions when project requirements are different from the routine. Although the owner may be able to take action to correct experience levels, knowledge deficiencies, and size of staff, this paper focuses on what actions the owner can take if staff limitations are a given.

A high degree of risk aversion is typical of public owners because public owners must be able to stand up to the scrutiny of the public and because of the inflexibility of the public budgeting process. This manifests itself through the choice of contracting strategy, which often disproportionately allocates risks among the contracting parties. If a risk is borne by a party that has no control over it and limited capacity to absorb it, the possible effects include high contingency costs, overly conservative design and construction methods, and an overly defensive posture [4]. A common example of this is the owner's insistence on a fixed-price contract for work, which is ill defined or subject to a large cost variability from unknown site conditions.

A large number of projects and/or geographically dispersed projects will tend to exacerbate communication problems between parts of the organization. It also magnifies the difficulty of project management for the program as a whole, including contract issues, cost, and schedule (not to mention the technical aspects of project management).

External factors such as legal restrictions and political/strategic considerations may limit the owner's choice of project management methods. In fact, they commonly prevent the manager from doing what this paper recommends: designing the means of executing a particular project based on the project's characteristics. The most obvious "external factors" for public owners are procurement rules (especially at the federal level) and political needs (especially at the local level). The project manager may need to advise the decision-maker on the potential benefits of relaxing a restriction in order to implement a particular right management practice.

Market-Specific Variables

Consequential market-specific variables include availability of appropriate contractors; availability of labor, material, and equipment; and current competitive state of the market.

Market conditions can have significant effects on project cost, timeliness, and quality. They can even affect a project manager's ability to execute a project as conceived by the owner. These are probably the variables that an owner has the least control over. Nonetheless, owners should seek ways to know of their existence and take mitigating actions whenever and wherever possible, even if it is only to budget additional funds.

Availability of appropriate contractors can be a problem in remote locations or when highly specialized work is required. This can have immediate and obvious impacts on quality, followed eventually by time and cost impacts.

Labor, material, and equipment availability will also affect cost and time and, in the extreme, could make a project unbuildable if design and contracting strategy are not adjusted appropriately. Similarly, the current competitive state of the market, in accordance with the law of supply and demand, will have a direct effect on prices and possibly on quality of expertise.

Conclusion

Our intuition is that when applied incorrectly in a functionally compartmentalized organization, current project management techniques do not effectively deal with the non-standard dimensions of the consequential project-, owner-, and market-specific variables described above. In the remainder of the paper, various ways of dealing with these variables will be explored.

"Right" Management Practices (RMP)

The authors have chosen to focus on five "right" management practices (RMPs) for dealing with project and contract management problems that arise when a FCO [functionally compartmentalized organization] encounters particular aspects and combinations of the consequential variables. They are:
- construction contracting strategy,
- feedback mechanisms during design and construction,
- cost management,
- schedule management, and
- dispute avoidance and resolution mechanisms.

Based on the authors' experiences, these RMPs are the current project management techniques that address the most enduring project management problems encountered on public projects today. The implementation of these RMPs is interdependent and order sensitive; the approach taken on one can have an effect on how the others should be treated. This is particularly true of the selection of contracting strategy, which will generally lead to a certain set of options with regard to the other RMPs. Some attempt will be made here to address this interdependence, but the project manager should consider it on a project-by-project basis and ensure that each RMP is compatible with the others. The authors assume that the reader is generally familiar with these RMPs and therefore will discuss them only briefly.

Construction Contracting Strategy

A properly matched contracting strategy increases project management's ability to effectively deal with the consequential variables. It is important to discuss the construction contracting strategy RMP [right management practice] first because it provides the foundation for the other RMPs. The construction contracting strategy RMP encompasses the type of contract, the method of selecting the contractor(s), and the means of determining and structuring contract price.
- There are six prevalent construction contracting strategies (each with variations) for public-sector construction, which are:
  - general contractor,
  - construction manager,
  - multiple primes,
  - design-build,
  - turnkey, and
  - build-operate transfer [6].
- Contract award methods range from lump-sum competitive bidding at one extreme to single-source negotiation at the other extreme, with variations between.
- There are two main groups of contracts: fixed price (such as lump-sum, unit prices, or a cap) and cost-reimbursable (such as cost-plus-percentage

or cost-plus-fixed-fee). A common hybrid is the guaranteed maximum price (GMP), in which the contractor is reimbursed only up to a predetermined point and is liable for any costs beyond.
- It is generally known that public owners find it very difficult (for funding and political reasons) to accept financial uncertainty and, therefore, prefer firm fixed-price contracts with restrictive provisions for price adjustments in which the contractor bears essentially all risks.
- Risk is often shifted within the major parties to construction contracts until it lands on someone willing to take the risk [7]. Proper allocation of risk should consider both a party's ability to absorb risk and its ability and incentive to manage risk, as well as the particular characteristics of the project contemplated. Often, public sector construction does an inadequate job in this regard. For instance, subway construction costs have rapidly escalated, largely as a result of the misallocation of risk through the use of inappropriate contracting strategies [3].
- The traditional approach involves a separate designer, a general contractor (responsible for construction only), and a fixed lump-sum contract arrived at by competitive bidding. This is the strategy preferred by the public sector, for it gives the public-sector owner control over the design, a fiduciary relationship with the designer to monitor the contractor, a single source of construction responsibility, a known total price before construction starts, price competition, and impartial selection [2]. It works quite well when the project objectives are clearly defined and unchanging, when the design is accurately and completely portrayed in the plans and specifications, and when the project has no tight time constraints.

Summary

When choosing a contracting strategy for a public-sector project, the owner should evaluate its own organization's abilities, the characteristics of the proposed project, and the components of the various contracting methods. The functional areas of the organization are more familiar with their roles and responsibilities under the traditional approach. A mistake made in the choice of a contracting strategy can be very expensive to correct if discovered after contracts are awarded.

Feedback Mechanisms

The term "feedback mechanisms" is used here to refer to practices that cause separate parts of the FCO [functionally compartmentalized organization] to assist, communicate with, and understand one another. This can help address both the "hand-off" and "limited perspective" problems described above as common to FCOs. Feedback mechanisms are critically important for assisting individuals to improve their ability to think system-wide and interdependently.

An organized feedback control system should operate throughout the life of a project from concept through design and construction to commissioning. It should measure, process, analyze, and report the most important information required for timely decision-making. The goal is to improve the quality of the information available for decision-making by minimizing the gathering and reporting time and maximizing the opportunity to examine options and alternatives. Documenting the reasonableness of decision-making is important in bureaucracies.

There is an abundance of project management software in the marketplace today, and there is no reason why progress or project status should not be measured in a timely fashion. For instance, elapsed time can be compared to estimated activity and project duration; money committed or expended can be compared to the estimate budget; resource use can be compared to the expected requirements for labor, material, and equipment; and earned value can be calculated by measuring the amount of work performed in terms of the budget established for that work.

The authors have categorized feedback mechanisms into three main categories, which are:
- feedback during the design process,
- feedback during the construction process, and
- feedback after construction is complete.

Feedback during the Design Process

The owner provides routine design process feedback by designating an individual project manager (or cross-functional project management "core" team) to interface with the designer at regular intervals and to evaluate the design alternatives as they are generated. It is this individual's (or team's) responsibility to involve the various functional elements of the organization on an as-needed basis.

When the design has evolved enough, an operability review may be performed. An operability review focuses on the ease with which a facility can be operated and maintained.

Design feedback is most often provided by value engineering (VE) studies. At pre-selected intervals, a team of specialists conducts a five-step workshop that develops a cost model for each item of the project, determines the function of each item, brainstorms new and creative ideas, evaluates and ranks the ideas generated, and recommends the best improvements for the project in a formal written report based on cost, time, or other utilization improvement standards.

Construction feedback during design is typically provided by way of constructability and "bidability" reviews. A constructability review focuses on how easily the project can be constructed. It examines such design concepts as: compatibility with the site, suitability of systems, materials selected, equipment availability, methods and techniques required for installation of materials and equipment, scheduling constraints, and field conditions. A bidability review focuses on how well a set of contract documents provides contractors with the information required to develop accurate estimates and to make bona fide bids. It examines the sufficiency and accuracy of the details described on the drawings and the language provided in the specifications. The purpose of bidability reviews is to identify and correct significant design errors, omissions, ambiguities, and inconsistencies. The principal issue is the completeness of the contract documents as compared to the suitability of design concepts.

A construction specialist may be involved early in the design process to evaluate the consequential market-specific variables. Opportunities may exist to positively influence the design by providing information on availability of appropriate contractors, labor, materials, and equipment availability, and current competitive state of the market.

Feedback during the Construction Process

If management is to have a clear vision of what lies ahead during the construction of a project, it should be able to anticipate problems before they arise. This requires forecasting and trending. Typically, a CPM [critical path method] schedule that is resource loaded (e.g., cost, labor, etc.) provides the vehicle for determining what effect a change in one operation will have on the project as a whole. Variances can be reported for deviations from planned or budgeted expenditures. Management-by-exception reports those variations that exceed certain predefined limits, focusing attention on those activities or operations most in need of control.

Regular involvement of designers, operators, and other stakeholders should occur during the construction phase to share relevant information, minimize misunderstandings, and maximize the opportunity to make good decisions. This can be accomplished through regular, structured contact with the project (such as regular attendance at site meetings, review of key submittals, distribution of key correspondence, daily use of E-mail, and so on).

Feedback after Construction Is Complete

After construction is complete, it is often useful to assess what went right or wrong and what lessons can be applied to future projects. This is especially true if the owner:

- expects more projects with the same or similar project variable,
- wants to explore options for dealing with the owner variables, or
- expects problematic market-specific variables to persist during other projects.

The "postmortem" should address which variables were present and which RMPs [right management practices] were or should have been employed. A team approach provides a good opportunity for the various parts of the FCO [functionally compartmentalized organization] to interface with each other. Design, construction, and procurement staff can each evaluate how their actions contributed to the end result and discover what each other's motivations were for the approach taken.

Summary

In the FCO, the best available information is often distributed among different parts of the organization. Feedback mechanisms provide a means for sharing specific knowledge among segmented groups, especially current knowledge of dynamic variables. Sometimes this knowledge takes the form of insight based on a different perspective or a more detached point of view. Optimum decisions require the best available information. For systemic reasons, FCOs have not been very good at acquiring the best available information.

Cost Management
- Cost management typically means cost control. The general purpose of a cost control program is to create an uncomplicated method of estimating, recording, and controlling costs.
- An important objective of cost management in an FCO [functionally compartmentalized organization] is to ensure that all alternatives have been explored before a project overrun is accepted. This is typically done by preparing a realistic budget in sufficient detail, regularly monitoring expenditures against that budget, and constantly evaluating the amount of work remaining.
- One of the basic tenets of effective cost management is realistically establishing and living within the project budget. The project budget is the amount of money an owner is willing to spend for a project. Many FCOs have difficulty preparing realistic budgets early in the capital appropriations process because it is seen as the responsibility of senior management, those most often removed from the crucial details. Early, formal involvement of all stakeholders, areas of specialization, and so on can help owners get a more accurate sense of project costs.
- Unfortunately, public-sector project managers are sometimes forced to carry unrealistically low contingencies in their budgets, either because higher contingencies are difficult to "sell" or to avoid committing funds to uncertain requirements. This can cause problems on large rehabilitation projects and on projects with long-time horizons.
- FCOs [functionally compartmentalized organizations] use established codes of accounts to serve the budgeting process as a sort of checklist so that each work effort and purchased item can be quantified and accounted for. It also provides the basis for routinely (e.g., monthly) updating all cost information. This is an important component for effective cost management. The project cost engineer must update the project budget. The project accountant must update the list of actual invoices received and the current manpower costs. The project purchasing agent must update project invoice predictions.
- Designers have a responsibility to provide a design that is within the owner's budget. Our experience suggests that this is easier said than done. The problem appears to lie with the objective of providing the "best" design. What is "best" is not always what is affordable. Designers, contractors, and owners alike must develop processes that allow decisions to be

made that depart from "best" designs due to budget considerations without feeling shortchanged.
- *Scope management is a vital part of cost management.* At each phase of the project, the manager should assess the certainty of defined project requirements and include an appropriate contingency to cover potential scope growth. This assessment should take into account the history of the owner regarding scope changes for similar projects. As the design evolves, the budget must be monitored and checked.
- When the project is in the construction phase, the pricing of changes is frequently a source of disagreement. Standardized form-type contract documents can be unnecessarily vague regarding the most common sources of disagreement: how labor productivity is determined, how construction equipment is priced, and what supplemental costs should be included in the fee. To reduce disagreements, reasonable pricing guidelines should be included in the contract documents.

Summary

All owners are cost sensitive to some degree, but some projects can benefit from extra attention to cost management. If the project, owner, and/or market exhibit characteristics that could have a substantial effect on cost, some combination of the precautions described above are required to effectively manage cost.

Schedule Management

- Schedules are used for planning the sequence and duration of the work, coordinating the actions of multiple participants, and monitoring progress. Other purposes may include tracking compliance with legal requirements, managing resources, assigning responsibility, planning and monitoring progress toward higher level objectives, and communicating with far-flung project stakeholders.
- FCOs [functionally compartmentalized organizations] typically fall into one of two camps regarding schedule management: hands-off or proactive involvement. A proactive owner involvement gives rise to a greater understanding of the contractor's plan, allows owner feedback to the contractor, and can help communicate a common understanding of project goals and responsibilities. In the event of a claim, it can contribute to a more rational basis for settlement.
- The decisions to be made in implementing a schedule management program revolve around what types of schedules and reports are needed, schedule content, who will prepare them and when they will be prepared, and how the owner will assign responsibilities to achieve the desired outcome. Matters to be decided regarding types of schedules and reports include multi-level schedules (e.g., program and project), *cost-loading*, the need for probabilistic activity durations and conditional paths, and critical path method (CPM) versus simple bar chart. Content decisions include

level of detail, intermediate (perhaps contractual) milestones, and treatment of float and contingency time. Schedules may be prepared by one of more of the following: planners, designers, contractors, scheduling consultants, or owner staff. Schedule-related roles should be carefully considered and defined in advance, considering the abilities, perspectives, and contractual arrangements of the parties. Reasonably detailed and prescriptive scheduling specifications help set the level of expectations in this regard.
- Evaluating construction scheduling requirements before bidding can increase project management effectiveness by reducing the probability of costly claims and changes with time-related components. These pre-bid evaluations focus on such issues as:
  - recommendations for contract time and level of liquidated damages (if applicable),
  - milestones for contract specific dates (such as notice to proceed),
  - recommended or required sequence of work constraints,
  - reasonable durations for owner and designer activities during construction (such as submittal review time),
  - requirements for contractor schedule submissions that correspond to the contract documents (such as monthly pay applications), and
  - long-lead procurement issues.
- In the general conditions of most standard contract documents, it is explicit that the designer is responsible for the administration of contract time, which involves reviewing contractor-submitted schedules. Many FCO [functionally compartmentalized organizations] owners prefer to provide schedule oversight themselves, removing designers from the process.
- For the most part, progress-monitoring activities are performed on critical path method (CPM) schedules. As a management tool, this is a vast improvement over the Gantt bar charts used previously. The good news is that, without a doubt, CPM has become the *preferred method for managing construction* schedules. The bad news is that CPM has become the favored tool of the construction litigation attorneys. There is a competing tension that results from this situation in which the CPM on the one hand is touted as a key management tool and on the other decried as a legal sword. In our opinion, administrators on public sector construction contracts would do well to understand what the implications of this dual character are.
- There is an intrinsic interdependence between the project cost and the project schedule, which should be made use of, if possible. *Cost- and resource-loaded CPM schedules* can provide important planning, monitoring, and cost containment advantages. They allow accurate assessment of the value of progress payments and cash flow projections to be forecast accurately. Additionally, they can facilitate the accumulation of accurate data for change-order negotiations, by measuring the actual expenditure of resources to accomplish specific activities.

Summary
Proactive schedule management requires that the owner recognize its primary role in project management. The careful delineation of responsibilities and consideration of the key aspects of the scheduling needs will result in benefits far outweighing the cost involved.

Dispute Avoidance and Resolution Mechanisms
The Construction Industry Institute has observed that the construction industry in the United States is "ill" and that litigation related to design and construction continues to increase. Industry observers lament the "awful litigious nature of the construction industry," blaming the situation of the "adversarial dance" between the parties at the construction site, which creates "a constant state of confrontation." The Center for Public Resources had observed that, "It is ironic that the one industry in the country which more than all others depends upon coordination, cooperation, and teamwork among multiple participants should be the country's most adversarial industry" [2].

- Resolving disputes on construction projects involves two axioms: (1) avoid unnecessarily adversarial situations; and (2) minimize the effects of the most common minor and moderate confrontational situations by providing appropriate mechanisms on a project to resolve disputes. Many FCOs [functionally compartmentalized organizations] accomplish this unilaterally by integrating conflict resolution mechanisms into the contract documents. Others may use voluntary partnering or team building to develop conflict resolution mechanisms on their projects in order to keep disputes on a professional level and not allow the participants to feel personally offended if conflicts escalate to higher authorities.
- In construction disputes, it is desirable to have the disputes resolved at the most efficient and appropriate organizational level. This level is determined by matching the people from the disputant groups that are most knowledgeable of the elements of the dispute and have the ability to commit resources to a settlement. This is difficult in an FCO because often the people who are most knowledgeable either lack the authority to enter into a binding agreement or have developed an adversarial attitude toward their counterpart that cannot easily be overcome. When disputes cannot be resolved at any given level of the project, it is important to recognize that negotiations do not have to cease or deadlock. An effective dispute resolution program should include a provision that does not allow disputes to become deadlocked or be left unresolved. Many FCOs have formal dispute resolution procedures already in place (e.g., United State Naval Facilities Engineering Command, United States Army Corps of Engineers).
- For purposes of this discussion, the dispute avoidance and resolution RMP [right management practice] includes a selected group of alternate dispute resolution (ADR) actions to be taken during contract performance, as follows:

1. *Explicitly Defined Risk Allocation*—This is generally done in the preparation of the contract documents and was discussed above. It requires an assessment of the risks present and assigning those risks to the party, which is best able to manage and bear them.

2. *Incentives/Disincentives*—These also are built into the contract documents. Performance incentives can be time, cost, or quality related. Although they can be very powerful tools, public bureaucracies commonly shy away from them unless a significant economic benefit to the public can be demonstrated.

3. *Partnering*—This is a voluntary approach to resolving disputes that is grounded in a facilitated team-building workshop and signed charter of specific behaviors between the parties which is established at the start of the contract. It can be helpful in preventing deterioration of relationships when conflict arises during project execution. Procedures for unassisted, internal negotiations are typically developed.

4. *Advisory Opinions and Neutral Experts*—These mechanisms involve external negotiation assistance. The parties bring in outside experts to analyze and provide opinions on reasonable resolution options. The intent is to reduce the emotional involvement of the analysis. These mechanisms are typically informal and non-binding.

5. *Mediation*—This is a more formal procedure wherein a neutral third party hears the arguments of both sides, may render an opinion as to the strengths and weaknesses of each side's arguments, and attempts to facilitate an amicable resolution.

6. *Dispute Review Boards*—The board generally consists of three people, one selected by each of the parties and the third agreed on by both parties. Formality and expense are higher than in mediation. After hearing each side's arguments, the board renders an opinion. No attempt is made to mediate the dispute to a resolution. Although not binding, it is expected that the credibility of the process and the psychological capital invested in it, will be adequate to produce a settlement of major issues.

7. *Arbitration*—This is a formal procedure wherein a third party hears the arguments of both sides and renders an opinion. There is no attempt made to resolve the dispute among the parties by facilitating negotiations. Arbitration is often binding on the parties. The first three of these methods tend to be preventative in nature. The last four are resolution mechanisms that lie on a continuum from maximum participant control and least cost (internal, unassisted negotiation) to minimum control and maximum cost (arbitration).

Summary

Because many FCOs [functionally compartmentalized organizations] are in the public sector, there is a tendency to adapt the judicial model to resolve disputes, which involves two adversaries making persuasive arguments to a knowledgeable arbiter. This model can be unnecessarily adversarial, especially if the dispute concerns a complex engineering issue. The intent of most ADR [alternate dispute resolution] methods is to resolve disputes in forums where more qualified participants can address the technical portions of the dispute, yet still negotiate mutually acceptable outcomes. Advisory opinions, neutral experts, mediation, review boards, and arbitration assist the disputants by providing them with the professional opinion and/or recommendation of knowledgeable construction professionals about the strengths and weaknesses of their case. However, if a particular dispute involves a complex legal issue, it should be litigated in court where the attorneys are the most qualified to deal with it.

Often speed of resolution is critical in situations where huge daily costs can be incurred while waiting for resolution. ADR can help resolve many technical disputes in a more timely fashion than litigation. It should be noted, however, that there are instances in which the owner's best interests are not served by a speedy dispute resolution process. In these cases, the checks and balances in the bureaucratic organization can slow the process to ensure that no resolution options are overlooked.

Public-sector FCOs [functionally compartmentalized organizations] have a duty to resolve disputes as economically as possible. Many believe that ADR [alternate dispute resolution] is more economical than litigation. However, it should not be overlooked that many FCOs have entire legal departments on the payroll. It can be tempting to rationalize that these "owner attorneys" can be used to fight with contractors at no cost. This is an unreasonable use of bureaucratic power if the intentions are vindictive and can be counterproductive to effective project management in the long run.

Assess the Situation and Select the Appropriate RMPs

In this section, various possible alternatives for dealing with the consequential variables will be presented. In reality, many of these variables can be present on one project. In order to develop an appropriate strategy for dealing with them, they must be prioritized or weighted against one another. Two variables may lead to the use of conflicting RMPs [right management practices], in which case the predominant variable will govern or a combination of RMPs should be used.

RMPs for Project-Specific Variables

If a time constraint is a governing variable, the traditional design-bid-build approach may not be the appropriate contracting strategy. Some version of "fast track" construction can be more appropriate. This typically involves packaging portions of the project for construction before the design is complete. Fast-tracking can cause problems if there is a financial constraint also involved because contractual commitments are made before the entire contract cost is known with any degree of certainty.

Consider the problem of an emergency repair. Project management effectiveness is reduced under the time constraints of an emergency repair, unless other constraints can be relaxed. In the public sector, an emergency repair project and a planned capital improvement project are at opposite ends of the price-certainty spectrum. Outsourcing emergency work under a predetermined agreement containing certain specific cost and schedule management guidelines can be an effective contracting strategy.

When a time constraint is coupled with staffing limitations, the design-build contracting strategy may be appropriate. The design-build approach can reduce the overall design-procure-construct duration because it allows for a closer coordination between design and construction and reduces the potential for conflicts between the designer and contractor. It is usually ineffective to use the design-build approach if the project is unique, complex, or involves uncertain and changing objectives. It appears to work best for "cookie-cutter," repeat-type projects (for instance, college dormitories, modular prisons, etc.).

FCOs [functionally compartmentalized organizations] appear to struggle with the design-build concept because of the tendency for FCO project managers to administer the projects as if they were using the traditional approach (with which they are more comfortable). It is difficult for the proactive FCO to maintain the hands-off approach required of design-build. Also, restrictive competitive procurement procedures can make the evaluation of design-build proposals difficult.

Enhanced schedule management becomes more valuable as project-specific and owner-specific variables become more critical. Design alternatives, real estate acquisition, permits, environmental documentation requirements, financing, and bid and award activities all have the potential to affect the project time. The authors believe that most FCOs can benefit from a proactive schedule management approach that attempts to manage the schedule to capture all the activities of the involved parties, not just the construction activities. Schedule enhancements include greater level of detail, more frequent updates, involvement by a wider range of team members, and the use of a scheduling expert.

For most large projects (say over United States $25 million) procured using the traditional approach, the authors believe that the benefits resulting from preparing and maintaining a cost-loaded schedule far outweigh the costs. Essentially, loading cost to schedule activities can be accommodated easily by most scheduling software available today, and provisions for cost loading can easily be included in the scheduling specification. It should be noted, however, that accurately allocating indirect costs and making adjustments to scope or adaptations of the schedule logic can be difficult. The effort involved to develop and maintain a cost-loaded schedule may not be prudent for small projects; straightforward linear-type projects (e.g., pipelines); or projects that will likely undergo significant changes during construction (e.g., rehabilitation projects).

Because FCOs [functionally compartmentalized organizations] must constantly be aware of documenting the reasonableness of the decisions they make, the necessity for feedback mechanisms is ever present. Time and financial constraints increase the need for enhanced feedback during the design phase. Contractors and VE [value engineering] teams are valuable sources of ideas to shorten time or reduce costs. Constructability, bidability, and operability reviews all tend to render the ultimate design more defensible. Concentrated initial planning effort by the project team and expanded geo-technical investigation can reduce the likelihood of later cost increases. The owner should also be involved to evaluate options and tradeoffs among time, cost, and other variables, which are identified during the design process. Sometimes, feedback mechanisms are eliminated in a misguided attempt to reduce costs. However, the payback during construction may well exceed the cost.

FCOs are typically weak when it comes to forecasting cash flow. Many rely too heavily on historical data for budgeting future projects. The cost and schedule RMPs [right management practices] are extremely useful here. Program schedules can be used to perform "what-if" analyses. Cash flow projections can be evaluated as various combinations of projects are time-shifted forward and backward.

Typically, an FCO [functionally compartmentalized organization] in the public sector does not have a problem defining why a specific project is being built. However, politics can change project objectives. FCOs are not particularly adept at handling these changes. Owner-requested changes during the construction phase are procured at a premium. Contractors have little incentive to minimize the cost of changes because public owners cannot generally prevent contractors from obtaining repeat business. Innovative contract language inserted into traditional lump-sum agreements can reduce the financial and schedule impacts of owner-requested changes. This involves including conditions for provisionary allowances that permit the owner to make changes up to a certain specified limit within the contract cost and/or time.

When project objectives are uncertain and evolving, and there is a time constraint present, an FCO may choose to split the procurement up so that the scope-certain portions are procured first while the uncertain scope portions are finalized. For example, a building shell could be built while the equipment or finishes are being designed and procured separately. If the general nature of potential changes is known, the contract bid structure could include unit prices for categories of work. The FCO should be very closely involved in the design process in order to continuously inject the latest thinking. An FCO with staffing limitations, financial constraints, and high accountability requirements will likely have difficulty with this approach.

Change-order pricing language assumes even more importance than usual under conditions of uncertainty. It should prescribe clear rules for pricing of labor, equipment, and overhead expenses. The language addressing treatment of delay issues should prescribe clear rules for determination of time extensions, such as through the use of CPM [critical path method] schedules, and for float sharing.

One of the problems caused by a project with time constraints, changing objectives, and a high level of technical difficulty is the adversarial relationship that often forms between the owner or owner's representative and the contractor because of differing perceptions of what constitutes a change and how it should be priced. While the owner may view contract time as an absolute, the contractor typically views it as a trade-off with cost. Cost reimbursable contracts can be a valuable tool for dealing with these pricing disagreements because they change the polar positions that owner and contractor occupy with regard to a fixed-price contract change order, particularly if the contractor is given a dollar incentive to minimize cost. However, cost-reimbursable contracts require significant owner staffing and expertise because of the high level of owner involvement in managing the project. Unit prices, alternates, and allowances can be helpful in managing uncertainty in scope.

An unusual degree of technical difficulty and dynamic complexity can lead to problems at the hand-off between designer and contractor. The antidote is feedback during design and construction. Contractor input and independent VE [value engineering] perspectives are particularly valuable as a "reality check" to the designer who is designing a technically complex project. A design-build contracting strategy may be appropriate if quality issues can be predetermined.

Dispute avoidance and resolution are so central to the practice of project management that it is difficult to find a project variable that does not have an impact on how this RMP [right management project] should be implemented. The project-specific variables are particularly important in this regard. In general, the more constrained the project is in terms of time, technical difficulty and complexity, and changing objectives and finances, the more likely disputes are, and the more beneficial these RMPs tend to be. For example, time and financial constraints might best be managed by heavy emphasis on preventive measures; the impact of uncertain scope could be ameliorated by a partnering agreement; and high degree of technical difficulty might require the use of a standing neutral expert from the beginning.

RMPs for Owner-Specific Variables

An owner with limited staffing, construction sophistication, or other capability shortfalls may be able to augment staff by contracting out some in-house functions, such as contract procurement, schedule management, and cost management. Professional construction management (CM for fee) is a variation on this theme wherein the owner hires a professional organization to act as the owner's representative, performing functions such as developing schedules, monitoring cost, negotiating changes, reviewing pay requests, coordinating multiple contracts, and responding to RFIs. CM for fee has had some success in the institutional construction market but had little success in the engineered construction market.

All outsourcing actions bring with them some risk; competitive procurement restrictions must be met, contracts must be clearly written, accountability expectations clearly identified, and qualifications must be carefully understood (especially regarding issues such as technical competence, a track record of trustworthy performance, and compatibility with existing FCO [functionally compartmentalized organization] staff). Our experience is that FCOs tend to outsource unusual, highly technical, or particularly risky projects and generally adopt a somewhat hands-off approach. However, if the FCO has a proprietary process involved or has the requisite staffing capabilities, it will likely adopt a very proactive and involved approach.

Risk aversion can take many forms. Consider the financial constraint variable. An owner may need a firm price early in the design phase or after design is complete or may be more interested in having an absolute assurance of quality. Clearly, the need for a firm price early on is not compatible with uncertain or changing objectives. A concerted cost-management effort will help control cost by spending the time and resources necessary to set up and monitor compliance with a detailed budget. VE [value engineering] studies, and constructability and bidability reviews at appropriate intervals, can help the uncertain project. Partnering may be useful for developing a quick-response procedure for handling problems so that they can be resolved before unacceptable costs accrue.

A large number of projects and/or geographical dispersion creates a unique set of challenges, particularly if owner staffing is not commensurate with the workload. From a contracting strategy standpoint, combining multiple projects into one contract is a possibility. One of the overriding difficulties relates to lack of communication among numerous contractors, designers, and owner staff who are geographically remote from one another. Perhaps the best RMP [right management practice] for an FCO [functionally compartmentalized organization] in this situation is a well-thought-out schedule-management program that can be used as an effective communication tool and responsibility matrix. Enhanced feedback mechanisms will also be valuable. A hierarchy of dispute resolution methods will help avoid stalemates at the job site level, which might be disastrous if left to fester.

External factors such as legal restrictions and political or strategic considerations are especially troublesome because they are often beyond the control of the owner or project manager. Some examples and possible responses to them are as follows.

- *Contracting Rules*—Prescriptive general conditions and proactive schedule management can help communicate the steps and time required to comply. Schedules should be tailored to provide the management information necessary to control the project.
- *Complex Environmental or Safety Rules*—Outsourcing to acquire technical expertise may be required. Design-build or build-operate-turnover may be appropriately contracting strategies for obtaining the needed expertise, if available in the market.

- *Political Pressure*—Lump-sum, competitively bid contracts may be used for openness in the award process, if there is that type of pressure. Proactive public relations programs should be considered for particularly high-profile projects. Accountability and decision-making should be supported by an organized document control program.
- *Strategic Desire to Develop a Particular Segment of the Construction Market*—Packaging work into smaller pieces or limiting bidders to local market; pre-qualification of bidders may be an alternative. The owner should be very closely involved in the design process in order to continuously supply the latest externally generated information to the design process. Projects with a high susceptibility to external influence justify an increased emphasis on dispute resolution mechanisms.

RMPs for Market-Specific Variables

FCOs [functionally compartmentalized organizations] in the public sector are particularly sensitive to market conditions, but have not been particularly effective at anticipating market problems. Construction market inadequacies, which in the United States are usually caused by sudden or short-term increases in demand for construction, require feedback mechanisms during the design phase. Contractor knowledge of market variables and strategies for responding to them should be obtained by using VE [value engineering] and constructability reviews.

If availability of appropriate contractors is a problem, contract packaging can be adjusted to segregate the work for which appropriate contractors are not available. Generally, FCOs prefer to package work in the largest possible pieces; however, the selective use of smaller work packages and contracts can help to overcome some availability problems. Another alternative is to assist the contractor in areas not familiar to it through hands-on technical assistance from the designer or owner or supplier technical representatives. Either of these approaches requires more involvement from the FCO staff.

The current competitive state of the market will affect prices positively or negatively, in accordance with the law of supply and demand. Unless the FCO's [functionally compartmentalized organization's] capital improvement program is large enough to affect the local market, there are limited courses of action. Additionally, limited labor, material, and equipment availability can cause significant time and cost impacts. Escalation and inflation are difficult to predict. FCOs should consider using outside experts for help in these areas.

Public-sector project management organizations tend to be functionally compartmentalized, with conservative, slow-response time, and bureaucratic cultures, for good reasons. Accountability to constituents, a clear chain of command, and a system of checks and balances often determine policies and procedures in the public sector.

It seems as if every three years, some project management consultant would have the FCO [functionally compartmentalized organization] reorganize to take better advantage of the current project management techniques available. The authors believe, on the other hand, that the FCO is here to stay and that the key to improving the effectiveness of project management in a FCO lies with helping the individuals within these organizations think more interdependently and system-wide. There are five right management practices that can assist in this endeavor. By adapting these project management techniques to fit a particular situation, as determined by an assessment of certain consequential variables, project management effectiveness can be improved.

The authors realize that this paper touches on only a few of the combinations and interdependencies that could be discussed regarding effective project management in bureaucracies, but it is our hope that this discussion will cause individuals to experiment themselves before embarking on a reorganization path. The authors intend to explore further the effectiveness of particular combinations of contracting strategies and feedback mechanisms.

References

1. Gordon, Christopher M. *Choosing Appropriate Construction Contracting Method.* **ASCE Journal of Construction Engineering** 120, no. 1 (March 1994): 196–210.

2. Keranen, Thomas M. *ADR in the Construction Industry: An Overview.* **The ADR Newsletter** 2, no. 3 Lansing, MI: State Bar of Michigan, Fall 1995.

3. Levitt, Raymond E., David B. Ashley, and Robert D. Logcher. *Allocating Risk and Incentive in Construction.* **ASCE Journal of the Construction Division** 106, no. C03 (September 1980): 297–305.

4. Naoum, Shamil G. *Critical Analysis of Time and Cost of Management and Traditional Contracts.* **Journal of Construction Engineering and Management** 120, no., 4 (December 1994): 687–705.

5. Senge, Peter M. **The Fifth Discipline**. New York: Bantam Doubleday Dell, 1994.

6. Sink, D. Scott. **Productivity Management: Planning, Measurement and Evaluation, Control and Improvement.** New York: John Wiley & Sons, 1985.

7. Stephenson, Ralph J. **Project Partnering for the Design and Construction Industry.** New York: John Wiley & Sons, 1996

Article reprinted with permission from 1996 AACE Transactions.

Appendix C: Project Manager's Book List

    Construction Contracting: Wiley, 1994
* *Project Management*: Wiley, 1996
* *CPM in Construction Management*: McGraw-Hill, 1993
* *The Implementation of Project Management*: PMI, 1981
    Project Management with CPM & PERT: McGraw-Hill
    Project Management Techniques: McGraw-Hill, 1983
    Essentials of Project Management: Petrocelli, 1991
    Contractor's Management Handbook: McGraw-Hill, 1991
    Managing Construction Contracts: Wiley, 1992
* *Construction Project Administration*: Wiley, 1988
    Construction Law in Contractors' Language: McGraw-Hill, 1990
    Construction Business Handbook: McGraw-Hill, 1985
* *The McGraw-Hill Professional Construction Management*: McGraw-Hill, 1992
    Project Management for Executives: Van Nostrand, 1981
    Project Management for the Design Professional: Whitney Library of Design, 1991
    Engineering & Construction Project Management: Gulf Publishing, 1986
    Managing Construction Projects: I10 Publications, 1995
* *Total Quality Through Project Management*: McGraw-Hill, 1994

* Available through PMI SourceGuide

Appendix D: PMI and Design-Procurement-Construction Specific Interest Group (SIG)

DPC SIG Action Teams

There has been a revolution in the business of organizing and managing design procurement construction (DPC) in the last few years. Our diverse and dispersed SIG action teams are working on projects right now to:
- Support member initiatives
- Research and solve industry wide problems
- Develop corporate support
- Support corporate sponsors
- Explore and perfect new methods of working
- Develop and test new communications paradigms
- Provide technical training and support for members.

DPC SIG Purpose

Provide a forum for education and professional development for members involved in the development, design, engineering, procurement, and construction processes for projects involving buildings and facilities to advance the field of project management while furthering the objectives of PMI.

DPC SIG Mission

Provide participants with the highest quality information, education, training, skills, and opportunities to successfully identify, plan, manage, and participate in design, procurement, and construction for projects involving buildings and facilities in the residential, commercial, and industrial sectors of the worldwide economy.

Project Management Institute

PMI is an international organization with over 30,000 members. It was formed in 1969 as a group of concerned managers who desired to improve the quality of management of project work. PMI members come from all industries. PMI offers membership in local chapters and specific interest groups (SIGs). Chapters offer members the ability to network with project management professionals from a variety of different industries on a regular basis in geographically determined areas. While local chapters provide the opportunity to network with peers in your community, SIGs give you access to project management professionals with special areas of interest.

SIGs enable members to share experiences with others managing similar types of projects and facing the same project management concerns that you face. These unique groups participate in a wide range of activities, publish newsletters, and contribute to the development of educational workshops and presentations for the Project Management Institute's prestigious Annual Seminars & Symposium.

DPC SIG Objectives

- Demonstrate and promote project management principles as the most effective means for planning and managing projects
- Establish a worldwide network of project management professionals in our industry
- Provide a forum for the free exchange of project management ideas, solutions, experiences, and applications
- Develop and disseminate consistent and appropriate standards of project management terminology, communications, and practice among project management professionals
- Identify and facilitate opportunities of all types for members and member organizations
- Provide project management information and education to DPC SIG professionals in industry, government, and educational institutions improving the overall delivery of processes and service as well as the quality and value of completed projects.

Interested?

Join with other leaders in design procurement construction as we shape the future of our industry.

Get Involved

To participate in an action team with other leaders in the industry; contact the PMI SIG coordinator at sig@pmi.org for more information.

Membership Benefits

Networking and Information Exchange. Take advantage of the opportunity to meet and talk with your peers in the design procurement construction arena either at the Annual Seminars & Symposium or anytime throughout the year. See the SIG pages at http://www.pmi.org

Project Management Journal *and* **PM Network.** When you become a member of PMI you receive the technical journal (four times/year) and the professional magazine (twelve times/year) with articles of specific and general interest to professionals. Share your successes and lessons learned by having your articles published in these prestigious publications.

SIG Annual Meetings. You have the opportunity to influence the future of the DPC SIG through its annual business meetings at the Annual Seminars & Symposium. Participate in regular and ongoing DPC Internet forums and local or regional events.

Special Projects. Participate in special projects to answer questions of concern to project management professionals.

Is the DPC SIG for Me?

If you work on projects involving design, procurement, or construction and want to be more effective at planning, organizing, controlling, or leading project work, PMI and the DPC SIG is for you! We can assist you in improving your professional development and in expanding your network of references and support. Your active participation is encouraged. You will find it most rewarding, both professionally and personally.

DPC SIG members pay a nominal fee to support DPC SIG activities. The DPC SIG member must be a member of PMI in good standing.

Join the DPC SIG Now
Associate with Winners!

PMI SIG Application
Design Procurement Construction

YES — Sign me up as a member of the DPC SIG!
　　　　I have enclosed my $15 annual DPC SIG fee payable to PMI (you must be a member of PMI to join).
　　　　I am not joining now but wish to receive additional information on PMI.
YES — I want my name in the SIG Directory.

NAME (LAST, FIRST, MIDDLE)

PROFESSIONAL DESIGNATIONS (PMP, OTHER)

JOB TITLE

ORGANIZATION

ADDRESS

CITY, STATE, ZIP

PHONE　　　　　　　　FAX　　　　　　　E-MAIL

PMI MEMBER #　　　　　PMI CHAPTER

I would like to participate in the following Action Teams:

Please complete, attach your check payable to PMI for $15 representing annual SIG dues and mail along with any additional information to:

　SIG Coordinator
　PMI, 130 S. State Road, Upper Darby, PA 19082 USA
　Phone: 610/734-3330　Fax: 610/734-3266
　Internet: http://www.pmi.org.
　E-mail: sig@pmi.org
　PMI's Fax on Demand Service:
　　　USA: 1-800-495-5201
　　　Canada: 1-303-804-1638
　　　International: 1-303-804-1638

Appendix E: The Authors

"Caution: Project Management Professional at Work!!!" by Mark Owen Mathieson, PMP, Sverdrup Corporation, Arlington, Virginia; "A Postal Point of View" by Steve H. Deeming, R.A., USPS, Project Manager, Major Facilities Office, Philadelphia, Pennsylvania, from *PM Network* (October 1993).

"Successful Utility Project Management from Lessons Learned" by Darrel G. Hubbard, P.E., Vice President, MAC Technical Services Co., from *Project Management Journal* XXI:3 (September 1990).

"Staff Responsibilities of the Project Manager" by Norman F. Jacobs Jr., Jacobs Consultant Services, Ashland, Virginia, unpublished.

"The Great Juggling Act" by Norman F. Jacobs Jr., Jacobs Consultant Services, Ashland, Virginia, unpublished.

"Job Set-Up by Project Manager" by Norman F. Jacobs Jr., Jacobs Consultant Services, Ashland, Virginia, unpublished.

"Project Management and Job Administration" by Norman F. Jacobs Jr., Jacobs Consultant Services, Ashland, Virginia, unpublished.

"Partnering: A Tool for Communications Management" by David E. Anderson, Department of Civil Engineering, The University of Texas at Austin, and G. Edward Gibson Jr., Ph.D., P.E., Department of Civil Engineering, The University of Texas at Austin, from *Project Management Institute 26th Annual Seminar/Symposium* (October 1995).

"Paperwork by Project Managers" by Norman F. Jacobs Jr., Jacobs Consultant Services, Ashland, Virginia, unpublished.

"Job Documentation: A Project Manager's Responsibility" by Norman F. Jacobs Jr., Jacobs Consultant Services, Ashland, Virginia, unpublished.

"Project Management Control, Computers, and Software" by Norman F. Jacobs Jr., Jacobs Consultant Services, Ashland, Virginia, unpublished.

"Pre-Project Planning for Capital Facilities" by Dennis G. King, P.E., P.Eng., The M.W. Kellogg Company; G. Edward Gibson Jr., Ph.D., P.E. The University of Texas at Austin; and Michele Hamilton, P.E., The University of Texas at Austin, from *Project Management Institute 25th Annual Seminar/Symposium* (October 1994).

"Communications for High Performing Project Teams" by Dennis G. King, Enron Engineering and Construction, and Joseph W. Synan, Leadingwell Associates, from *Project Management Institute 26th Annual Seminar/Symposium* (October 1995).

"Philosophy and Critical Path Method Communications" by Norman F. Jacobs Jr., Jacobs Consultant Services, Ashland, Virginia, unpublished.

"Critical Path Method Updates and Control" by Norman F. Jacobs Jr., Jacobs Consultant Services, Ashland, Virginia, unpublished.

"Today's Needs in Project Management" by Norman F. Jacobs Jr., Jacobs Consultant Services, Ashland, Virginia, unpublished.

"Using Project Finance to Help Manage Project Risks" by Carl R. Beidleman, DuBois Professor of Finance, and David Veshosky and Donna Fletcher, Research Scholars, Lehigh University, Bethlehem, Pennsylvania, from *Project Management Journal* XXII:2 (June 1991).

"Assuring Excellence in Execution in Construction Project Management" by Henry J. McCabe, PMP, Fluor Daniel's Health Sciences Center Project, King Abdul Aziz University, Jeddah, Saudi Arabia, from *PM Network* (October 1995).

"The Residual Costs of Inferior Project Management" by N.D. Henry, Morrison Knudsen Engineers, Inc., Fort Lauderdale, Florida, and J.M. Moore, Stone & Webster Engineers, Inc., Fort Lauderdale, Florida, from *Project Management Institute Seminar/Symposium* (October 1990).

"An Architect's View" by Derek Neale, MAIBC, Neale, Staniszkis, Doll Architects, and Michael A. Ernest, MAIBC, PMI, Michael A. Ernest & Associates, from *PM Network* (February 1990).

"Construction Delay Communication Computer System" by Dr. Janet K. Yates, San Jose State University, and Hisham Aoude, Polytechnic University, from *Project Management Institute 26th Annual Seminar/Symposium* (October 1995).

AIA Document A201-1997: General Conditions of the Contract for Construction by the American Institute of Architects, Washington D.C.

"Effective Project Management in Bureaucracies" by John R. Spittler, P.E., and Courtney J. McCracken, P.E., from *1996 AACE Transactions*.